Open Scientific Data - Why Choosing and Reusing the RIGHT DATA Matters

Authored by Vera J. Lipton

Published in London, United Kingdom

IntechOpen

Supporting open minds since 2005

Open Scientific Data - Why Choosing and Reusing the RIGHT DATA Matters
http://dx.doi.org/10.5772/intechopen.87201
Authored by Vera J. Lipton

First published in London, United Kingdom, 2020 by IntechOpen
IntechOpen is the global imprint of INTECHOPEN LIMITED, registered in England and Wales, registration number: 11086078, 7th floor, 10 Lower Thames Street, London, EC3R 6AF, United Kingdom
Printed in Croatia

British Library Cataloguing-in-Publication Data
A catalogue record for this book is available from the British Library

Additional hard and PDF copies can be obtained from orders@intechopen.com

Open Scientific Data - Why Choosing and Reusing the RIGHT DATA Matters
Authored by Vera J. Lipton
p. cm.
Print ISBN 978-1-83880-984-3
Online ISBN 978-1-83880-985-0
eBook (PDF) ISBN 978-1-83880-986-7

An electronic version of this book is freely available, thanks to the support of libraries working with Knowledge Unlatched. KU is a collaborative initiative designed to make high quality books Open Access for the public good. More information about the initiative and links to the Open Access version can be found at www.knowledgeunlatched.org

For EU product safety concerns:
IN TECH d.o.o., Prolaz Marije Krucifikse Kozulić 3, 51000 Rijeka, Croatia, info@intechopen.com or visit our website at intechopen.com.

Meet the author

Dr. Vera J. Lipton is an advocate of open innovation, a data analyst, and an intellectual property counsel with over 15 years' experience gained in Australia, Europe, and Asia. She is currently a researcher with the Zvi Meitar Institute for Legal Implications of Emerging Technologies at IDC in Herzliya, the heart of data science in Israel. Previously, she founded the National Patent Analytics Hub at IP Australia and, before that, worked as a technology transfer consultant for a medical software company. Vera's research focuses on the intersection between law, information technologies, and digital rights — especially open knowledge and data, automation, and technology ethics. She lives in Cyprus and works in Israel and internationally.

To my late father, my eternal source of inspiration

Acknowledgements

Many people have contributed to this book and encouraged me in the course of my research.

My greatest thanks go to Professor Brian Fitzgerald, one of the most amazing leaders and finest human beings with whom I have ever had the opportunity to cross paths.

I first met Brian at the Queensland University of Technology in 2009 when I was working on IP Australia's submission to the National Innovation System Review. Brian and his sister, Dr. Anne Fitzgerald, sounded like a breeze of fresh air—talking with passion and determination about open innovation, free sharing of knowledge, and collaboration in online spaces. And there I was—coming from the Patent Office, where the prescribed narrative was the protection of ideas with intellectual property and making money from them. A whole new world opened up to me at that Brisbane meeting.

Nine years later, with this book finally complete, I remain eternally grateful for Brian's wise counsel and support along the way.

I am also profusely thankful to Dr. John Gilchrist. Without John, this book would have never become a reality. His patient and steady approach and diligent comments on the numerous revisions of the text were consistently professional and thoughtful.

I am deeply indebted to Dr. Hans Peter Beck, Senior Physicist at the Atlas Collaboration at CERN, President of the Swiss Physics Society, and Co-chair of the International Particle Outreach Group at CERN. I was fortunate to be one of the first people to visit the Large Hadron Collider at CERN immediately after its opening in early 2009. Hans Peter was there to show me around and has provided me with a great deal of support ever since.

Hans Peter also facilitated connections with so many others at CERN who have shared with me their knowledge and experiences with open data—namely Jens Vigen and Dr. Suenje Dallmeier-Tiessen from the CERN Library; Tibor Simko, Head Developer of the Invenio digital library software; Dr. Achim Geiser, Senior Physicist working in the CMS Collaboration; and his colleague Achintya Rao, also from the CMS collaboration.

I much appreciate the encouragement of Dr. David Secher, the world's leading university technology transfer expert and the former Senior Bursar at Gonville & Caius College at the University of Cambridge. I first met David at the Praxis Unico technology transfer training in Melbourne in 2010 and we have managed to keep in touch over the years. Communications with David have helped me to internally reconcile some of the seemingly opposing approaches between open sharing of scientific knowledge and the protection of public research with intellectual property.

I gratefully acknowledge all the time, support, and encouragement I have received from my good friend, linguist, "resident philosopher," and accomplished broadcaster Dr. Heinrich Stefanik OAM. When I first came to Canberra in 2002, I had little notion of what it takes to communicate with ease and to write with clarity, and how to make technical writings more accessible to diverse audiences. Heinrich spent hundreds of hours listening to me, discussing, and editing my writings over and over again. He also reviewed the early chapters of this book.

I thank Professor Anne-Laure Mention of the Royal Melbourne Institute of Technology. The founding Co-editor of the Journal of Innovation Management, Anne-Laure provided me with the opportunity to act as a guest editor of the journal and the opportunity to publish portions of this study in the book *Open Innovation: A Multifaceted Perspective* (World Press Scientific/Imperial College Press).

Next, I acknowledge the assistance I received from IP Australia in 2009 to study changing models of intellectual property management in the context of open innovation. This professional development project informed early stages of my research. I particularly thank my former colleagues Geoff Sadlier, Ian Goss, and Brendan Bourke for helping me organize the study tour and, more recently, sharing references to latest reports and developments in the field.

I thank Professor Dov Greenbaum, Dr. Ben Atkinson, Dr. Kylie Pappalardo, Dr. Cheryl Foong, Mr. Brett Walker, Mr. Dimitris Pierides and Dr. Barbara Petropoulou-Lillikas for their continued support on my academic journey.

I thank IntechOpen for recognising this book as part of the Woman in Science program.

The list of people who have contributed to this book would not be complete without Martin Freckmann. I am grateful for his professional and timely feedback and edits.

My thoughts and blessings go to my colleagues and quiet supporters all over the world, especially in Australia, Israel, United States, Cyprus, Slovakia, the Netherlands, Germany, and New Zealand.

My warmest thanks go to Nicos. It is so wonderful to share life with you in Cyprus.

Last but not least, I would like to honor my mother, and appreciate her boundless love and vast competence. I would have never had the time and the means to do what I have done in life without the generous support and understanding I have received from her.

Vera Lipton

Contents

Foreword

Our lives and our societies are being transformed, thanks to digital technologies, social media, data, algorithms and artificial intelligence. Most of us use the Internet, mobile phones and computers, and most of us are familiar with Facebook, Amazon and Google. These and other technologies are changing forever how we do business and engage in politics, how we conduct academic research, produce and disseminate science and how we teach and learn in online spaces.

As digital technologies have become increasingly integrated into our society, they are generating unprecedented quantities of data, sometimes called big data. Such data is now available more widely and through ever-faster access points. Such data have greater coverage and they include new types of collections and measurements that were previously not available [1]. For example, in medicine alone, the annual rate of increase of digital healthcare data has stood at around 50% over the past 5 years, according to Stanford University.[1] It is becoming clear that digital data is a dynamic force that can drive science forward, especially if the data is openly available.

Much has been written about enabling open access to research data for further study, and researchers are not alone in thinking about how to share research data in electronic formats. They have been recently joined by research funders, librarians and science policymakers. At the same time, many issues surrounding digital scientific data remain unknown, and new problems and questions are emerging as we address the old ones—issues such as the legal, ethical, cultural and technical impediments to open data sharing. Some of the questions that arise are the following: What would motivate researchers to share their own data and to reuse data produced by others? How can the data be curated and shared efficiently and cost-effectively? Who should be responsible for data sharing? What are the optimal ways of enabling access while protecting research integrity and confidentiality? How can we balance the commercial interest of universities with providing open access to research data? Who should pay for open research data?

This book offers pragmatic answers to many of these questions. Rather than emphasising the future ideal of open scientific data, it deals with the current realities and practical aspects of open data sharing. Rather than focusing on data across all scientific disciplines, it draws on lessons learned at CERN and in the use of open clinical trial data. Rather than dwelling on the expectations of funders and publishers, it deals with the challenges posed to researchers—challenges that also present many opportunities. These are clearly articulated in the 'staged model' for open scientific data that the author proposes as a 'flexible template' for future data sharing in other scientific disciplines.

---

[1] Almost 2500 exabites (one exabite = one million gigabites) will be produced in 2020, according to the Stanford University School of Medicine. Compare this with just 153 exabites produced in 2013. See Ref. [2].

It often happens that a research publication is strong on analysis but weak on the proposals. Not this one. The 'staged model' for open scientific data is illustrated in detail in Chapter 8; but this is really the full enunciation of multiple, and complementary, strands of research and data sharing principles.

The principles emerge in logical progression over several chapters—the identification of the ways in which the open data present challenges different from those in open publications (Chapter 7) and raise reuse issues that, in turn, are entirely different from the issues presented by access (Chapter 1); how the open data mandates, adopted on the wings of success of open access publications, fall short of dealing with the specificities of the issued raised by data (Chapter 3); how research data management at CERN (Chapter 5) and in clinical trial data (Chapter 6) offer templates for the 'staged model' that is to be understood as a general frame of reference rather than a single optimal solution. In short, the thoughts and concepts examined in all these chapters seamlessly converge into the 'staged model' introduced in Chapter 8 and is then summarised again from the perspective of providing answers to the research questions posed in the concluding Chapter 9.

The contribution of this book to the open scientific data debate is not only original but is also well-timed. Much of the zeal towards extending the success of open access publishing to open research data often fails to take into account the peculiarities of the latter field. This book takes a fresh look at the main critical points—including the importance of the criterion of data reuse over the goal of access, the multiple fine implementation issues, the importance of getting right the incentives for the different stakeholders such as researchers. The lessons learnt from CERN practice in addressing these issues are especially welcome.

I highly commend the determination of the author and IntechOpen to make this book available as an open access publication. This will, no doubt, enable an expansion of its readership outside the science, research and policy spheres. Yet, as the author rightly points out, for open scientific data to be successful, it needs to be first embraced by researchers. Only then, the general public can follow and engage in open science projects.

I hope this book will bring many illuminating insights into open scientific data to all.

Professor Marco Ricolfi
Chair, Intellectual Property, Department of Law, University of Turin
Co-founder, The NEXA Center for Internet and Society

Open Scientific Data

Why Choosing and Reusing the Right Data Matters

Vera J. Lipton

Abstract

Public science is critical to the economy and to society. However, much of the beneficial impact of scientific research only occurs when scientific knowledge is disseminated broadly and is used by others. This book examines the emerging policy, law and practice of facilitating open access to scientific research data. One particular focus is to examine the open data policies recently introduced by research funders and publishers, and the potential in these for driving the practice of open scientific data into the future.

This study identifies five major stumbling blocks to sustainable open scientific data. Firstly, it is the *prevailing mindset* that facilitating open access to data is analogous to facilitating open access to publications and, therefore, research data can easily be shared, with research funders and librarians effectively leading the process. Secondly, it is the unclear meaning of the term *data* which causes confusion among stakeholders. Thirdly, it is the *misunderstood incentives* for data sharing and the additional inputs required from researchers. Fourthly, *data privacy*—an issue that only applies to selected research datasets, and yet appears to dominate the discussion about open research data. Finally, there is a *copyright law*, which poses challenges at different stages of data release and reuse.

In this book, it is argued that the above problems can be addressed using a staged model for open scientific data. I draw specifically on the practice with open scientific data at CERN (the European Organization for Nuclear Research) and the practice of sharing clinical trial data to argue that open data can be shared at various stages of processing and diversification. This model is supplemented by recommendations proposing changes to existing open data mandates and the introduction of a text and data mining exemption into Australian copyright law.

Keywords: open data, open science, open research, research data, scientific data, big databig, science, Science 2.0, digital science, open access, data access, data reuse, data management, research data management, data mining, metadata, legal issues in open data, copyright and open data, big data, privacy of research subjects, confidentiality, open data licencing, data exemptions, data quality, data exclusivity, data ownership, data science, e-research, data service, research data product

Chapter 1

Introduction: Opening Up Data in Scientific Research

"Imagine a world in which every single human being can freely share in the sum of all knowledge."

Wikimedia Foundation

1.1 Why open access to scientific outcomes matters

The need to effectively disseminate and share science outcomes is pressing. As nearly every region feels the effects of climate change, as food insecurity is rising, and as the demand for natural resources is increasing, the world looks to science for solutions. In this interconnected globe where over 50% of its population can access the Internet,[2] science offers hope. It offers hope for those living in prosperous societies and for the remaining half of the world—over 3 billion people—who live on less than US$2.50 a day.[3]

In this age of communication, if anything is to secure the future of our planet and the well-being of its civilisation, then it is likely to be science, as Australian science commentator Julian Cribb noted. Yet it will not be science alone, rather the knowledge that it imparts and the learning that it yields when it is shared broadly and applied wisely. If science is to deliver its full value to society, it must be easily and freely accessible [5].

But the majority of science is not accessible easily, and only a fraction of it is accessible freely. This is despite the fact that scientific knowledge is plentiful and is growing rapidly—doubling, on average, every 15 years.[4] Much of the knowledge and research data underpinning science remains guarded by elites; much of it stays locked in institutional repositories or costly scientific journals.[5]

The low accessibility and subsequent uptake of scientific knowledge are not ideal for researchers who produce and use science and who are unable to access in a timely manner the scientific outputs produced by their peers.[6] The situation is also not ideal for universities and public research organisations that train and employ researchers or for governments that fund the majority of basic research.[7]

---

[2] Statistics sourced from Internet Source Stats [3].

[3] Statistics sourced from Shah [4].

[4] See Larsen and von Ins [6]. The rate of doubling of the body of scientific knowledge was calculated as an average number of scientific records included in the following databases: Web of Science (owned by Thomson Reuters), Scopus (owned by LexisNexis), and Google Scholar. Duplicate entries were removed.

[5] In a consultation carried out in 2012, the European Commission determined that there were huge barriers to accessing research data. Of the 1140 subjects questioned, 87% contradicted the statement that there was no access problem to research data in Europe. See European Commission [7]. See also McCain [8].

[6] In a study conducted in 2011 by Tenopir et al. [9], 67% of 1300 researchers pointed to a lack of access to data generated by other researchers or institutions. See also point 4 above.

[7] According to the OECD, industry in 2014 funded just over 1% of gross domestic expenditure on basic research in Australia, Austria, Belgium, Denmark, France, Germany, Sweden, and the United States. The figure was less than 1% in Canada, Chile, Czech Republic, Greece, Hungary, Italy, New Zealand, and the United Kingdom. Source: OECD Main Science and Technology Indicators [10].

Equally, the low availability of scientific knowledge is not ideal for taxpayers and citizens whose hope for improved living standards increasingly depends on the development and application of science and technology. And it is not an ideal scenario for technology companies that require timely access to knowledge as they increasingly innovate by combining research outputs from external and internal sources [11, 12]. Nobody benefits from science that stays limited to those who initially create it. Such science is lost—lost to follow-on innovation and lost to society at large.

Fortunately, there are ways to increase access to scientific knowledge and opportunities to accelerate scientific discovery.

The open access movement has developed over the past two decades. It advocates the sharing of scientific knowledge over the Internet by challenging the application of exclusive property rights over scientific outputs.[8] This movement further promotes 'digital openness' in the conduct of science and of scientific communication, facilitating online access to scientific publications and the underlying research data. The open scientific content that results from this movement and emerging online communities are shaping the fundamental processes of science creation and dissemination. These processes are taking place alongside—and are intimately connected with—the evolution of digital technologies and interactive communications. Open science is developing and building upon the body of digital knowledge, data and infrastructure that it inherently generates.

More recently, an increasing number of governments, research funders and publishers have mandated the release of research data over the Internet with a view to making scientific results more easily and more broadly available for research, innovation, education, technology development and other applications. In 2010, the National Science Foundation in the United States announced that grant proposals would require a data management plan and that the plan would be subject to peer review [16]. The policy was a tipping point leading to similar mandates emerging in other nations.

In 2011, the Research Councils in the United Kingdom (RCUK)[9] released *Common Principles on Data Policy* [18] and, subsequently, many RCUK funders have mandated the requirements for data management plans with new grant applications. The principles encourage research data to be made openly available with as few restrictions as possible in a timely and responsible manner.[10] Similarly, the *Recommendation of the European Commission on Access to and Preservation of Scientific Information* [19] encouraged the European Union member states to develop policies for open access to scientific results, including research data and information [20]. This was followed with the Open Research Data Pilot in 2014, aimed at exploring the digital sharing of research data resulting from the Horizon 2020 research grants [21].

The Australian Government was among the first to invest in the development of research data infrastructures. The Australian National Data Service (ANDS) was established in 2008 to develop an Australian Research Data Commons platform [22] —an Internet-based discovery service designed to provide rich connections

[8] The term 'digital science' is often referred to as 'open science' or 'Science 2.0'. Its roots go back to the emergence of the Internet and communication technologies. In general terms, open science refers to changing scientific practice based on cooperative work facilitated by diffusing knowledge by using digital technologies. See, for example, European Commission [13]; Fecher and Friesike [14]. The concept of digital science is discussed in Chapter 2, Section 2.2 of this study. For a good overview of the evolution of open access movement, see Suber [15].

[9] Integrated in April 2018 into a new body [17].

[10] *Ibid.*, point 2.

between data, projects, researchers and institutions. Funding was also allocated for the development of metadata tools through the 'Seeding the Commons' initiative[11]. Open research data is a priority area for the Data to Decisions Cooperative Research Centre established in July 2014.[12] The two principal research funders in Australia—the Australian Research Council (ARC) and the National Health and Medical Research Council (NHMRC)—both 'strongly encourage' the recipients of their grants to share data and metadata arising from their research.[13]

Many private research funders also require the public release of data resulting from the research they fund.[14] The open data mandates introduced by governments and research funders follow similar policies promoting open access to publications[15] and public sector information.[16] The mandates were first introduced in the United States, Europe and Australia and quickly spread to other parts of the world. The sharing of scientific data in electronic formats has a long tradition in medical research, biotechnology and geospatial sciences. Within a span of 6 years, the policies mandating open access to scientific data have expanded to all fields of research, including humanities and social sciences.

At a multilateral level, the United Nations Educational, Scientific and Cultural Organization (UNESCO) adopted the *Revised Draft Strategy on UNESCO's Contribution to the Promotion of Open Access to Scientific Information and Research* in 2011 [29]. The strategy was established to promote open access to scientific information and research[17], and it called for examining the feasibility of developing a UNESCO convention on open access to scientific information and research.[18] In recent years, the UNESCO has viewed open access to research results as a prerequisite for reaching its Sustainable Development Goals.[19] As such, the UNESCO believes that open science has a fundamental role in supporting poverty reduction. The organisation is committed to making open access to research one of its central supporting agendas.[20]

The open data policies vary in their scope and among research funders, yet they share some common objectives—to advance science by making research data available to others more quickly and more broadly; to enable reproducibility of scientific outcomes; and to increase the uptake, use and quality of scientific knowledge, including in developing countries. Such arguments reflect the desire to tackle some of the big challenges facing humanity and the planet today. Building upon and reusing open scientific knowledge can expedite these global efforts [31].

---

[11] Seeding the Commons was a programme funded by the Australian National Data Service to improve discoverability and use of university research data. Full description of associated university projects is available at: https://projects.ands.org.au/getAllProjects.php?start=sc.

[12] The centre brings together researchers and industry to contribute to the development of Australia's big data capability. See Data to Decisions CRC [23].

[13] The National Health and Medical Research Council (NHMRC)'s [24]. *Open Access Policy* (previously also referred to as the *NHMRC Policy on the Dissemination of Research*) took effect from 15 January 2018, 7.

[14] One of the earliest advocates of open research data was the Wellcome Trust. See Wellcome Trust [25, 26].

[15] For a good overview of open access to publications, see Swam [27].

[16] For a good overview of OA policies for public sector information, see Fitzgerald [28].

[17] *Ibid*, Par. 1.1.

[18] *Ibid*, Annex 3.

[19] The UNESCO states at least 10 out of the 17 Sustainable Development Goals comprising the 2030 Agenda for Sustainable Development require constant scientific input. See UNESCO [30].

[20] *Ibid.*

1.2 The early challenges facing open scientific data

The arguments put forward for open scientific data certainly are plausible. At the same time, understanding the requirements for responsible data sharing and ensuring compliance with these requirements pose fresh challenges to research organisations. Indeed, making research data available, legible and useful to unknown audiences, and for unanticipated purposes, may not be an easy task. Maintaining the privacy of subjects involved in data collection, particularly in clinical trials, is an additional concern for medical research institutes. Furthermore, digital curation of research data requires substantial investments in data infrastructures, human resources and new business models. Many research organisations point out that open scientific data cannot be covered from research budgets. Further still, the very nature of scientific research is changing profoundly as open scientific data is increasingly being curated and shared. In the face of these challenges, some stakeholders feel that the future of open scientific data is uncertain.

This book argues, however, that these challenges help us understand how best to achieve open access to scientific data. Open scientific data is not only desirable, it is possible. Yet it requires careful balancing of the needs of all stakeholders and especially the need to balance 'collective benefits' with 'individual responsibilities'. The 'collective benefits' are likely to accrue from the provision of open data to society, while 'individual responsibilities' for curating open data and developing supporting infrastructures are vested in researchers and their organisations. Those tensions between 'individual responsibilities' and 'collective benefits' form an overarching theme of this book. I investigate the ways in which the two concepts are merged and confused and what might be done to clarify them.

Ultimately, it is argued that the responsibility for open data cannot be placed on researchers if their efforts for data curation are not recognised and rewarded and if open data cannot be reused successfully. I suggest that 'collective societal benefit' and 'individual responsibility' would be best balanced within a staged model for releasing scientific data as open data.

The proposed model is researcher-centric and puts a major emphasis on data quality, which is the key prerequisite for data reuse. The model rests on the observation that even organisations fully committed to openness, such as the European Organization for Nuclear Research (CERN), are unable to share all of their research data as open data at this point.

However, CERN has developed a useful classification model for research data based on the levels of data granularity and processing. I adopt and slightly adjust the CERN classifications to propose the stages of open data release for all research organisations and across all scientific disciplines. I specifically acknowledge that the definitions of 'research data' and the timing of data release will vary not only among research disciplines but even among the defined data stages and among individual research projects. This reasoning is consistent with a major finding of this book that the opening up of research data requires an open mindset while acknowledging that 'one size does not fit all'. The open data mindset finds the practice of open scientific data to be a diverse, ongoing and ever-evolving process that is as important a driver of research practice as are the scientific results and the data that underpin them.

Central to the proposed model is an understanding of the social context in which scientific knowledge is created and used. Historically, science has had a role in creating data and assessing validity of the data. As science develops and changes over time, the meaning and relevance of data also change.

This study finds that the nature, dissemination and use of scientific knowledge are profoundly changing in the context of the digital revolution. However, the core theories of knowledge production and dissemination in the digital age—namely, the theories of a knowledge society[21]—envisage that merely releasing scientific data into the public domain is sufficient for the economic and social benefits of open data to accrue.

The model proposed in this book rebuts this argument, positing that simply providing *access* to data in the public domain is useless to society and that only data *reuse* can realise the envisaged benefits.

At present, the scientific community is the sole community sector that appears capable of the competent reuse of scientific data. Consequently, it is argued the rationale for open scientific data should be narrowed to focus on data-enabled science, rather than data-enabled society. This argument rests on the fact that science is a form of social organisation in its own right [34, 35]. Therefore, the first task is to facilitate improved data sharing and reuse of open scientific data among relevant researchers. Once researchers embrace open scientific data and learn how to better describe and embed the data into their daily research practice, only then the benefits can spill over to a wider society.

At the same time, open scientific data is profoundly changing the economic context in which power and control over science are distributed in society. In today's world, where knowledge means power[22] and where science regulates cutting-edge knowledge,[23] the control of science is also becoming more important. Open access is a response to a trend towards the commodification of knowledge.

Looking at different scientific disciplines, we see that commodification is pervasive in engineering, in the biological and medical sciences, and—on a somewhat smaller scale—in the physical sciences [37]. Although these trends have roots in policy changes in intellectual property and the economics of information, critical data mass has led to new markets. Some of the data can be exchanged only within academia, but some have commercial value and can lead to new partnerships with industry, just as commercial data can lead to academic research. However, such data exchanges lead to new tensions [38–40].

Open scientific data empowers researchers, not markets, to control scientific knowledge into the future. Open scientific data thus leads towards a more transparent and accountable governance of science that, in turn, advances a more open, collaborative and democratic society.

To summarise how things stand today—while attempts at sharing research data in electronic formats go back to the late 1950s—rapid and pervasive technological changes have enabled the storing, processing and transmitting of large volumes of data and have stimulated collaboration among scientists. The recent and successful practice of enabling open access to scientific publications and government data

---

[21] There is a range of definitions of the term 'knowledge society' but, broadly speaking, a knowledge society is one that generates, processes, shares, and makes knowledge that may be used to improve the human condition available to all its members [32]. Also in 1994, Gibbons et al. [33] examined changes in forms of scientific knowledge production. This is one of the key theories examined in this study.

[22] Castells argues that the rise of networks that link people, institutions, and countries characterise contemporary society. The purpose of these networks is for information to flow in what Castells defines as an 'informationalised society'—one in which 'information generation, processing, and transmission become the fundamental sources of power and productivity.' See Castells [36].

[23] Nowotny and others ([33], pp. 12–13) observed that specialised knowledge plays a crucial role in many dynamic markets. Specialised knowledge is an important source of created comparative advantage for both its producers and users of all kinds, and not only in industry. As a result, the demand for specialist knowledge is increasing.

(public sector information) brought a new impetus to digital research data and has inspired new methods for scientific research in online spaces. Such data-led science holds promise for the development of new scientific knowledge and is transforming the conduct of science and the communication of scientific outcomes.

1.3 Exploring a way forward

This book investigates how the open data policies recently introduced by research funders are being implemented in practice. Drawing on early experiences with open data at CERN and experiences with data resulting from clinical trials—two scientific fields in which the sharing of research data in digital formats is already well-established—this study aims to determine whether open data policies can achieve open access to scientific data. More specifically, the principal goal of this study is to investigate optimal ways to tackle the challenges associated with the practical implementation of open scientific data.

In the context of this study, 'open scientific data' refers to the evidence that underpins scientific knowledge produced by publicly funded organisations[24] and that meets the FAIR standards for openness—data that are findable, accessible, interoperable and reusable.[25]

This book contributes to the ongoing discussion and considers four principal research questions.

Firstly, I examine the objectives and benefits stated for open scientific data.

Secondly, I analyse the open data policies and seek to establish whether open scientific data is an achievable objective.

Thirdly, I ask how selected data-centric public research organisations are implementing open data in practice. Specifically, in this context, I enquire about the legal and other challenges emerging in the process of open data implementation and investigate how data-centric research organisations are dealing with these challenges.

Finally, I seek to establish what can be done to promote open access to data and whether the open data mandates need to be revised.

For the purposes of clarity, the research questions are summarised as follows:

1. *Vision.* What are the expected benefits associated with the curation and release of scientific data?

2. *Policy*. What is the scope of the open data policies?

3. *Practice.* How are selected data-centric public research organisations implementing open data? What are the legal and other challenges emerging in the process of implementation? Is open scientific data an achievable objective?

4. *A way forward.* What can be done to promote open access to scientific data across different research disciplines? Is there a need to revise the open data mandates?

The research questions are answered in the specific chapters of the book as depicted in **Figure 1**.

In answering the stated research questions, I provide a theoretical framework based on the social theories of innovation—especially the models of science and

[24] The reasons for this focus on publicly-funded organisations are discussed at 1.4: 'Matters beyond the scope of this study'.

[25] See Wilkinson et al. [31] at point 27. The meaning of 'open scientific data' and the parameters of 'openness' are discussed in detail in Chapter 4 and described in **Table 1**.

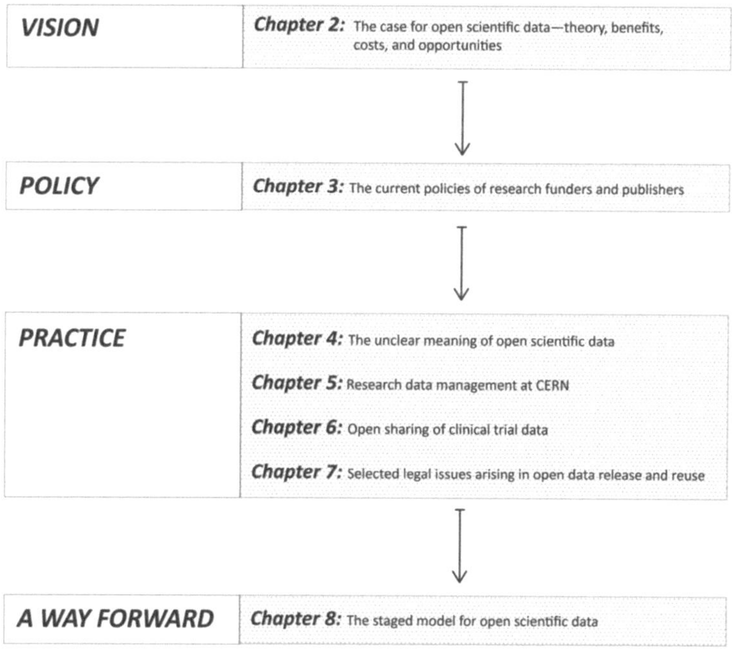

Figure 1.
Structure of this book.

knowledge production and how these are changing in the context of the digital revolution. I place a special emphasis on the reusability of open research data and the reproducibility of research findings, which are the primary stated objectives of open scientific data. I then analyse the open data mandates and the requirements they place on researchers and research organisations. I further discuss and conceptualise the meaning of 'open scientific data' and examine how stakeholders understand the term.

This inquiry helps to identify the many facets of open scientific data and the lack of clarity among stakeholders regarding the meaning of 'research data' and associated terms such as 'data use' and 'data reuse'. The meaning of 'data' is also discussed in the context of copyright law and the parameters that 'data', 'datasets' and 'databases' need to meet to be protected by copyright. The discussion informs the proposed staged model for open scientific data, but that model is also largely informed by the experiences with research data management at CERN and with clinical trial data.

The purpose of the present study is to bring together the existing research into open scientific data, its practice and the challenges that have occurred in its implementation over the past decade. In this regard, it is a survey of theoretical work, policy and legal documents and practical experiences with open data in two scientific fields.

Specifically, this study documents the implementation of the open data mandates recently introduced by research funders and publishers. Further, it evaluates the potential of the mandates for driving open scientific data into the future.

1.4 What this book contributes

Open scientific data is a recent and vast subject—spanning many scientific and scholarly disciplines and various types of research data. To date, all efforts to study open scientific data have been piecemeal—focusing on specific initiatives, successful case studies, desired objectives and the envisaged benefits of open science, the evolving parameters for data openness and factors that may motivate researchers to release their research data to other users. Such issues have been assessed through the lenses of specific research disciplines or data initiatives or through individual technical issues that were deemed necessary to successfully implement open data. Scholarly research that is more systematic and that brings together the practice of open scientific data across various scientific disciplines is in short supply.

At the same time, research funders, government officials and librarians tend to approach the treatment of open scientific data with the same methods that proved successful in the implementation of open access to scientific publications. Such established approaches have been embedded in open data mandates. However, it is not clear, at this point, whether the current open data mandates can achieve the desired objectives.

There are significant differences evident in the implementation of open access processes. While the implementation of open publication mandates has been achieved within a few years, implementing open access to research data does not appear to be as straightforward. The rates of data deposit in online repositories remain low, and the implementation of the mandates in practice is lagging, as documented in Chapter 6 of this book. Some of the impediments to data sharing are known but have not been systematically studied to date. Other challenges have only become apparent as research organisations have begun the process of implementing the mandates. These last challenges are less known and are not well-documented. Apart from its newness as a concept, open data is proving to hold far more complexity in its execution than does the practice of open scientific publications.

Examining the challenges faced by open scientific data practice is a much-needed contribution to the ongoing debate. This book looks in detail at challenges in policy, data management and legal administration. It draws upon research and experiences with open data at CERN and in clinical trial data—two data-intensive fields at the frontline of the debate regarding open data. It is hoped that lessons learnt in these fields may help other research disciplines to adopt open data policies.

This investigation is significant because many key stakeholders are not aware of the challenges in implementing open data. And even when they are interested in applying the principles of it, many smaller research organisations appear to struggle with the concepts and definitions of open research data and its management, curation and funding. Some organisations yet to embrace open data are questioning not only the costs but whether the broad mandates for open data are fit for purpose. At the same time, while many research funders have introduced open data mandates, others appear to be backtracking from earlier commitments to do the same.

With regard to stakeholders, this book focuses mainly on those matters predominantly raised by researchers and others who execute open data mandates in research practice. Their voices are important and need to be heard by those who believe, mistakenly, that open scientific data requires nothing but the publishing of research data in public repositories.

In this uncertainty, it is hoped that a coherent exploration of the early experiences and challenges with open data in one of the largest data-centric research organisations in the world can bring fresh insights and unearth areas of best practice that, together, may help refine approaches to open data mandates.

1.5 The research methodology

The research in this book is interdisciplinary due to the diverse nature of open scientific data ([41], p. 2). The concept incorporates information, perspectives, concepts, practices and theories from several fields—science, public policy, science policy, law, data management, information technology, scientific communications and library scholarship, among others.

This book focuses on the policy, law and data management practice aspects of open scientific data.

The primary approach adopted in the present study is the problem–solution method. Firstly, I identify and analyse the relevant policies, theoretical concepts and international legal mechanisms adopted in support of open scientific data (Chapters 2 and 3). This is followed by a detailed examination of data management practices and by identifying issues that arose in putting into practice the adopted instrument (Chapters 4–7). The final two chapters propose a solution in the form of a staged model for open scientific data that addresses the issues identified in the preceding chapters. The proposed model, along with eight recommendations, presents a roadmap towards more achievable and sustainable open scientific data.

The main objective of the above methodological framework was to develop a greater degree of shared understanding of the legal, policy and conceptual framework that is appropriate for the current level of technological development; the experience of researchers with the digital sharing of scientific outputs; and the proclaimed social and policy objectives of open science.

This study used both doctrinal and empirical research.

Doctrinal research involved analysis of both legal and non-legal documents—including international declarations and instruments guiding open scientific data; the open data policies of research funders and publishers; statutes and case law governing the notion of data; copyright in data; ownership of data; confidentiality; and privacy of the research subjects. This analysis is supported by secondary sources such as monographs, peer-reviewed articles and reports underpinning the benefits of sharing data and scientific knowledge in the context of the digital revolution.

This research, to make the claim impersonal research goes beyond legal scholarship in that it considers the theories of science and knowledge production and the social functions of science. Historical records regarding the emergence of early data-sharing initiatives and projects have provided the context and background. This combination of multiple literature sources provides a more comprehensive and insightful discussion of the challenges arising in the implementation of open scientific data.

The staged model for open scientific data presented in this book was developed with a view to presenting a pragmatic and achievable approach to open scientific data—taking into account resource and technology constraints, established culture, current research practice and legal impediments to open data. The proposed model is less ambitious in its scope than the current open data mandates of research funders and publishers. Yet, if adopted, the proposed model would provide a basis for improved online data sharing among both researchers and non-researchers and also serve as a springboard for realising the vision for improved access to research data across all scientific disciplines.

1.6 Matters beyond the scope of this book

This book is not an exhaustive review of the current practices in making available open scientific data. It examines specific developments in the area of research data mandates and how these are implemented. To keep within reasonable bounds and for the sake of cohesion, the research in this study focuses on open scientific data as implemented by public research organisations that conduct applied and basic scientific research, including medical research institutes. In this context, a research organisation is considered to be publicly funded if it receives more than 50% of its income from public sources. The primary focus is on research institutes, and not on universities, mainly because universities are relatively late entrants and have far less experience with research data management and data sharing than data-intensive research organisations.

This book is not intended to cover the experiences with data sharing in the private sector. However, I draw on certain experiences of private sector organisations in regulating access to data from clinical trials to examine how they manage the ethical, privacy and research integrity issues arising in data sharing in digital formats.

While open data now covers all domains of research, including humanities and, to some extent, social sciences, this study only considers experiences with open data in the STEM disciplines—science, technology, engineering and medicine. Specifically, this book focuses on particle physics and clinical trial data and, to a lesser extent, geospatial sciences.

Open scientific data spans many jurisdictions, with rules emanating from different sources of law. As such, open data can be governed by various regimes. This book does not study the transnational operability of open data. However, Chapter 7 considers some cross-jurisdictional issues arising in the reuse and mining of open scientific data across national boundaries. The legal definitions of 'data' and 'databases' are analysed in selected English-speaking jurisdictions, including Australia and the United States, and within the context of the European Union's General Data Protection Regulation.[26]

Finally, there are many issues arising in the context of open scientific data, and every one of them can probably lead to a separate monograph. This book covers only selected issues associated with open scientific data, focusing on research data mandates and their implementation, especially with regard to research data management. The study also focuses on the legal issues arising in the release and reuse of open data.

The technical parameters and infrastructures that make open data findable, accessible, interoperable and reusable are not substantially covered in this book.

Nor is the question of the economics of open scientific data covered extensively, even though recent research on this matter is touched upon in this study. The economics of open data is a nascent area and the relevant economic models for quantifying the components of open data infrastructures and the methods for evaluating the benefits and costs of open scientific data are just starting to emerge.

The legal and other developments discussed in this book are those available to me as at 1 December 2017, but significant changes that have occurred after this date have been included where possible.

1.7 The structure of this book

This book consists of nine chapters, including *Introduction* (Chapter 1) and *Conclusion* (Chapter 9).

---

[26] Regulation (EU) 2016/679 of the European Parliament of the Council of 27 April 2016 on the protection of natural persons with regard to the processing of personal data and on the free movement of such data and repealing Directive 95/46/EC (General Data Protection Regulation). *Official Journal* L 119/2, 04/052015, 1–88. The European data protection framework is complemented by Directive 2002/58/EC on privacy and electronic communication [42–44].

Chapter 2. The Case for Open Scientific Data: Theory, Benefits, Costs and Opportunities

Chapter 2 examines why the idea of open data has been taken up by research funders, research organisations, the broader scientific community and civil society. It first considers whether the activities of these actors constitute a social movement seeking to mobilise open scientific data and whether the move towards openness in science is fostering a transition to a knowledge economy. In order to assess such broad questions, this chapter reviews the theories underpinning open knowledge-based and knowledge-based society as well as the role of open access in fostering the dissemination and reuse of scientific data. It also discusses the ways in which scientific knowledge has been produced historically and how it is produced today.

Chapter 3. The Current Policies of Research Funders and Publishers

This chapter analyses the policies mandating open access to scientific data. These policies are primarily focused on research funders and vary in their scope and format, which make any comparative analysis difficult. None of the policies under evaluation are more than 7 or 8 years old. Despite these limitations, the preliminary analyses are positive. The chapter finds that in addition to early entrants—that is, the English-speaking world—more than one third of the 28 European Union members had mandates for open scientific data in place at the end of 2017. Many Latin American countries have also adopted open access to research data, and similar mandates were under consideration in countries with large scientific output such as China. Some European countries—notably Italy, Spain, Germany and the Netherlands—have legislated open access to scientific data.

Chapter 4. The Unclear Meaning of Open Scientific Data

The problematic notion of 'data' is further examined in Chapter 4. Each term such as 'open data' and 'research data' has multiple meanings in the open data mandates and practice. Key concepts are often conflated or used interchangeably. 'Data' mean different things to different stakeholders, all at the same time, this chapter concludes. Researchers often like to share 'datasets', another contested term. Settling on criteria that define 'data' raises more questions. Chapter 4 provides background on each of these terms although every one of them warrants a lengthy study.

Chapter 5. Research Data Management at CERN

This key chapter deals with some of the evolving aspects of research data management. It examines data-driven experiments at the European Organization for Nuclear Research (CERN), acknowledging that it is not feasible to address, within the purview of a single chapter, all unfolding issues associated with the curation and reuse of open scientific data. The experiences with open data at CERN demonstrate efforts to reconcile the interests of all relevant parties. A major finding is that the data management process is a continuously evolving process and that this and the thinking around data preservation, curation and open sharing have proved to be challenging in most organisations, including CERN.

Finally, Chapter 5 explores efforts to define data in operational terms, based on levels of data processing and granularity and concludes by offering a working definition of the stages of open scientific data that is further canvassed in Chapter 6 and then embedded in the staged model proposed in Chapter 8.

Chapter 6. Open Sharing of Clinical Trial Data

Chapter 6 outlines the research data management process in the context of sharing data that results from clinical trials. The principal focus is on the specific protocols for data sharing—particularly data quality protocols at various levels of data processing, the risks in sharing data and the approaches used to mitigate the risks. This chapter argues that the risks arising from data sharing (as opposed to non-sharing) can be addressed though controls of data access. This exploration reveals that the application of soft tools, such as professional code of conduct and data use agreements, can be a means for reducing concerns that create disincentives for sharing clinical trial data as open data. Finally, Chapter 6 considers the motivation of researchers to share their own data and their willingness to reuse data produced by others.

Chapter 7. Key Legal Issues Arising in Open Data Release and Reuse

This chapter discusses the legal issues arising at two critical stages, namely, data release and data reuse.

The first part examines the legal issues arising in data release. The focus is on intellectual property rights, especially copyright in data and databases. This is followed by consideration of the uncertainty around data ownership—identified as the cause of subsequent problems affecting data licencing—along with a potential lack of interoperability and unclear conditions governing data reuse. There is an examination of some relevant licencing issues.

The second part is dedicated to analysis of different types of data reuse, such as linking or mining, and whether these types of reuse can infringe copyright. Other issues that need specific attention in the reuse of open scientific data include ensuring the privacy of research subjects, the ethics of research, and managing the risks associated with possible disclosure of confidential information.

Chapter 8. The Staged Model for Open Scientific Data

Drawing on the findings of the three preceding chapters, Chapter 8 proposes a model to address problems arising in their implementation.

This chapter consists of three main parts. It first outlines the policy setting within which the policies mandating open access to scientific data have emerged. This is followed by an overview of the main features of the mandates and identification of their drawbacks. The final section discusses the shortcomings in more detail and introduces a staged model for open scientific data, along with eight recommendations.

It is argued that the open data mandates have created a momentum for data release globally. At the same time, the mandates alone are insufficient to effectively drive open data into the future because the digital curation of research data for public release poses many challenges. The open data mandates, as they stand today, fail to acknowledge and address these challenges and thus should be revised. The recommendations in the proposed model suggest options for dealing with the issues arising in implementation so as to ensure sustainability of open scientific data into the future.

Chapter 9. Conclusion: Towards Achievable and Sustainable Open Scientific Data

The final chapter answers the research questions posed in this study. It summarises the core findings and contributions. The chapter concludes with a call to revise the open data mandates and so initiate changes in data management practices across different scientific disciplines to move towards the staged model.

Chapter 2

The Case for Open Scientific Data: Theory, Benefits, Costs and Opportunities

This chapter provides the theoretical, historical and economic background for the study of open scientific data. It consists of five key sections:

1. The emergence of open scientific data
2. Science and scientific data in the evolving knowledge economy
3. The envisaged benefits of open scientific data
4. The costs of developing open data infrastructures
5. Open data and commercialisation of public research

Introduction

This chapter reviews the theories underpinning open scientific data and explains when and why the concept of open scientific data has been adopted by the research community, funders, policymakers and broader civil society. The author first considers the historical developments and the role of scientific data in the evolving knowledge-based economy. This chapter then outlines the theories that advocate open science and the open flow of data in the economy and the role of open access in fostering the dissemination and development of science.

The chapter concludes by analysing the economic arguments put forward for open scientific data—including the economic, social and scientific benefits that open sharing of scientific data is likely to generate into the future and the tensions between open science and commercialisation of public research. These benefits and tensions are illustrated in three case studies showcasing the application of open scientific data—the Human Genome Project, the *E. coli* epidemic in Germany in 2011 and the Global Positioning System.

2.1 The emergence of open scientific data

Scientists were instrumental in developing the Internet and other communication technologies, and now scientists are leading the way in applying these technologies to the creation, communication and dissemination online of the results of their work. Across many disciplines, and from many locations, researchers are using digital technologies to share tasks, knowledge and research outcomes. Working in real time, digital technologies help to speed the creation of knowledge and its dissemination. This revolution in scientific communications and these new means for collaboration open the way to a dramatic increase in the social value of science.

Good data enables good science, and digital technologies provide the means for acquiring, transmitting, storing, analysing and reusing massive volumes of data. In embracing these technologies, research organisations and researchers are extending the frontiers of science. This is open innovation in science, or open science.

Open science is part of the broader access to knowledge movement that advocates the distribution of educational, intellectual, scientific, creative and government works online through permissive licences by the right holders (open access) [45–51]. More specifically, open science refers to online scientific resources, whether data or a publication, that anyone can access, use, reuse and distribute without permission from any other party. It may be that those resources have been placed in the public domain and so are not subject to any legal control. Or it may be that permission has already been granted to use, reuse and distribute the resources. Whichever case applies, the ability to use and build upon such resources simply requires access to them.[27]

While the definition and licencing mechanisms for open access are new, the sharing of scientific data in digital formats predates the emergence of the open access to knowledge movement and also predates the World Wide Web [54].

Open access publishing has roots in electronic publishing experiments that began in the 1970s [55] and led to the adoption of the Budapest Open Access Declaration in 2002 [56]. The origins of open access to data go back even further. The World Data Center was established in 1955 to collect and to distribute data generated by the observational programs of the 1957–1958 International Geophysical Year. Scientists from 67 countries participated in the data collection that year and agreed to share data generated from cosmic ray, climatology, oceanography, Earth's atmosphere and magnetic research, with a view to making the data available in machine-readable formats [57, 58]. One year later, in 1959, representatives of 13 governments agreed on scientific collaboration enabled by a free sharing of scientific observations and results from Antarctica [59]. In 1966, the Committee on Data in Science and Technology (CODATA) was founded by the International Council for Science to promote cooperation in data management and use [60].

In 1982, the Internet era began and the open research data made a giant leap forward shortly thereafter. In the 1990s, several Internet-based open research data initiatives were introduced—The Committee on Earth Observation Satellites (1990), International Geosphere-Biosphere Programme (1990), US Global Change Research Program [61], Inter-American Institute for Global Change Research (1992), United Nations Framework Convention on Climate Change (1992), Intergovernmental Oceanographic Commission of UNESCO (1993), Global Climate Observing System (1993), International Social Science Council (1994), World Meteorological Organization (1994), University Corporation for Atmospheric Research (1995), Human Genome Project (1996) and American Geophysical Union (1997) [62].

The success of the Human Genome Project has also drawn the attention of governments, funding agencies and scientific organisations. In 2003, the Human Genome Project was completed. The same year marked the adoption of the Berlin Declaration on Open Access to Knowledge in the Sciences and Humanities, which called for open access 'to original scientific research results, raw data and metadata,

---

[27] See Lessig [52]. There are many ways to enable open access, including through publications and data repositories, dedicated websites, journal websites, etc. The two prevalent methods of delivery are (i) publication in open access journals and (ii) self-archiving in open access repositories (Green Road). See Harnad et al. [53].

source materials and digital representations of pictorial and graphical and scholarly multimedia materials' [63]. The open science story continued to unfold.

An important earlier milestone was the launch of arXiv, originally developed as a repository of preprint publications in high energy physics, in 1991. The arXiv model was developed on an existing infrastructure that supported the flow of information within networks of close colleagues, known as invisible colleges [64]. Hosted by Cornell University, the model later expanded to other scientific fields and established the culture of exchange of preprint publications that later inspired the principle of open access to publications as we know it today.

Previously, many journals refused to consider papers posted online on the grounds that such posting constituted 'prior publication'. Over the years, the practice became more readily accepted by publishers, and arXiv has expanded to other fields to science. Competing platforms have emerged, such as the Sponsoring Consortium for Open Access Publishing in Particle Physics[28] developed by CERN, the European Organization for Nuclear Research and Inspire [65], an overarching High Energy Physics information system also developed by CERN and interconnected with arXiv.

The movement for open access to research data is built on those early foundations with open access to scholarly publications. In the 1990s, calls for recognition of open scientific data by key international organisations came, such as the OECD. In the Declaration on Access to Research Data from Public Funding adopted on 30 January 2004, the OECD recognised 'that open access to and unrestricted use of data promotes scientific progress and facilitates the training of researchers' [66, 67]. Three years later, the OECD codified the principles for access to research data from public funding [68].

Similar declarations and statements came later from the European Commission (2008) and were followed by mandates for open access to scientific data introduced by research funders, with the National Institutes of Health being the first in 2003. In 2010 the National Science Foundation announced that all future grant proposals would require a two-page data management plan and that the plan would be subject to peer review [69]. The policy was a tipping point in stimulating similar mandates outside the United States. In the following years, similar policies mushroomed in other parts of the world. Some countries have even legislated to require open access to research data. The policies and mandates of research funders are examined more fully in the next chapter.

Another driver for the movement in support of open access to data is the increasing use of 'e-research'[29]—the application of digital technologies to research and to research practice, whether in current or new forms. E-research is forcing some rethinking of the means for producing and sharing scientific and scholarly knowledge. The development of digital communications and novel ways of creating and handling data are creating an interest in 'data-led science' [71]. Generally, e-research refers to large-scale science involving global collaborations. Enabled by

---

[28] After several pilot projects, SCOAP was formally launched in January 2014 and was extended at least until 2019. From January 2018 SCOAP will also support HEP publications in three journals of the American Physical Society.

[29] The term e-science is most popular in the United Kingdom, continental Europe, Australia, and some other parts of Asia. In the United States, other parts of Asia, and other parts of the Americas, the concept of cyberinfrastructure for research is more common. The difference between these terms is interesting. One stresses the practice of research, the other the infrastructural condition for that practice, but both concepts are understood to refer to a shared view of computationally intensive research as a qualitatively novel way of doing research. See Jankowski [70].

the Internet, these typically require access to very large data collections and high-performance computing and visualisation capabilities that the originating scientists can access. Dominant in e-science are the disciplines of physicists, computer scientists, life scientists and some computational social sciences [72]. Yet the prospect of e-research has spread out across the entire scholarly community, including the interpretative social sciences and humanities.

Clearly, open access to publicly funded research data is a mainstream development associated with broader moves towards open science or Science 2.0, an approach that attempts to open up the process of scientific research for review and broader uptake. Open science advocates the sharing of scientific knowledge over the Internet by challenging the application of exclusive property rights over scholarly outputs. This movement further promotes 'digital openness' in the conduct of science and scientific communication, facilitating online access to scientific publications and research data. The resulting open scientific content and emerging online communities are reshaping the fundamental processes of science creation and dissemination.

In general terms, policymakers and open data advocates are seeking to drive changes in the ways data is created, managed, shared and reused. Adoption of these practices will require a shift in the behaviour of researchers and in established practices of research, including data sharing and data preservation practices. These processes are taking place alongside and are intimately connected with the evolution of digital technologies and interactive communications. Open science is developing and building upon the body of digital knowledge, data and infrastructure that it inherently generates. Central to these changes is a developing ecosystem, with novel means for creating and using scientific data to generate knowledge and to use this knowledge for social and economic benefits.

2.2 Open scientific data in the evolving knowledge economy

To understand the role of data and science in the changing knowledge economy, it is necessary to look at the approaches for producing and disseminating scientific knowledge and how these have developed over time and also at how science and scientific knowledge relate to other areas of society. This social role of science is important, because the characteristics of scientific data are shaped in the context of the production and use of scientific knowledge. Indeed, data, information and knowledge have become the central features of an evolving knowledge economy in which innovation plays a central role [36, 73–75]. The terms data, information and knowledge are often used interchangeably, even though many scholars have studied the evolution of these expressions and the differences among them, resulting in many books devoted to this subject [76–87].

2.2.1 Defining and differentiating the terms

Broadly speaking, data consists of figures without any interpretation or analysis [88]. Information captures data at a single point—in other words, the data has been interpreted to provide meaning for the user. And information can lead to knowledge, by combining it with experience and insight.[30] As such, data involves a lower level of abstraction from which information and then knowledge are derived [89]. A detailed discussion of concepts of 'data' and 'open data' is provided in Chapter 4 of this book.[31]

---

30 *Ibid.*

31 See Chapter 4, especially Sections 4.2 and 4.5.

In reality, however, the boundaries between data, information and knowledge are not always clear. What is data to one person can be information to someone else. What seems to matter, though, is the capacity of humans to use data and information to develop meaningful knowledge. Also important is the capacity of humans to interpret data as well as to process and absorb knowledge developed by others. These attributes have been identified to be crucial to knowledge and technology transfer [90–92]. They are also crucial factors in the development and adaptation of computer-assisted data processing and artificial intelligence.

In the operational context, the Reference Model for an Open Archival Information System defines information as 'any type of knowledge that can be exchanged. In an exchange, the knowledge is represented by data' [93, 94]. However, data can change over time. The mistake people often make is to think that the information presented is always an accurate reflection of data. Yet that information can only be as accurate as the data underpinning it, and as data changes so can the information derived from it. Buckland [86] looked at the subtle differences in further detail and distinguished between information as process, as knowledge, or as a thing [86].

The differentiation between 'information' and 'knowledge' is also apparent in the theories underpinning the creation of knowledge in society. There are subtle differences between the information society and the knowledge society, the two terms most commonly used. Although the term 'knowledge society' was coined by Drucker back in 1969 [95], further development occurred only in the 1990s by Mansell & Wehn [96] and Stehr [97]. According to Wessels et al. [89] and Castelfranchi [32], knowledge society produces, extracts value from, and makes data available to all its members. The key objective of the knowledge society is to improve the human condition [32].

However, a knowledge society cannot be achieved simply by providing universal education, nor can it be achieved by making information technologies available to everyone, or by making information previously accessible only to selected circles available freely to all.

Castelfranchi argues that the driving force of a knowledge society is its 'cognitive capital'—that knowledge has become an actively productive factor of economic development.[32] He also notes that knowledge itself is 'intrinsically motivated' and that a real knowledge society would be a society guided by this value—meaning that the motivation to engage in knowledge consumption and production would arise from within the society and its members because knowledge is naturally satisfying to them. But this is exactly what is not happening, Castelfranchi notes. The proposed vision for a knowledge society is one of an instrumental and subordinated activity; it is a society in which knowledge has to justify its utility and in which science is no longer a curiosity-driven activity. He goes on to say that today even virtues have to demonstrate they are 'useful'.[33]

In this sense, the definition of a knowledge society is similar to the theory of an 'information society' that treats information as the key commodity in production, consumption, and innovation. Information can be used to create knowledge to fuel innovation and economic growth. However, knowledge in an 'information society' circulates within selected economic, political and social networks and has a more limited social agenda of inclusion than a knowledge society.[34]

A knowledge society is distinct from an information society and a knowledge economy because

---

[32] *Ibid*, 1.

[33] *Ibid.*

[34] Wessels, at point 24.

> *... it sees information and knowledge as open to all. Its central value is openness, which means that data, information and knowledge are seen as a 'commons' or shared asset in society. This has the potential to allow any member of society to use data to engage and participate in economic, social, political and cultural projects.*[35]

Both theories—a knowledge society and an information society—posit that the creation and accumulation of knowledge can lead to economic growth. As such, the vision of both theories is the creation of a knowledge economy.

To understand the role of data and science in this evolving knowledge economy, it is necessary to briefly look at the ways of production and dissemination of scientific knowledge and how these have developed over time and how science and scientific knowledge relate to other areas of the society. The social role of science is important, because the characteristics of scientific data are shaped in the context of the production and the use of scientific knowledge. This approach was also advocated by American sociologist Robert K. Merton, who argued that the production and role of knowledge need to be understood through the 'modes of interplay between society, culture and science' [98]. Specifically, he studied the relationship between science and religion.

2.2.2 Mertonian science

Following on from the claim by Max Weber that the Protestant work ethic drove the emergence of the capitalist economy, Merton argued that the ascendance of Protestantism and the arrival of experimental science were similarly interwoven [98, 99]. Merton held that science became popular in seventeenth century England and was taken up by the Royal Society, which at that time was dominated by Puritans and other Protestants, because Protestant values corresponded with the emergence of new scientific values, resulting in 'modern science'. Merton separated science from religion, which was a major shift in understanding the position science has in society. In particular, Merton differentiated between science as 'handmaiden' to theology during the Middle Ages and the 'modern science' emerging from the seventeenth century onwards. This shift from science as an adjunct of theology to 'modern science' is also known as the Scientific Revolution.[36]

Merton also defined the four sets of norms of modern science as the following:

- *Communalism*—the common ownership of scientific discoveries, according to which scientists give up intellectual property in exchange for recognition and esteem.
- *Universalism*—according to which claims to truth are evaluated in terms of universal or impersonal criteria, and not on the basis of race, class, gender, religion, or nationality.

---

[35] *Ibid.*

[36] The transformation of science into an autonomous discipline began in Europe towards the end of the Renaissance period and continued through the late eighteenth century. This scientific turn also influenced the Enlightenment. The 'modern science' included mathematics, physics, astronomy, biology (including human anatomy), and chemistry. The institutionalisation of modern science was marked by the establishment of the Royal Society in England in the 1660s and the Academy of Sciences in France in 1666.

- *Disinterestedness*—according to which scientists are rewarded for acting in ways that outwardly appear to be selfless.
- *Organised scepticism*—all ideas must be tested and be subject to rigorous, structured community scrutiny.[37]

These four characteristics are often referred to as the principles of the Mertonian sociology of science and are often put forward for the development of open science.

2.2.3 Modern science

Thomas Kuhn elaborated on the concept of scientific revolutions in 1962. In his seminal work *The Structure of Scientific Revolutions,* commonly viewed as one of the most influential books of the twentieth century, Kuhn challenged the Mertonian view of progress with what he called 'normal science'. In Kuhn's view, scientific change occurs as a process with a number of stages, leading to paradigm change. He argued that 'normal' scientific progress occurs through the accumulation of generally agreed facts and the theories built on them. Kuhn argued that progress occurs episodically—periods of conceptual continuity, or 'normal science', are disrupted by episodes of 'revolutionary science'. During such revolutionary periods, anomalies are discovered that challenge established theories and lead to new paradigms requiring that old data be questioned in new ways. Consequently, a new paradigm moves from the 'puzzle-solving' function of its precursor and so changes the rules of the game by motivating renewed research activity.[38]

As in any community, Kuhn argued that some scientists are bolder than their colleagues. Whether because they see that a problem exists or for some other purposes, these pursue 'revolutionary science' to explore alternatives to established assumptions. From time to time, such activity creates a rival framework of scientific thought. The candidate paradigm, being new and incomplete, may appear to have numerous anomalies and will meet opposition from the general scientific community. However, at some point, the attitudes of scientists will change, and the anomalies will finally be resolved. Those with the ability to recognise a new theory's potential will be the early adopters of the challenging paradigm, Kuhn said. Over time, as the challenger paradigm is tested and as views unify, it will replace the old model. Thus, a 'paradigm shift' occurs.[39]

2.2.4 Digital science

One of the paradigm shifts in science envisaged by Kuhn was the emergence of the Internet and communication technologies. Toffler [102] coined the term the 'Third Wave', which he saw as the Information Age that succeeded Industrial Age society (the 'Second Wave') in developed countries [102, 103]. The new society characterised the combination of knowledge and information as the principal factor in the exercise and distribution of power, replacing wealth. The era is further

---

[37] Merton, at point 33.

[38] See Kuhn [100]. Asking new questions of old data on pages 139, 159. Moving beyond 'puzzle-solving' on pages 37, 144. Change in rule sets on pages 40, 41, 52, 175. A similar view was expressed by Bronowski in [101], that is, all fundamental scientific discovery 'opens the system again' and 'to some extent are errors with respect to the norm' on pages 108 and 111.

[39] *Ibid,* Kuhn [100].

characterised by the emergence of novel technologies and scientific fields such as global communications networks, DNA analysis and nanotechnology.

Toffler also predicted that the rise of the Internet will transform the very nature of democracy. In an interview discussing his book, Toffler said that the centralised, top-down management and planning used in industry would be replaced by a style that he called anticipatory democracy—more open, democratic and decentralised.[40] However, Toffler was aware of the limitations of the Information Wave. He was convinced that a society needs more than just cognitive skills: it needs skills that are emotional and affectional. He said that a society cannot be run on data and computers alone [104].

At the same time, the emergence of the Information Wave has ushered in a new era in scientific communications and impacted the production and practice of science. Previously, modern science had become the exclusive system in society for knowledge production, with few opportunities for lay people and amateur scientists to participate in science utilisation and production [105].

This has changed with the evolution of the Internet, which is:

> *... shaping the move away from traditional science and research while, at the same time, developing further ... not least influenced by the development it has originally initiated [106].*

In the second stage, the changes induced by new communication technologies have led to digital science, sometimes also referred to as cyberscience, or open science, as qualitatively distinct from 'modern science'. Nentwich [106] has argued that this model leads to a qualitative 'trend extrapolation'[41] and to the more or less complete replacement of old ways of practising science as the result of enabling by new cybertools.

Similarly, in the book *The New Production of Knowledge: The Dynamics of Science and Research in Contemporary Societies* published in 1994, a team of authors proposed that there had been a shift in the production of scientific knowledge from what they termed 'Mode 1' to 'Mode 2'.

Mode 1 was *characterised by the hegemony of theoretical or, at any rate, experimental science, by an internally driven taxonomy of disciplines and by the autonomy of scientists and their host institutions, the universities* [33].

Mode 2 is a new approach to knowledge production that is *socially distributed, application-oriented, transdisciplinary, and subject to multiple accountabilities*.[42]

As a result of the emergence of digital communications, the production of scientific knowledge in *Mode 2* is more centrally located within social relations. This also means that data is viewed in a different way to that found in *Mode 1*. The key difference is that if data is produced through publicly funded research, then the broader public should have a right to access it. Furthermore, according to *Mode 2* knowledge production, data is seen as having value through its reuse by a broader range of users than just the research community that produced the data.[43] Data users include researchers, policymakers, businesses and citizens, and there is a belief that each of these users will advance within their own domains through the democratisation of science. This, in turn, will lead to a more informed public that is better able to participate in social debates and the development of the society [27].

---

[40] *Ibid*, Toffler [103].

[41] *Ibid*, 48.

[42] *Ibid*.

[43] Wessels, at point 24, 56.

At the same time, research practices are also becoming more complex and include input from societal actors such as business and research funders (whatever their motives), among others.[44] So it can be argued that the users of scientific data are likely to include two types of external actors—transdisciplinary users applying scientific data to advance their own fields of endeavour, such as new technology development, and scientific users applying the data to advance science. However, the increasing number of stakeholders and groups also means that they may hold differing views of what data is and what it means for knowledge production, and this may complicate the process of making data open.[45]

Yet another issue arising in *Mode 2* of scientific knowledge production is in the form of the market forces that influence society and the production of science. Science is rarely characterised by the open paradigm, Fuller argued [107]. Researchers have the tendency to organise themselves in competitive networks, each seeking to control funding, academic appointments and the conduct of associations and journals. Much of the history of science documents those struggles and the displacement of one network by another.[46] These pressures are likely to continue into the future, even though digital science makes research more transparent and enables checking of research quality.

In *Mode 2*, the criteria that determine quality are indicative of a broadening social composition in the system of review. The implication is that 'good science' becomes more complex to assess; it is no longer confined to the judgements of peers within the discipline. Broadening the review system does not, however, necessarily mean that the research becomes of lesser value. Instead, it gains complexity ([33], p. 8).

Other market influences on the mode of scientific production are the increasing linkages between industry and academia and the push to commoditise and commercialise research. These are further discussed in the section below dealing with the inherent tensions between open data and commercialisation of scientific knowledge.

For now, I will outline the issues raised by Nowotny et al. [33] who observed that specialised knowledge plays a crucial role in many dynamic markets.[47] Specialised knowledge holds a vital place as a source of created advantage—both for its producers and users of all kinds. As a result, the demand for specialist knowledge is increasing. The core of the thesis of science production introduced by Nowotny et al. is that the expanding numbers of potential knowledge producers run in parallel with the expanding demands for specialist knowledge. The effect is to create the settings for the evolution to a new model for scientific knowledge production.

This and the push to commoditise and commercialise research have implications for all institutions—whether in the academic world or as private sector research stakeholders—that have an interest in the production of scientific knowledge. As markets for specialised knowledge emerge, so must the game change for all these institutions, albeit not necessarily all at the same pace.[48] The economic aspect of these developments is that knowledge-based innovation enables companies to generate market power and monopoly rents because, even though knowledge is nonrivalrous (can be used simultaneously by many agents without detracting from its

[44] Wessel at point 24, 119.
[45] *Ibid.*
[46] *Ibid.*
[47] *Ibid*, 12.
[48] *Ibid*, 13.

utility), it is at least partially excludable (innovating firms can restrict access to the novel features of their inventions) [108]. This causes problems in that public knowledge can be easily appropriated as a private good, the economic returns of which may not later return to the broader society. For these reasons, the cultivation and preservation of the scientific commons are of outmost importance.

From the discussion above, it is clear that the changing modes of both science production and science utilisation in the Internet era have had a significant impact on the ways scientific knowledge and data are created and utilised. It is clear that the combination of a proliferation of data and the open data movement is a significant feature in advancing a knowledge society and the attendant knowledge-based economy.[49] The actions of many actors, who organise themselves in networks and interact with a range of public and private level stakeholders with whom they exchange digital data, are a key aspect of this process. To increase these linkages and knowledge utilisation, it is necessary to make the data widely available. Open scientific data can bridge this gap while contributing economic and social benefits.

However, to achieve this goal, the data will have to be provided in a manner that permits not just sharing but also reuse across society.[50] This aspect is not well covered in the theories of knowledge society, which for the most part envisage that merely releasing scientific data into the public domain is sufficient for the benefits of open data to accrue. The model proposed in this book rebuts this argument, positing that simply providing *access* to data in the public domain is useless to the society and that only data *reuse* can realise the envisaged benefits. These aspects are canvassed in Chapter 8.

2.3 The envisaged benefits of open scientific data

Of the many benefits put forward for the adoption of open science in general and open scientific data in particular, some can already be seen in practice, while others will only become apparent as open data collection increases.

2.3.1 Solving great problems facing humanity

Open scientific data is important because the need to share scientific outcomes has perhaps never been greater. As nearly every region feels the effects of climate change, as conflict and food insecurity are rising, and as the demand for natural resources increases, the world looks to science for solutions. This world is interconnected—over 40% of its population was able to access the Internet in 2013, and the number of users online is growing exponentially ([109], p. 3). In this global digital village, open science offers hope—hope for those living in prosperous societies and hope for the remaining half of the globe, over 3 billion people, who live on less than US$2.50 a day [110].

Ease of access to scientific data, knowledge and application will play an enormously significant role in the planet's future well-being. Yet it may not be science alone, but rather the knowledge and discipline that it imparts and the learning that it yields when shared broadly and applied wisely. For science to deliver its full value to the society, it must be easily and freely accessible [5].

---

49 Wessels at point 24, 14.

50 *Ibid.*

2.3.2 Increased dissemination and impact of research

At present the majority of science is not easily accessible, and only a fraction of it is freely accessible despite the fact that scientific knowledge is plentiful and growing rapidly—doubling, on average, every 15 years.[51] Indeed, the current system of science generates massive volumes of knowledge and data. Yet much of the knowledge and data stays locked in institutional repositories, costly scientific journals, or patent applications. Locking up knowledge does not contribute to the greater good. Statistics confirm this—90% of scientific publications are *never cited*, and up to half of the world's scientific papers are *never read* by anyone other than their authors, referees, or editors [111, 112], while 98.5% of patents are *never asserted* [113]. Many scientific outcomes are lost because of the failure to make them available to those who could use them and add value. This gap between the capacity for science creation and its dissemination is a 'dual tragedy'—a tragedy of science and a tragedy of society—as Australian science commentator Julian Cribb put it.[52]

Open science can help bridge this gap. The Internet, Web and social networking have created new opportunities for disseminating scientific research, by sharing research data sooner and more widely. Much science is publicly funded, and the society increasingly expects that the outcomes of public science will be freely available. In the United Kingdom, Australia and in many other countries, universities constitute the primary recipients of government funding for research. In recent years, governments in these countries have taken considerable steps to develop mechanisms to increase the economic, social and environmental impact of science. Releasing research data is a logical step.

The 2009 study of the economic effects of open access to Australian public research found that a one-off increase in accessibility to public sector research and development produces an estimated return to the national economy of A$9 billion over 20 years.[53] The potential economic benefits of open research data are immense, indeed. In addition, there is an increased research impact realised from investing in curated research data activity. Early evidence shows that when researchers make their well-managed and curated data accessible along with publications, they can expect an increase of up to 69% in the number of citations.[54]

2.3.3 Reduced duplication of research effort

Open scientific data has the potential for significant savings to be realised through better targeting of scientific effort and reduced duplication of research. Scientists, especially early career scientists, devote a great deal of their time to data collection. Moreover, the cost of collecting data for multiple research projects can be high, especially for clinical trials and drug testing [116]. If projects complement or build on one another, why would it be necessary to provide funding for a research team to generate new datasets when another existing dataset could shed light on the problem? Further, is it really necessary to create a dataset that would be used just by one research team for a single project and then be discarded?

---

[51] See Larsen and von Ins [6]. The rate of doubling of the body of scientific knowledge was calculated as an average number of scientific records included in the following databases: Web of Science (owned by Thomson Reuters), Scopus (owned by LexisNexis), and Google Scholar. Duplicate entries were removed.

[52] Cribb, at point 62.

[53] See Houghton and Sheehan [114]. Public sector R&D was defined as 'the proportion of R&D stock available to firms that will use it' and 'the proportion of R&D stock that generates useful knowledge'.

[54] See Piwowar et al. [115]. Their subsequent research found that cancer clinical trials that share their microarray data are cited about 70% more frequently than clinical trials that do not.

Data that is shared, reused and recycled can achieve savings or free resources for new research. It is important that both scientists and research funders recognise this. Given the wealth of information collected in clinical trials, it is apparent that there is a variety of secondary uses that could enhance scientific advances in ways not foreseen by original authors. Indeed, the ability to access and reuse existing research can enable follow-on research and discoveries faster and more cheaply and can also facilitate the reproducibility of results.

2.3.4 Enhanced quality of scientific outcomes and methods

Openness has been the core principle of scientific enquiry since the early days of modern science. Henry Oldenburg, a German theologian and the first secretary of the Royal Society, pioneered the peer review of scientific publications. In 1655 he referred to the printing press as:

> *... the most proper way to gratify those [who] ... delight in the advancement of Learning and profitable Discoveries [and who are] invited and encouraged to search, try, and find out new things, impart their knowledge to one another, and contribute what they can to ... the Universal Good of Mankind [117].*

Oldenburg's contemporary, Irish scientist Robert Boyle, sets two other precedents that shaped the future of science. Boyle published his results in lively English, making them accessible to those who did not speak Latin or were not trained as scientists. He also described his experiments in great detail so that others could reproduce them. In short, Boyle believed that science belonged to everyone and the principles of science could be tested and repeated by anyone [118].

The vision of open science is to enable scientists and the general public to access and scrutinise scientific results—to 'search for the truth'—as double Nobel Laureate Linus Pauling famously defined science. And the truth is often interpreted to be an evidence. Science is based on the best evidence we have at the time. Evidence identifies what is true and what can be trusted. As science develops, new evidence confirms or rebuts previous evidence, resulting in self-correction. But often circumstances do not allow scientists to be 100% certain that their findings are true. They work with the best evidence available.

Scientific data typically presents the evidence. This needs to be assessed as to its degree of reliability, which then determines the degree of confidence that can be invested in the conclusion. In borderline cases, computer algorithms and replicated computer analyses can be used to probe the results. More often than not, computers can do science faster and more accurately than humans. Increasingly, they can perform computations that humans cannot. Open scientific data can serve as the springboard for computational science, or e-science. Such science brings high integration of modelling and simulations into the methodologies in particle physics, bioinformatics, earth, geospatial and social sciences.

2.3.5 Enhanced education

The long-term stewardship and open availability of research data also present better educational opportunities across all ages, all disciplines and all around the world. At the secondary education levels, students can use open data repositories to further their scientific understanding and skills. University students need open data to experiment with or to learn the latest data management techniques. In the digital era, the development of data science and data management and curation skills, which require a good educational foundation, is of particular interest to governments. These are growth areas for employment in an era of shrinking job opportunities [119].

2.3.6 Improved governance

Open research data repositories can play a role in supporting good governance. Openness of scientific information empowers non-scientific communities and the wider public to participate in knowledge creation and utilisation. Open datasets also enhance public decision-making [120], and open data policies can broaden the influence of governments [121]. Countries with limited public resources for devoting to science can benefit even more from access to public data resources [122]. In the context of increasing commoditisation of science, the governance of scientific data will become more important. Open scientific data empowers researchers, not markets, to control scientific knowledge into the future. Open scientific data thus leads towards a more transparent and accountable governance of science that, in turn, advances a more open, collaborative and democratic society.

2.3.7 Envisaged economic benefits and costs of open scientific data

Quite rapidly, data is becoming 'the lifeblood of the global economy' and represents 'a new type of economic asset'—the European Commission has recently stated [123].[55] Between 2008 and 2012, worldwide cross-border trade in data increased by 49%, while trade in goods or services rose by just 2.4% [124]. As the world adopts new technologies facilitated by data—technologies such as artificial intelligence, blockchain and robotics—open scientific data presents enormous opportunities to reap economic benefits. Governments and industry recognise that knowledge of the use of these technologies provides a decisive competitive advantage—in better performance; in providing products better tailored to the user, through new services; and in fostering innovation.[56]

Data holds the enormous potential to create jobs and increase our wealth. In the European Union alone, 100,000 new data-related jobs will be created between 2014 and 2020 [125]. Another recent study found that big data analytics solutions have the potential to unlock an additional £241 billion (2015 prices) in economic benefits for the United Kingdom over the period 2015–2020.[57] This is equivalent to an average of 2.0% of that country's gross domestic product (GDP) per year. The global market for data-related hardware, software and professional services is booming at even faster rate and is predicted to reach €43.7 billion by 2019, or 10 times that of 2010 [127].

Such statistics demonstrate the impressive economic value of data in our society. Those data-related services predicted to grow dramatically include data-centre computing, networking, storage, information management and analytics. Public research organisations, including universities, are very well positioned to provide such services. Open scientific data can therefore be a precursor for such organisations seeking to expand into these areas. In the first place, however, the infrastructures for open scientific data need development. In addition to direct economic benefits in terms of employment opportunities for researchers and analysts, such infrastructures will generate additional economic benefits derived from supporting

---

[55] European Commission (2017).

[56] *Ibid.*

[57] From 2015 to 2020, the total benefit to the UK economy of big data analytics is expected to amount to £241 billion or £40 billion on average per year [126].

the goals of research and innovation. It may take some time to identify and to measure those wider benefits, however.

In the context of open data, economic studies that have established the benefits of public sector information (PSI) and, more recently, open research data exist. The studies measuring the economic benefits of PSI [128–133] all concluded that the benefits accrued would exceed the revenue received from charging users for data. In Europe, the direct PSI reuse market was quantified to represent €32 billion in 2010 and was growing at the rate of 7% annually [130].

The experience of the Australian Bureau of Statistics (ABS) provides a specific, documented example from a data-intensive government institution, one of only a few to compare the before-and-after effects of moving from a user-pays model to an open access policy. The study showed that after adopting a CC-BY common-use licence, the ABS saved the costs of sales transactions and sales staffing and experienced far fewer licence inquiries and so less demand on staff resources, as well as broad social uptake. The savings for the ABS amounted to about A$3.5 million per year and for users around A$5 million, among other efficiencies and accrued benefits.[58]

2.4 The costs of developing open data infrastructures

A major shortcoming of the economic studies measuring the impact of PSI is their inability to quantify, or at least to estimate, the level of public investments required to develop the underlying infrastructures for data release. In many cases, such infrastructures would have been well established before open access to data was introduced. In other cases, the infrastructures evolved over time and required modernisation or just a simple upgrade to enable packaging of data products, as was the case with the ABS [134]. However, the costs of developing open data infrastructures should not be underestimated.

With regard to research data repositories, several recent studies in the United Kingdom and Australia combined qualitative and quantitative approaches to measure the value of research data and measure its impact [135–140]. These studies have covered several research fields and organisations—including the Economic and Social Data Service (ESDS), the Archaeology Data Service (ADS), the British Atmospheric Data Centre (BADC) and the European Bioinformatics Institute (EBI). All the studies are based on the economic evaluation framework, incorporating both quantitative and qualitative methods, developed by Beagrie and Houghton. The economic methods are based on estimating a range of values—from those focusing on minimum values to methods that measure some wider impacts.

They incorporate two ways of expressing return on investment in the data centres—firstly, the ratio of users' value to investment in the centres, and secondly, the ratio of value of the additional reuse of the data hosted to investment in the centres, as depicted in **Figure 2**.[59,60] The proposed model is interesting and useful because it captures not only the user value (economic benefit) but also the investment value (economic costs).

Four interesting findings of the economic studies stand out.

Firstly, the value of research data to users was found to exceed the investment made in data sharing and curation in all the studies.[61] Secondly, research data have had substantial and positive efficiency impacts, not only in terms of reducing the

58 *Ibid.*

59 Beagrie and Houghton [138] at point 86.

60 *Ibid*, 9.

61 *Ibid.*

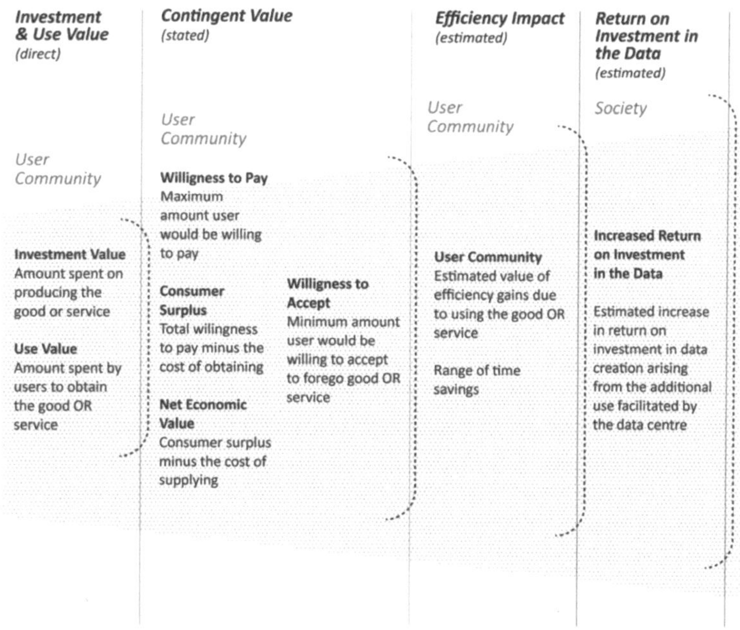

Figure 2.
The model estimating the value of open scientific data.

cost of conducting research but also enabling more research to be done—to the benefit of researchers, research organisations, their funders and society more widely. Thirdly, substantial additional reuse of the stored data was documented, with between 44 and 58% of surveyed users across the studies saying they could neither have created the data themselves nor obtained it from elsewhere.[62] Finally, the evaluation indicated that research data stored in repositories is reused by a wide range of stakeholders. Close to 20% of respondents to the ESDS and EBI user surveys, around 40% of the BADC user survey, and almost 70% of the ADS survey were from the government, non-profit and commercial sectors. Consequently, the value of public research data is being realised well beyond the academic sector.[63]

A unique feature of the ADS Impact Study was the inclusion of an analysis of the evolving, cumulative value of its archive, while other studies only provide a snapshot of the repository's value (which, the authors argue, can be affected by the scale, age and prominence of the data). In this regard, Beagrie and Houghton noted that in most cases data archives are appreciating rather than depreciating assets. Most of the economic impact is cumulative, and it grows in value over time. It will be important to capture this cumulative appreciative effect in future studies. Like libraries, data collections become more valuable as they grow, provided that the data remain accessible, usable and used.[64]

The early evaluations show that the economic benefits of open research data are already felt across many sectors. At the same time, the costs of developing open data infrastructures can be high, too. As Stallman has said, open is more akin to free speech than to free beer [141].[65]

Moreover, the responsibility for developing such infrastructures is not clear, which can lead to tensions. While the economic value of data grows over time, data

---

62 *Ibid*, 4–5.

63 *Ibid.*

64 *Ibid.*

65 Stallman (2002).

also needs to be curated over time, with significant costs. At present, most research grants only appear to cover data curation in the course of a research project and do not provide for ongoing curation. This aspect is not covered in the methodology developed by Beagrie and Houghton and needs to be explored further.

Berman and Cerf [142] discussed possible ways of funding open data infrastructures and concluded that there is no obvious actor to cover the costs [142]. Their assessment was that public research organisations are unlikely to allocate enough resources to support open data. The costs of infrastructure would absorb a great portion of their research budgets, and this is clearly not a sustainable option. The private sector has the capacity to develop such infrastructures; however, the business case and incentives for that involvement appear to be lacking.

One example of this difficulty is Google, a brand that is synonymous with data access. In early 2008 the company announced the Google Research Datasets program to store and make freely available open source scientific datasets, but by the end of that same year, the company had decided to end the project, diverting those resources elsewhere.[66] University libraries do not have the funds to curate open data, either. The solution, according to Berman and Cerf, might be an increased focus on developing partnerships and linkages[67] between the public and private sectors.

Another model is to develop supranational or national data infrastructures as is the case of the European Open Science Cloud spearheaded by the European Commission [144]. While the Commission is still working with member states on the definition of governance and financing for the initiative, the project is gaining a momentum. It is envisaged that over time, a co-funding mechanism mixing different revenue streams will be set up to increase the accountability, build trust, share resources and build long-term capacity for European research data [145].

One further economic challenge associated with the implementation of open research data is the restriction on data sharing because commercialisation appears to be a greater priority for policymakers, as discussed in the following sections.

2.5 Open data and commercialisation of public research

Open science challenges the application of exclusive property rights over scholarly outputs and calls for free access and reuse of scientific outputs. However, the open science movement has emerged at the time when major governments are decreasing their funding for research[68] and when there is a shift in the private

---

[66] *Ibid.* See also Google Blogoscoped [143].

[67] *Ibid.*

[68] Spending on R&D in government and higher education institutions in OECD countries fell in 2014 for the first time since the data was first collected in 1981. Countries with declining public R&D budgets include Australia, France, Germany, Israel, the Netherlands, Poland, Sweden, the United Kingdom, and the United States. See OECD [146].
In the United States, for the first time in the post-World War II era, the federal government no longer funds a majority of the basic research carried out in the country. Data from ongoing surveys by the National Science Foundation (NSF) show that federal agencies provided only 44% of the US$86 billion spent on basic research in 2015. The federal share, which topped 70% throughout the 1960s and 1970s, stood at 61% as recently as 2004 before falling below 50% in 2013. Also, in the United States, investments in research and development as a percentage of discretionary public spending have fallen from a 17% high at the height of the space race in 1962 to about 9% today, reflecting a shift in priorities of the government. The biggest decline has taken place in civilian research and development, which has dropped significantly as a proportion of both GDP and federal spending. See Mervis [147].
In the United Kingdom, the research funding slumped below 0.5% GDP in 2015 and has been declining steadily since 2009. See Rohn et al. [148].

sector to increasingly draw on public research.[69] Many governments now require publicly funded research organisations to increase the impact of public research and generate income through the protection and commercialisation of intellectual property, including through the creation of start-up enterprises.[70] The need for commercialisation has affected the goals of government research funding, causing public sector research agencies to justify the success of their research by proving or providing a convincing argument for the future economic value of their science and technology bases [151]. In countries such as Australia and the United Kingdom, universities supplement a vast portion of their income from tuition fees received from international students.[71]

The push towards commoditisation and commercialisation of public research leads to new tensions [38, 40]. Data from publicly funded research can have commercial value and lead to new partnerships with industry. Open access to research data also leads to new business models that will enable significant economic returns to be realised a few years down the track, as was the case with the open genomic data, as illustrated below.

The seemingly opposing trends towards opening research data and increasing the commercial returns from public research appear to be closely connected to the development of new technologies. On the one hand, policymakers are trying to open up research data to speed up innovation and the development of new technologies; on the other hand, they are trying to privatise and protect more and more research and emerging technologies with intellectual property, thus preventing the data and research from being shared in the future. These tensions were already pronounced in the early stages, as demonstrated in the project to map human genes.

2.5.1 Human Genome Project

In 1984, the US government started planning for a grand scientific project looking to map and decipher the entire human genome. But instead of doing it in secret laboratories in one country alone, this project brought together genome sequencing institutions from around the world. In the early 1980s scientists in many

---

[69] For example, in the pharmaceutical sector in the United States alone, roughly 75% of the most innovative drugs, the so-called new molecular entities with priority rating, trace their existence to the National Institutes of Health (NIH). See Angell [149].
Chesbrough has shown that technology companies require timely access to knowledge as they increasingly innovate by combining research outputs from external and internal sources and increasingly draw on research from universities and other public research organisations [11, 12].

[70] The policy measures advocated by the OECD in this regard focus on balancing stable institutional funding with a fair level of pressure from competitive R&D project grants, on encouraging the commercialisation of public research, and on improving science-industry relations and other linkages within the national innovation system and internationally. Increasing public research links with industry and their contribution to innovation is another main policy objective, because there is increasing pressure for public investments in research to be held accountable for their contribution to innovation and growth. Two types of measures are typically used—one is to link public research organisations and universities to other innovation system actors, particularly firms, through collaborative R&D programmes, technology platforms, cluster initiatives, and technology diffusion schemes and another is to better commercialise the results of public research through science and technology parks, technology incubators, and risk capital measures in support of spin-offs, technology transfer offices, and policies on intellectual property of public research. Source: OECD Public Research Policy [150].

[71] In 2016, over 20% of revenue of Australian universities, 6.25 billion AUD was received from fee-paying overseas students. See Department of Education and Training [152].

countries started to use computer technology in researching genetics and DNA sequences—developing processes for generating such data in digital formats.

Encouraged by these early experiments, the Human Genome Project got underway in 1990 and was initially funded by the Department of Energy and the National Institutes of Health in the United States. Their laboratories were joined by over 20 collaborating institutions from across the globe, including from the United Kingdom, France, Germany, Japan and China [153]. In 2003 the International Human Genome Sequencing Consortium announced that its project was complete —2 years ahead of schedule, under budget, and with 99.99% accuracy.[72]

The success of the Human Genome Project resulted from the convergence of science, technology and society in recording one entire human DNA sequence—around 3 billion letters of genetic code. This is the code that opened doors to improved understanding of human health as well as the detection and diagnosis of many diseases.

An important accelerator was a meeting in 1996 of representatives from sequencing centres around the world. At that meeting in Bermuda, scientists committed to make genomic data publicly available prior to publishing their findings in a scientific journal. Agreement on that principle was among the major achievements of the Human Genome Project and has, it is argued, had as much influence as the sequencing outputs themselves.[73] Over the years, sharing of genomic data has become a more established practice and biological research has exploded. The practice of data sharing demonstrated the enormous capacity of the research community to mobilise—a shift in how scientists work together as a global community to create knowledge.

The commitment to data sharing resulted from a fierce battle over the nature and ownership, and ultimately control, of the human genome. Two years after the Bermuda meeting a private gene sequencing company called Celera Genomics was set up in California. Celera owned a sizeable number of genome sequencing machines and aimed to build its own human genomic database, which it would only make available to subscribers. Celera also intended to claim ownership of 300 clinically-important genes and, at some stage, filed over 6000 patent applications to this end.[74] The emergence of this powerful competitor created a fresh impetus for the Human Genome Project. In the United Kingdom, one of the key scientists in the field later suggested that 'it has not been a race but a battle to ensure that the tools to speed biomedical research were available to all' [155].

The battle went on for about 3 years. On 26 June 2000 the White House hosted a press conference that changed the rules. In front of representatives of the International Human Genome Consortium and Celera Genomics, President Bill Clinton announced that both public and private research teams were committed to publishing their genomic data simultaneously, for the benefit of researchers in every corner of the globe.[75] Later that year, the Human Genome Sequencing Consortium published in

---

[72] *Ibid.*

[73] *Ibid.*

[74] Dr. Craig Venter, the Managing Director of Celera, later abandoned most of these applications, in response to promises made at US Congress in 1998. Releasing the entire human genome into the public domain extinguished patentability of all applications filed after the release date. A patent search conducted in 2009 revealed only 4 patents granted to Celera. See Cook-Deegan and Heaney [154].

[75] Office of the Press Secretary, *Remarks Made by the President, Prime Minister Tony Blair of England (via satellite), Dr. Francis Collins, Director of the National Human Genome Research Institute, and Dr. Craig Venter, President and Chief Scientific Officer, Celera Genomics Corporation, on the Completion of the First Survey of the Entire Human Genome Project*, media release, The White House, Washington, 26 June 2000 (http://www.genome.gov/10001356).

Nature while Celera's findings appeared in *Science*. The methodology presented by Celera was criticised by many scientists, who argued that the company's assembly of the genome would not have been possible at the time without the data released by the Human Genome Consortium. In retrospect, Celera may have well been the first commercial user of open genomic data published in GenBank—a distributed database that stores the DNA sequence in various locations around the world.

The sequencing of the human genome, as a single undertaking, had a scale unmatched in the history of biological science. The resulting dataset spearheaded the democratisation of science and has transformed medicine, renewable energy development and food production across the globe [156]. Open genomic data brought together an understanding of the whole of humanity for the benefit of all. And the United States, the key investor in the project, has reaped the majority of the economic benefits of the project.

Today, GenBank supports a multi-million dollar genomics research industry to develop DNA-based products. The initial investment of the US government of approximately US$3.8 billion, or approximately 0.075% of the country's GDP, has developed the critical tools to help identify, treat and prevent the causes of many diseases. The project further created huge growth opportunities for the high-tech American biotechnology industry, which accounted for more than three-quarters of US$1 trillion in economic output, or 5.4% of GDP, in 2010 [157]. The project further created over 300,000 jobs in the United States alone.[76] A single private-sector actor would have never succeeded in creating such a spillover of knowledge and innovation—government funding of open data infrastructures did.

In the Human Genome Project, government-funded research has played an active role in innovation and the creation of new markets for that innovation, with the resultant economic growth. It is this kind of innovation-led, 'smart' growth that requires strategic investments in innovation and mission-oriented projects, as leading innovation economist Mazzucato has argued [158, 159]. However, a common economic narrative regarding market creation positions the private sector as the principal force for innovation, with contributions from the public sector only important in setting the conditions for that private sector activity. Government investments in open data projects and infrastructures can actively shape and create new lucrative markets, while enabling the more equitable and sustainable sharing of the fruits of public research. These types of government investments can spur genuine innovation and create breakthrough technologies, Mazzucato argues.[77]

There are other examples in which public investments in scientific open data infrastructures have generated new and substantial economic returns and business opportunities, as illustrated later in this chapter by the well-known Global Positioning System technology. Open data can also enable enormous savings of public money by facilitating swift responses to public health emergencies. This capacity of open scientific data was powerfully demonstrated during the outbreak of a highly virulent *E. coli*-strain bacterium in Germany in May 2011.

2.5.2 *E coli* epidemic, Germany 2011

In May and June of 2011, almost 4000 people in 16 countries mysteriously fell ill with digestive symptoms. Almost a quarter of them suffered haemolytic uremic syndrome. In many cases, the syndrome led to kidney failure. Of those who were affected, 54 people died. The highly virulent *E. coli*-strain bacterium was found to

[76] *Ibid*, at point 111.
[77] *Ibid*.

be resistant to common antibiotics. There appeared to be no cure and the source of the infections was not known either. These dramatic events brought together scientists from four continents to work on what later became known as the 'world's first open source analysis of a microbial genome' [160].

Researchers from the Beijing Genomics Institute had first analysed the strain, working closely with their colleagues in Hamburg. Three days later a full genomic sequence of the bacterium was published [161]. By enabling free sharing[78] and permanent access to the original results[79] the Chinese microbiologists spurred dynamic international collaboration. Just 1 day later the genome was assembled and within a week over 20 reports were filed on a website dedicated to crowdsourced analysis of the bacterium.[80] The reports were crucial to identifying the strain's virulence, resistance genes and effective treatment. These efforts, along with concentrated measures taken by public authorities and doctors, resulted in the epidemic being averted.

Thanks to open data, the cure for the epidemic became known earlier than the source of the epidemic. Open data revealed that the epidemic was caused by an enteroaggregative *E. coli* strain, not an enterohemorrhagic strain, as originally thought. Open data further revealed that the strain had acquired the genes that produce Shiga toxins present in organic fenugreek sprouts. This hint led to the source of the epidemics being discovered. The agriculture minister of Lower Saxony identified an organic farm in Bienenbuettel that produced a variety of sprouted foods to be a source of the epidemic. The farm was immediately closed.

The value of human lives saved is priceless. The costs associated with the epidemic being averted cannot even be estimated. Every day of waiting would have resulted in more people falling sick and more people dying. The key economic benefits of dealing with public health emergencies like this lies in the swift response. In this case, open data was the key.

2.5.3 The global positioning system

The global positioning system (GPS) is a space-based radio navigation system owned by the US government and operated by the United States Air Force. According to the National Aeronautic Space Agency, GPS originated in the 1950s during the time of the Soviet Union's first Sputnik satellite mission. Scientists in the United States found they could track the satellite by monitoring its radio transmissions and measuring the shifts in those signals, analysing the Doppler effect that an observer experiences as an object moves past. In the mid-1960s, the United States Navy is built on this experience to conduct experiments with satellite navigation for the purpose of tracking US submarines carrying nuclear missiles. The submarines observed the Doppler changes of six satellites that orbited the poles and were able to pinpoint their locations within minutes [162].

When the Department of Defence sought to build a robust, stable, satellite navigation system in the 1970s, it decided to use those satellites to support a navigation system that took on the earlier ideas and experiences of Navy scientists. The result was the launch in 1978 of the first Navigation Satellite Time and Ranging system. Comprising 24 satellites, the system became fully operational in 1993.

---

[78] The original strain was published under the Creative Commons Zero licence.

[79] EHEC Genome with a DOI name [http://datacite.wordpress.com/2011/06/15/ehec-genome-with-a-doi-name/ (15 June 2011)]. The genome data is available at: http://gigadb.org/dataset/100001.

[80] GitHub Inc. is a sharing platform principally used by computer programmers. See the page: ehec-outbreak-crowdsourced/BGI-data-analysis. https://github.com/ehec-outbreak-crowdsourced/BGI-data-analysis/wiki/_pages.

Meanwhile, in 1985, the GPS technology became available to any user as a GPS receiver. That service[81] remains available worldwide to all users with no direct charges.

The GPS technology rapidly became a subject of intensive innovation, especially as it was infused with other applications. Over time, GPS became embedded in virtually every communication device. The economic benefits of GPS accrued to the United States up until 2013 were estimated at about US$56 billion, or 0.3% of national GDP.[82]

From the case studies listed above, it is clear that the development of open technologies and open data infrastructures has an enormous economic potential to harness greater returns from public research. It appears that the benefits reaped from open data and open technologies surpass, by some distance, the economic benefits received from licencing and IP commercialisation of public research[83], especially in the university sector where many patents are 'sleeping patents'—meaning that they remain commercially unexploited, are neither licenced nor used internally, and are not held for purely defensive purposes.[84] The effect is that the patented knowledge cannot be shared but, at the same time, is not generating any economic or other benefits. The result is a net loss associated with the cost of IP protection.

Open data and open technologies can lead to substantial economic benefits, and the value of open data assets and collections will further appreciate over time [166, 167]. For these reasons, scientific open data assets have a far greater potential to generate economic returns from public research than the returns received from commercialisation of public intellectual property.

The public function of research is best upheld in collaborative spaces that are open to all stakeholders—researchers working in the public and private sectors—all around the world. There is also ample evidence showing that open data and open scientific knowledge can effectively spur collaborations with the private sector and lead to the development of new technologies faster.[85]

---

[81] GPS currently provides two levels of service: Standard Positioning Service (SPS) that uses the coarse acquisition (C/A) code on the L1 frequency and Precise Positioning Service (PPS) that uses the P(Y) code on both the L1 and L2 frequencies. Access to the PPS is restricted to the US Armed Forces, US federal agencies, and selected allied armed forces and governments. The SPS is available to any user globally. Source: NASA [162].

[82] Results of a 2015 study commissioned by the National Executive Committee for Space-Based Positioning, Navigation and Timing. See GPS World Staff [163].

[83] According to the OECD, in Australia, Europe, and the United Kingdom, the licencing revenue received from IP hovers around 1% of R&D expenditure and appears to be declining. In the United States, the figure stood at 4% in 2011 and the revenue was also declining. A study by the Brookings Institution found that 84–87% of US universities do not realise enough income to cover the costs of running their technology transfer office. See Valdivia [164].
In the United States, the top 15 universities with the highest income received from intellectual property received only US$1 billion from licencing revenue in 2015. Just over US$400 million of commercial income was received from intellectual property licencing by the top 15 biomedical research institutes. See Hugget [165].
Patents, licencing income, and spin-offs are frequently used indicators to assess an institution's or a country's capabilities to turn public research into innovation. In terms of patent applications filed by universities in the United States, the average annual growth rate fell from 11.8% (2001–2005) to 1.3% (2006–2010), while other public research organisations experienced a negative growth of −1.3% over the latter period, compared with 5.3% growth recorded between 2001 and 2005. Source: Cervantes and Meissner [166].

[84] *Ibid, 77.*

[85] For example, Chesbrough argued that an important element of 'open innovation' is the use of purposive inflows and outflows of knowledge to accelerate internal innovation [12, 168].

Conclusion

The nature, dissemination and use of scientific knowledge are profoundly changing in the context of the digital revolution. Digital technologies have provided the means to collect, process, analyse, store and disseminate vast amounts of data. These technological advances are changing the core processes of science production, with a shift away from the modern science espoused by Thomas Kuhn towards the digital science emerging in collaborative online spaces.

For open science, data has a role that has changed from how it was treated in earlier contexts of science creation. The key among the differences is the principle that data produced in publicly funded research should be openly available. In addition, there is a growing view that the value of data is multiplied when it is shared with a range of stakeholders beyond the research community that initially collected it. In this changing context, as data becomes more accessible, it opens the way to uses that can create new knowledge and fuel innovation and economic growth, thus furthering the aims of a knowledge-based society. Open scientific data aims to encourage, for the first time in history, the participation in science creation, validation and dissemination by both scientists and non-scientists.

As digital formats increasingly become the preferred means for data storage and distribution, computers alone now have the capacity to validate and generate scientific outcomes—a capacity that will grow further with advances in artificial intelligence and quantum computing, along with the development of algorithms that can rapidly process and calculate vast amounts of data to solve problems. Consequently, there is a strengthening argument to the effect that open scientific data challenges established research and science conduct and related communication practices. At the same time, open scientific data promises to beak the monopoly held by researchers over the validation and creation of scientific outcomes. This transformative social role of science is important and needs to be understood in the interplay between evolving technologies, advanced communication, changing culture and increasing education.

However, the calls for sharing of research data in electronic formats came well before modern digital technologies. The World Data Center was established in 1955, and major international scientific data projects emerged in the 1960s. Digital sharing of scientific data builds on these early foundations and took a huge leap forward in 2003 when the Human Genome Project was completed. The year 2003 also loosely marks the emergence of the open access movement, which brought renewed calls for greater availability of scientific data with the adoption of the Berlin Declaration on Open Access to Knowledge in the Sciences and Humanities.

The benefits of open data are well covered in the theories of innovation and in economic literature. Clearly, open data in general, and open scientific data in particular, holds an enormous potential to increase the social and economic benefits of public research. The economic benefits are already felt in those fields that adopted open scientific data early—fields such as genomic and geospatial research. As data has rapidly become a commodity in the global economy, scientific data represents a new type of economic asset. There is a decisive competitive advantage for those who know how to use open scientific knowledge. However, the increased demand for scientific knowledge also poses a risk to public science in the form of the increased privatisation of public research. The open science movement counterbalances these developments by placing a renewed emphasis on the broader dissemination and free sharing of scientific outcomes in the public domain.

At the same time, the benefits of open scientific data can only be realised if the infrastructures for open science are developed and if the data is not only openly shared but also gets reused. The reuse aspect is not well covered in the theories of knowledge society and digital science production. These theories view the release of scientific data into the public domain as sufficient for the economic and social benefits of open data to accrue. This chapter argues that while data sharing is a prerequisite, only data reuse can harness the envisaged returns on investments in open scientific data.

The three parameters identified in this chapter—the changing role of scientific knowledge in society, the possible benefits of scientific data and the necessity to reuse the data to realise the benefits—need to be viewed in relation to one another, Chapter 2 concludes.

In the next chapter, I follow up this thinking by examining the open data policies recently introduced by research funders and the potential of these policies to drive the release and reuse of open scientific data into the future.

Chapter 3

The Current Policies of Research Funders and Publishers

This chapter provides a review of the principles underpinning open scientific data and the policies mandating open access to scientific data. It has a specific focus on the policies of research funders and journal publishers.

The chapter consists of five parts, as follows:

1. Main international developments
2. Key policies of research funders
3. Selected policies of publishers
4. Issues covered in the open data policies
5. Open scientific data in emerging and developing countries

Introduction

Increased data sharing among scientists and with non-scientists can generate vast benefits to society and to the economy. Yet creating conditions conducive to data sharing remains a challenge. Inspired by the positive experience with open publications, similar policies have been introduced in recent years with a view to facilitating greater sharing of research data.

This chapter surveys open data policies, paying particular attention to the scope of the open data mandates. It starts with an overview of major international developments and declarations that have inspired governments and research funders to introduce open data policies. This is followed by an analysis of the policies of research funders and publishers in several jurisdictions. Next is identification of the components of ideal data sharing policies. The final section surveys the open data landscape in emerging and developing countries.

3.1 Main international developments

3.1.1 Early policies in the United States

Some of the world's leading research organisations are based in the United States. Many of them were also among the first in the world to recognise the potential of open science. The first policy statement for open access to research data consists of the Bromley Principles issued by the United States Global Change Research Program in 1991 [169]. Five years later the Bermuda Principles—developed as part of the Human Genome Project—established an international practice in the sharing of genomic data prior to publication of research findings in scientific journals [170]. These principles of free release and data sharing have been one of the major outputs of the Human Genome Project and have established the practice of genomic data sharing globally.

The *Access to Databases Principles* first published by the International Council for Science/Committee on Data for Science and Technology (ICSU/CODATA) in 2002 provided a further impetus for promoting open access to scientific data among policymakers [171]. The principles were developed to facilitate the evaluation of legislative proposals that may affect the use of scientific databases.

3.1.2 The Berlin Declaration

The Human Genome Project was declared complete in 2003. In the same year, open access to scientific data was first codified internationally, in the Berlin Declaration on Open Access to Knowledge in the Sciences and Humanities. The declaration emerged from a conference hosted by the Max Planck Institute in Munich and represents a landmark statement on open access to scientific contributions[86] including:

> *... original scientific research results, raw data and metadata, source materials, digital representations of pictorial and graphical materials and scholarly multimedia material [63].*

Such scientific contributions need to satisfy two conditions to quality as 'open':

First, the author(s) and right holder(s) of such contributions grant(s) to all users a free, irrevocable, worldwide, right of access to, and a licence to copy, use, distribute, transmit and display the work publicly and to make and distribute derivative works, in any digital medium for any responsible purpose, subject to proper attribution of authorship ... as well as the right to make small numbers of printed copies for their personal use.

Second, a complete version of the work and all supplemental materials, including a copy of the permission as stated above, in an appropriate standard electronic format is deposited (and thus published) in at least one online repository using suitable technical standards (such as the Open Archive definitions) that is supported and maintained by an academic institution, scholarly society, government agency, or other well-established organisation that seeks to enable open access, unrestricted distribution, interoperability and long-term archiving.[87]

Organisations committed to implementing these objectives and the two key principles can sign the declaration. As of October 2007, there were over 240 signatories, mostly research organisations. As of early June 2018, the number of signatories had reached 620 [172].

3.1.3 UNESCO and open science

The United Nations Educational, Scientific and Cultural Organization (UNESCO) is the only UN agency with a specific mandate for science. One of its main functions, articulated in the UNESCO constitution, is to:

---

[86] The Berlin Declaration does not use the term 'open research data' but rather refers to 'open knowledge contributions' which represent a broad definition of open research data. See also discussion concerning the definition of research data in the next chapter.

[87] *Ibid.* This definition of open data and open access is further discussed in Chapters 4 (Section 4.5) and Chapter 7 (Section 7.3) of this book.

> *... maintain, increase and diffuse knowledge: by assuring the conservation and protection of the world's inheritance of books, works of art and monuments of history and science, and recommending to the nations concerned the necessary international conventions.*[88]

At the same time, facilitating the sharing of scientific outcomes is only one of the many responsibilities assigned to UNESCO. Perhaps for this reason the organisation has not played a pivotal role in recommending any international conventions for open science in recent years. Many provisions of the UNESCO Declaration on Science and the Use of Scientific Knowledge—adopted in 1999—are now outdated due to rapid technological developments and changing methods of science production and dissemination.[89]

Having said that, one of the key objectives articulated in the Strategy on UNESCO Contribution to the Promotion of Open Access to Scientific Information and Research is to convene an international congress on scholarly communication to examine the feasibility of developing a UNESCO convention on open access for scientific information and research ([29], p. 13).

More recently, UNESCO endorsed several open science initiatives, including the Open Science for the 21st Century Declaration by All European Academies,[90] which encourage scientists and their organisations, particularly publicly funded organisations, to apply open-sharing principles to the data underpinning research publications, including negative results. The Declaration also calls for measures to ensure data quality and preservation to enable future reuse.[91]

In addition, UNESCO supports several public education projects aimed at raising awareness of open access, including in developing countries. In 2012, UNESCO issued Policy Guidelines for the Development and Promotion of Open Access written by Swan [27]. The report notes that:

> *Research data are increasingly covered by policies and often these policies are being implemented by smaller, niche players as well as large research funders. These policies are not usually, however, the same (Open Access) policies that cover the text-based literature. Data are exceptional because policies must take into account issues of privacy and special cases where data cannot be released for other reasons. Developing and wording Open Data policies is therefore a specialised issue that is not as straightforward as developing polices for Open Access to the literature. Where*

[88] Article 1, Clause 2 of the UNESCO Constitution.

[89] Article 38 of the Declaration states: 'Intellectual property rights need to be appropriately protected on a global basis, and access to data and information is essential for undertaking scientific work and for translating the results of scientific research into tangible benefits for society. Measures should be taken to enhance those relationships between the protection of intellectual property rights and the dissemination of scientific knowledge that are mutually supportive. There is a need to consider the scope, extent and application of intellectual property rights in relation to the equitable production, distribution and use of knowledge. There is also a need to further develop appropriate national legal frameworks to accommodate the specific requirements of developing countries and traditional knowledge and its sources and products, to ensure their recognition and adequate protection on the basis of the informed consent of the customary or traditional owners of this knowledge'.

[90] A declaration of ALL European Academies (ALLEA) presented at a special session with Mme Neelie Kroes, Vice-President of the European Commission, and Commissioner in charge of the Digital Agenda on occasion of the ALLEA General Assembly held at Accademia Nazionale dei Lincei, Rome, on 11–12 April 2012.

[91] *Ibid*, 5.

> *there is Open Access policy development now, Open Data policy development will follow.*[92]

In recent years, UNESCO has taken a more active role in developing open scientific repositories. One recent example is the World Library of Science [173], an online repository of short e-books and articles, developed in partnership with the publishers Nature Education and the pharmaceutical company Roche. This currently contains resources in the field of genetics intended for university undergraduate faculties and students. The platform enables science teachers and students from all parts of the world to exchange views, information and knowledge.

3.1.4 The OECD principles for access to research data from public funding

In January 2004, the ministers of science and technology from OECD countries and from China, Israel, Russia and South Africa adopted a Declaration on Access to Research Data from Public Funding. They also called on the OECD to develop a set of guidelines based on commonly agreed principles to facilitate optimal cost-effective access to digital research data [174]. The OECD responded with such a set of principles, published in late 2006, which highlighted the importance of open access to publicly funded research data.[93] The principles held that open access has a vast potential to improve the scientific and social return on public investment [175]. The OECD noted, however, that the level of public research funding varies significantly across countries, as do data access policies and practices at the national, disciplinary and institutional levels. The OECD Principles, summarised below, were developed with a view to providing broad policy recommendations to governments, research organisations and funding bodies:

Principle A. Openness—access on equal terms and at the lowest possible cost. Open access to research data should be easy, timely, user-friendly and preferably Internet-based.

Principle B. Flexibility—recognising the rapid and often unpredictable changes in information technologies, the characteristics of each research field and the diversity of research systems, legal systems and cultures of each member country.

Principle C. Transparency—information on research data and data-producing organisations and the conditions attached to the use of the data should be available in a transparent way, ideally through the Internet.

Principle D. Legal conformity—data access arrangements should respect the legal rights and legitimate interests of all stakeholders in a public research enterprise. Subscribing to professional codes of conduct may facilitate meeting legal requirements.

Principle E. Protection of intellectual property—data access arrangements should consider the applicability of copyright and other intellectual property laws that may be relevant to research databases. At the same time, the fact that there is private sector involvement in the data collection or that the data may be protected by intellectual property laws should not be used as a reason to restrict access to the data.

Principle F. Formal responsibility—formal institutional practices should be promoted. These include rules and regulations regarding the responsibilities of the

---

[92] *Ibid*, 47.

[93] The Principles define research data from public funding as the research data obtained from research conducted by government agencies or departments or conducted using public funds provided by any level of government.

various parties involved in data-related activities. The issues to be covered include authorship, producer credits, ownership, dissemination, usage restrictions, financial arrangements, ethical rules, licencing terms, liability and sustainable archiving.

Principle G. Professionalism—institutional arrangements for the management of research data should be based on relevant professional standards and values embodied in the codes of conduct of the scientific communities involved.

Principle H. Interoperability—technological and semantic interoperability is the key consideration in enabling and promoting international and interdisciplinary access to, and use of, research data. Member countries and research institutions should cooperate with international organisations in developing data documentation standards.

Principle I. Quality—data managers and data collection organisations should pay particular attention to ensuring compliance with explicit data quality standards.

Principle J. Security—supporting the use of techniques and instruments to guarantee the integrity and security of research data. Data integrity means completeness of the data and absence of errors. Security means that the data, along with relevant metadata and descriptions, should be protected against intentional or unintentional loss, destruction, modification and unauthorised access.

Principle K. Efficiency—improve the overall efficiency of publicly funded scientific research by avoiding unnecessary duplication of data collection efforts.

Principle L. Accountability—data access arrangements should be subject to periodic evaluation by user groups, responsible institutions and research funding agencies.

Principle M. Sustainability—research funders and research institutions should consider long-term preservation of data at the outset of each new project and determine appropriate archiving mechanisms for the data.

These core OECD Principles were the early guidelines for policymakers to promote open data, including open research data. These principles have been widely adopted. However, the definition of research data in this source is very narrow, referring to research data as:

> *…factual records used in primary sources … that are commonly accepted in the scientific community as necessary to validate research findings.*

Later documents have adopted a far broader approach to research data. These more recent policies are discussed in the following sections.

3.1.5 The Denton Declaration (2012)

In May 2012 [176], at the University of North Texas, a group of technologists and librarians, scholars, researchers and university administrators gathered to discuss best practices and emerging trends in research data management. Resulting from this discussion was a vision for openness in research data titled 'The Denton Declaration: An Open Data Manifesto'. The declaration includes 6 declarations, 13 principles and 7 intentions.

The principles set out general guidelines for open data in science:

1. Open access to research data benefits society and facilitates decision-making for public policy.

2. Publicly available research data helps promote a more cost-effective and efficient research environment by reducing redundancy of efforts.

3. Access to research data ensures transparency in the deployment of public funds for research and helps safeguard public goodwill towards research.

4. Open access to research data facilitates validation of research results, allows data to be improved by identifying errors and enables the reuse and analysis of legacy data using new techniques developed through advances and changing perceptions.

5. Funding entities should support reliable long-term access to research data as a component of research grants due to the benefits that accrue from the availability of research data.

6. Data preservation should involve sufficient identifying characteristics and descriptive information so that others besides the data producer can use and analyse the data.

7. Data should be made available in a timely manner: neither too soon to ensure that researchers benefit from their labour nor too late to allow for verification of the results.

8. A reasonable plan for the disposition of research data should be established as part of data management planning, rather than arbitrarily claiming the need for preservation in perpetuity.

9. Open access to research data should be a central goal of the lifecycle approach to data management, with consideration given at each stage of the data lifecycle to what metadata, data architecture, and infrastructure will be necessary to support data discoverability, accessibility and long-term stewardship.

10. The costs of cyberinfrastructure should be distributed among the stakeholders—including researchers, agencies and institutions—in a way that supports a long-term strategy for research data acquisition, collection, preservation and access.

11. The academy should adapt existing frameworks for tenure and promotion and merit-based incentives to account for alternative forms of publication and research output including data papers, public datasets and digital products. Value inheres in data as a stand-alone research output.

12. The principles of open access should not be in conflict with the intellectual property rights of researchers, and a culture of citation and acknowledgement should be cultivated rigorously and conscientiously among all practitioners.

13. Open access should not compromise the confidentiality of research subjects and will comply with principles of data security, HIPAA, FERPA [177, 178], and other privacy guidelines.

The intentions articulated the issues of most importance to librarians at the time. They include developing a culture of openness in research, building the infrastructure that is extensible and sustainable for archiving and making the data discoverable, developing metadata standards and recognising and supporting the intellectual property rights of researchers.

The principles are widely known among librarians in the United States and in other countries.

3.1.6 Other statements and policies supporting open scientific data

Several statements and policies have emerged promoting the dissemination of scientific data in online spaces following adoption of the Berlin Declaration and the OECD Open Access Principles. In 2009 the Toronto Statement reaffirmed earlier principles relating to the prepublication release of genomic data and recommended these principles be extended to other types of large biological datasets [179]. The Rome Agenda called for scientific data to be released immediately after the publication of journal articles [180]. The Panton Principle for Open Data in Science—developed in 2010—provides guidelines on licencing of open scientific data [181]. In early 2015, the Research Data Alliance released draft principles on the legal interoperability of research data [182]. These initiatives have facilitated broadening the scope and coverage of open access to research data to include prepublished, published and unpublished data—particularly data generated from publicly funded research.

Many attempts to define the principles of open scientific data also incorporate the challenges associated with implementation, thus restraining the scope for data sharing. These include legal, ethical and commercial limitations on data release; early availability and long-term preservation of research data; the management and curation of the data, metadata and software; sharing the costs of developing research data infrastructures; developing incentives and reward structures; facilitating searchability of the data; and respecting the privacy of research subjects. The challenges are clearly articulated in more recent and more comprehensive sets of principles for open scientific data, summarised below and canvassed in Chapters 4–7.

3.2 Key policies of research funders

For several years now, leading funders of research have required grant recipients to share their data with other investigators. However, originally they had no policies on how this should be accomplished. The game has changed completely in recent years, with many funders requiring the recipients of grants to enable open access to research data and, often, requiring the submission of research data management plans at the grant proposal stage. Such policies ensure that data resulting from publicly funded research is retained and can be reused over time—usually 3–10 years.

Research organisations and universities are largely dependent on grant funding. Suddenly, these institutions realised that to enable researchers to successfully compete for grants, they had to provide support in the formulation of data management plans. Libraries, too, have taken up this approach, and researchers are changing their research data management practices as a result. Within the past decade, the policies introduced by research funders appear to have built a momentum for significant organisational and behavioural changes, and these changes are driving the retention and sharing of research data globally.

3.2.1 The United States

The funders of research in the United States are the leaders when it comes to open research data. The National Institutes of Health (NIH) were among the first to introduce open access deposit of peer-reviewed journal articles in PubMed Central as a condition of receipt of grant funds.[94] The NIH also:

> *... expects a data sharing plan for all proposals over $500,000 per year in direct costs. Some research communities have developed their own policies [183] in which sharing is expected—and executed—for all grants, not just those over the $500,000 threshold [184].*

Awareness of the need to develop data management infrastructure took a leap forward in 2010 when the National Science Foundation (NSF) announced that it, too, would begin requiring data management plans with applications. Proposals submitted to NSF on or after 18 January 2011:

> *... must include a supplementary document of no more than two pages labelled 'Data Management Plan'. This supplementary document should describe how the proposal will conform to NSF policy on the dissemination and sharing of research results [185].*

Importantly, the data management plan is to be included with every application for NSF funding, even if the plan is a statement that 'no detailed plan is needed'. According to the NSF policy:

> *Investigators are expected to share with other researchers, at no more than incremental cost and within a reasonable time, the primary data, samples, physical collections and other supporting materials created or gathered in the course of work under NSF grants. Grantees are expected to encourage and facilitate such sharing. Investigators and grantees are encouraged to share software and inventions created under the grant or otherwise make them or their products widely available and usable.*[95]

The US government has taken significant steps to enable the dissemination of scientific outcomes arising from public research. On 22 February 2013, the Office of Science and Technology Policy at the White House issued the memo 'Increasing Access to the Results of Federally Funded Scientific Research'. It directed each federal agency with over US$100 million in annual research and development expenditure to develop plans to make 'the results of unclassified research arising from public funding publicly accessible to search, retrieve and analyse and to store such results for long-term preservation'.[96] The research results include peer-reviewed publications, publication metadata and digitally formatted scientific data. The major shortcoming is that the memo does not mention metadata associated with research data. This omission is unfortunate because, in many cases, scientific data without metadata is unlikely to be reusable.

The memo also directed agencies to ensure that intramural researchers and all extramural researchers receiving federal grants and contracts for scientific research

[94] The NHS requires that 'an electronic version of all final peer-reviewed journal articles accepted for publication on and after 7 April 2008 be made publicly available no later than 12 months after the date of publication'.

[95] See NSF Award and Administration Guide, Chapter VI—Other Post Award Requirements and Considerations, points 4(b) and (c). Available at: http://www.nsf.gov/pubs/policydocs/pappguide/nsf13001/aag_6.jsp#VID4

[96] *Ibid*, p. 3.

have data management plans in place along with mechanisms to ensure compliance with the plans. To support the implementation of data management plans, grant proposals may include appropriate costs for data management and access. Further, agencies are to promote the deposit of data in publicly accessible repositories and develop approaches for identifying and providing appropriate attribution to scientific datasets.

The memo builds on the NIH and NSF open data mandates and covers all larger federally funded organisations. Prior to the memorandum, only six federal funders of research had in place policies requiring the retention and sharing of research data —NIH, NSF, the National Aeronautics and Space Administration, the National Oceanic and Atmospheric Organisation, and the National Endowment for the Humanities, Office of Digital Humanities [186].

3.2.2 The European Union

The European Commission was one of the first major research funders to recognise open access to research data. The Commission considers that facilitating broader access to scientific publication and data can improve the quality of research results, foster collaboration, avoid duplication of research effort and improve the transparency of scientific enquiry—including through increased involvement by citizens [187]. Increasing access to the outcomes of publicly funded research lies at the core of the European policies. Underlying this vision is realisation that research outcomes originating from public sources should not require payment with each access or use. Instead, the outcomes should be preserved and made freely available for the benefit of all.

Open access to science falls broadly under three flagship initiatives of the Commission—namely the Digital Agenda for Europe [188], the Innovation Union Policy [189], and the European Research Area Partnership [190]. The Recommendation on Access to and Preservation of Scientific Information [191], published in July 2012, encourages European Union member states to develop policies for open access to scientific results, including research data and information. The Commission further stated that such policies should include concrete objectives and indicators of progress, implementation plans and appropriate funding mechanisms.[97] The Communication of the Commission regarding open access is not binding on European Union member states, and they are free to adopt any policy that best suits the needs of their own scientific communities. Some countries—Germany, Spain and the Netherlands—have legislated open access to scientific publications and data [192].

The European Commission was among the first large funders to test funding arrangements that encourage open access to publicly funded research. In 2008, the Commission launched the Open Access Pilot as part of its Framework Program 7 (later replaced by the Horizon 2020 Pilot) for data underlying publications, including curated data and raw data [21]. The Rules of Participation [193] represent the legal basis for open access to research data funded by the European Commission under Horizon 2020:

> *With regard to the dissemination of research data, the grant agreement may, in the context of the open access to and the preservation of research data, lay down terms and conditions under which open access to such results shall be provided, in particular in ERC (European Research Council) frontier research and FET (Future and Emerging Technologies) research or in other appropriate areas, and taking into*

[97] *Ibid*, Recommendation 3.

consideration the legitimate interests of the participants and any constraints pertaining to data protection rules, security rules or intellectual property rights. In such cases, the work programme or work plan shall indicate if the dissemination of research data through open access is required.[98]

These principles are translated into specific requirements in the Model Grant Agreement[99] under the Horizon 2020 Work Programme. The Commission has also developed a user guide that explains the provisions of the Model Grant Agreement to applicants and beneficiaries, including guidance for open scientific data, as follows:

Regarding the digital research data generated in the action, the beneficiaries [participating in the open research data pilot] must:

a. Deposit in a research data repository and take measures to make it possible for third parties to access, mine, exploit, reproduce and disseminate—free of charge for any user—the following:

   i. The data, including associated metadata, needed to validate the results presented in scientific publications as soon as possible

   ii. Other data, including associated metadata, as specified and within the deadlines laid down in the 'data management plan'

b. Provide information—via the repository—about tools and instruments at the disposal of the beneficiaries and necessary for validating the results (and, where possible, provide the tools and instruments themselves).[100]

The guidelines also define exceptions to data sharing. These include the obligation to protect research results with intellectual property, confidentiality and security obligations and the need to protect personal data and specific cases in which open access might jeopardise the project. If any of these exceptions is applied, then the data research management plan must state the reasons for not giving or restricting access.

3.2.3 European Research Council

The European Research Council (ERC) is a leading funder of research in the sciences and humanities. The ERC regards open access as the most effective way for ensuring that the fruits of the research it funds can be accessed, read and used in further research. On that basis, the ERC:

> *... considers it essential that primary data, as well as data-related products such as computer codes, is deposited in the relevant databases as soon as possible, preferably immediately after publication and in any case not later than 6 months after the date of publication [194].*

The guidelines also list discipline-specific repositories. The recommended repository for life sciences is the Europe PubMed Central [195] (formerly known as

[98] *Ibid.*

[99] Multi-beneficiary General Model Grant Agreement, Version 1.0 11 December 2013.

[100] Annotated Model Grant Agreement, Version 1.7, 19 December 2014, 215.

UK PubMed Central), and for physical sciences and engineering, the recommendation is to use ArXiv [196].

3.2.4 The United Kingdom

The peak body for research councils in the United Kingdom, Research Councils UK (RCUK, now transitioned into UK Research and Innovation),[101] instituted policies on open access in 2005 and their Common Principles for Open Data [198] that took account of the evolving global policy landscape. These Principles encouraged the practice of making research data openly available, with as few restrictions as possible, in a timely and responsible manner.[102] The Principles further addressed a number of important issues.

Firstly, data management policies and plans should be in accordance with community best practice and relevant standards set by research institutions themselves.[103] The onus for ensuring that legal, ethical and commercial issues are considered lies with research institutions, and these issues should be considered at all stages in the research process.[104]

Secondly, published results should always include information on how to access the supporting data. Metadata should be recorded and made openly available.[105]

Thirdly, the principles allow for the delay in data release to enable the original data collectors to publish the results of their research.[106]

Finally, public funds can be used to support the management and sharing of publicly funded research data.[107] At the same time, research organisations are responsible for ensuring there are enough resources allocated to research data management—for example, from research grants. RCUK clarified in 2013 that all costs associated with research data management are eligible expenditure of research grant funds, but the expenditure must be incurred before the end date of the grant [199].

Open data is thus defined as an integral part of doing research, and the costs are front-loaded into that research. This can initially make the conduct of research more expensive, but significant savings are realised down the track through the recycling of research data and improved quality of research outcomes. These principles are important as they address the concerns raised by several organisations and scientists who pointed out that open scientific data should not be an unfunded mandate [200].

Since the release of RCUK Common Principles on Data Policy in 2011, many member funding organisations have mandated the requirement for a data management plan with each new application. Most research funders in the United Kingdom have issued data policies; however, the extent and coverage of these vary greatly [201].

The RCUK policy on open access states:

Peer-reviewed research papers which result from research that is wholly or partially funded by the research councils:

---

[101] Subsumed into UK Research and Innovation in [197].
[102] *Ibid*, bullet point 2.
[103] *Ibid*, bullet point 3.
[104] *Ibid*, bullet point 5.
[105] *Ibid*, bullet point 4.
[106] *Ibid*, bullet point 6.
[107] *Ibid*, bullet point 8.

1. *Must be published in journals which are compliant with Research Council policy on Open Access*

2. *Must include details of the funding that supported the research and a statement on how the underlying research materials—such as data, samples, or models—can be accessed* [202]

Unlike the United States, where institutional approaches to research data management are developing, most research councils in the United Kingdom 'place the responsibility on individual researchers to provide evidence that data management and sharing issues have been considered' [203].

However, one research council—the Engineering and Physical Sciences Research Council (EPSRC)—took a different approach. The EPSRC encouraged research organisations to develop their specific approaches to data management, appropriate to their own structures and cultures. At the same time, these approaches were required to align with the EPSRC's expectations. To that end, EPSRC requested that applicant institutions develop road maps for open data management. These requirements appear to have acted as a catalyst for developing data management policies and support systems in many UK research organisations.

In 2015, RCUK provided publicly funded research institutions and investigators with explanatory text on each of the seven 'common principles' first developed in 2005. This guidance was intended to inform the RCUK consultation on a draft Concordat on Open Research Data[108]—a broader network of stakeholders and interested parties in open data. The Concordat committed to the seven 'common principles' adopted by the RCUK.

3.2.5 Australia

The Australian Government was among the first to invest in the development of research data infrastructure. The Australian National Data Service (ANDS) was established in 2008 to develop an Australian Research Data Commons platform [204]—an Internet-based discovery service designed to provide rich connections between data, projects, researchers and institutions. Funding was also allocated for the development of metadata tools through the 'Seeding the Commons' initiative.

Open research data is a priority area for the Data to Decisions Cooperative Research Centre established in July 2014. The centre brings together researchers and industry to contribute to the development of Australia's big data capability.

The Australian data management framework, which has emerged over time, is based on four principles:

1. The institutional data management framework is in accordance with the Australian Code for the Responsible Conduct of Research and other external legal and regulatory frameworks.

2. The research institution will support all aspects of the data lifecycle, through creation and collection, storage, manipulation, sharing and collaboration, publishing, archiving and reuse.

3. Data management is an essential part of doing good research and supporting the research community of which each researcher is a part.

[108] The Concordat on Open Research Data includes a broader coalition of UK funders and university stakeholders.

4. Effective data management is best achieved through teamwork and collaboration between researchers, research offices, information specialists and technical support staff.

While the principles were originally drafted to outline how responsibilities between research institutions and researchers should be divided, it is now clear that increasing the availability of open scientific data is a collective endeavour. At the same time, accountability for the preparation and curation of such data must be clearly assigned. It is for this reason that research funders, providers and researchers themselves are likely to remain the key stakeholders in this process. The Australian Code for the Responsible Conduct of Research (revised in 2007) remains the principal document guiding Australian research organisations and researchers in data management. The code states:

> *Each institution must have a policy on the retention of materials and research data. It is important that institutions acknowledge their continuing role in the management of research material and data [205].*

The Australian Research Council (ARC) and National Health and Medical Research Council (NHMRC)—two principal funders of national research—mandated open access to peer-reviewed publications in 2012. Starting from 2014, the ARC requires data publication for selected grants. The ARC Centre of Excellence funding agreement:

> *... strongly encourages ... the depositing of data and any publications arising from a Project in an appropriate subject and/or institutional repository [206].*

The NHMRC mandate did not extend to open data until early 2018. These very recent developments are covered in Chapter 8, Section 8.2.

3.2.6 Canada

The principal funders of research in Canada—the Canadian Institutes of Health Research (CIHR), the Natural Sciences and Engineering Research Council and the Social Sciences and Humanities Research Council—all adhere to open access practices in research. Following a long consultation process, the final version of their Tri-Agency Open Access Policy was released in March 2015. With regard to open data, several submissions suggested that all three agencies should practice long-term preservation and digital release. Yet only the CIHR has committed to a policy on open research data at this stage:

Recipients of CIHR funding are required to adhere with the following responsibilities:

1. Deposit bioinformatics and atomic and molecular coordinate data into the appropriate public database (e.g. gene sequences deposited in GenBank) immediately upon publication of research results.

2. Retain original datasets for a minimum of 5 years after the end of the grant (or longer if other policies apply). This applies to all data, whether published or not. The grant recipient's institution and research ethics board may have additional policies and practices regarding the preservation, retention and protection of research data that must be respected.[109]

[109] Article 3.2 of Ref. [207].

This policy applies to all CIHR grants awarded from 1 January 2008 and onwards. An important aspect that the data deposit is required (not just encouraged) for all CIHR grants.

3.3 Selected policies of publishers

Meanwhile, publishers are also having a profound influence, with changes to how they provide scholarly communications. Journal publication is the primary mode of disseminating scientific research. However, recent years have seen the emergence of data journals and of open access data repositories for holding the data associated with journal articles.

The best-known example of the latter is perhaps the Dryad Digital Repository [208], governed by a consortium of scientific members who collaboratively promote data archiving, free access, reusability and citation. Membership of Dryad is open to any stakeholder organisation—including journals, scientific societies, publishers, research institutions and libraries. Dryad initially covered biosciences and ecology studies and, in recent years, has expanded to other disciplines. Many libraries and research organisations now refer to Dryad as a generic data repository and recommend it for deposit in all instances where discipline-specific online repositories do not exist.

As a result of these practices, Dryad is increasingly becoming an interdisciplinary resource covering data from a variety of scientific fields and international sources. Data repositories such as Dryad can provide quicker access to findings in advance of results published in paper journals or e-journals.

The growing significance of data publications has prompted established journals to expand their offerings. In early 2014 the Nature Publishing Group announced a new peer-reviewed open data publication, *Scientific Data*. The journal introduces data descriptors—a combination of traditional content and structured data and information to be curated in-house. Such descriptors may include articles and data from multiple journals. The actual datasets will not be stored in-house but in a recognised discipline data repository[110] or, in the absence of such repository, in a more generic data repository such as Dryad. The initial focus of *Scientific Data* is on biomedical, life and environmental sciences—subject matter that appears to overlap with the initial collecting priorities at Dryad. It will be interesting to see how Dryad and *Scientific Data* differentiate themselves and develop into the future.

Another important driver of open research data is the changing policy among traditional journal publishers who increasingly require that underlying data be made available to both peer reviewers and readers. In many cases, the publishers also specify the requirements for sufficient data description so as to facilitate reuse and validation of the research findings. For instance, the policy of *Journal of the Royal Society Interface* states:

> *To allow others to verify and build on the work published in Royal Society journals it is a condition of publication that authors make available the data and research materials supporting the results in the article. Datasets should be deposited in an appropriate, recognised repository and the associated accession number, link, or digital object identifier (DOI) to the datasets must be included in the methods section of the article. Reference(s) to datasets should also be included in the reference list of the article with DOIs (where available). Where no discipline-specific data repository exists authors should deposit their datasets in a general repository such as Dryad [210].*

Similarly, the journal *Nature* has a policy on the availability of data and materials that implies that the data should be described sufficiently to allow for validation and reuse:

---

[110] *Nature* lists publicly-recognised data repositories on its website [209].

> *An inherent principle of publication is that others should be able to replicate and build upon the authors' published claims. Therefore, a condition of publication in a Nature journal is that authors are required to make materials, data and associated protocols promptly available to readers without undue qualifications.*[111]

Importantly, *Nature* reserves the right to refuse publication to authors who fail to comply with the journal's requirements on data availability.

This open data policy is far more specific and stringent than similar policies introduced by other publishers. An authoritative study by Vasilevsky et al. published in 2017 evaluated the open data policies of 318 biomedical journals [211]. That investigation found that only 12% of these journals required data sharing as a condition of publication—a policy similar to that of *Nature*.[112] Out of the journals surveyed, 23% explicitly encouraged or addressed data sharing, but did not require it as a condition of publication, while 9% required data sharing but made no explicit statement regarding the effect on publication. Additionally, 15% only addressed data sharing for specific subsets of genomic data. Sadly, 32% of all journals did not mention anything about data sharing.[113] The study confirmed earlier findings by the same authors that fewer than 50% of journals require data sharing [212].

However, in 2017–2018 many publishers introduced changes to their editorial policies that provide for greater transparency and openness, including statements on expectations for data sharing. Publishers typically choose one of the following approaches for implementing data transparency:

- **Option 1: Duty to disclose.** Published articles must state whether the data upon which they are based is available and must provide information on how to access it. The wording of publisher policies typically includes "sharing upon reasonable request" or "expects data sharing".

- **Option 2: Mandate to deposit.** Authors of articles must include in a trusted repository for the underlying data for sharing. If any portion of such data cannot be shared, this must be clearly identified while the authors must provide as much of the remaining data as can be reasonably shared. This type of policy typically focuses on creating "open data" or even "open FAIR data".

- **Option 3: Verification of reproducibility.** Open data must be verified by a third party to establish whether the data enable the replication of findings as represented in the article. This type of data is typically referred to as "peer-reviewed data".

The introduction of 2017–2018 policies by leading publishers, such as Springer Nature, Elsevier, Taylor and Francis, and Wiley, has appeared to have increased the expectations not only for the digital availability of research data, but also for the credibility and veracity of that data.

3.4 Issues covered in the open data policies

Reflecting on the above analysis of the emergent principles and policies in this chapter, it becomes clear that open scientific data extends open access to scientific

---

111 *Nature* at point 65.

112 *Ibid*, 18.

113 *Ibid.*

publications. Several issues need consideration when developing policies for open research data, specifically:

1. The 'data' that should be covered by the policy
2. The timeframe for releasing research data into the public domain and who is responsible for the data deposit
3. The period for storing the data in digital archives
4. Whether research data management policies should be required and, if so, whether they should be submitted at the grant proposal stage or later
5. How open access to research data should be provided and under what conditions
6. Whether to recommend specific data repositories or whether to leave the decision with the project participants
7. When data sharing may not be required and whether the reasons for not sharing should be known to the broader research community
8. Whether and how data deposits should be embedded in the rewards and recognition frameworks for researchers and their organisations
9. Whether compliance with the policies should be monitored and, if so, whether penalties should apply
10. How to foster an environment that enables researchers and the public to maximise the value of research data
11. How to encourage the sharing of the best practices and experiences with research data management, including data transparency, code transparency, design and citation standards, and replication policies.

While the above points represent an ideal open data policy, the current policies of research funders and journal publishers are highly fragmented, covering only selected aspects of the data preservation, sharing and reuse process. This gap leaves those aiming to implement open data in a position of experimentation. The gap also makes any comparative analyses difficult. Nevertheless, it is apparent that the open data mandates have created a momentum driving the release of research data in many parts of the world.

At the same time, the policies are more like high-level statements of principles and expectations rather than detailed guidelines for researchers. One particular concern is the unclear meaning of research data in the policies. At best, the list of possible research data outputs included in the policies is incomplete and lacks a level of detail. At worst, the definitions of 'data' provided do not appear to match the notions of data commonly used by the key stakeholders across different scientific disciplines. The inability to clearly acknowledge and articulate the heterogenous nature of research data is a major shortcoming of the open data mandates.

The above overview of policy statements supporting access to scientific data shows that all major players in the system have shown a commitment to open data. The policies also illustrate, however, that concerns about implementing open scientific data remain and require further attention. And while policies may state clearly what challenges exist, the solutions and best practices are only just starting to emerge.

Nevertheless, open scientific content is increasingly becoming readily available, largely due to policies recently introduced by research funders and publishers.

3.5 Open scientific data in emerging and developing countries

Elsewhere in Europe and Asia, open scientific data practice is already in place, and it is emerging in many Latin American countries. Yet these policies are not readily available in English and therefore are not analysed in this chapter. The awareness of open access has increased rapidly in recent years, with countries including China introducing open access mandates.

3.5.1 China

Chinese research output has increased rapidly—from 48,000 articles in 2003, or 5.6% of the global total, to more than 186,000 articles in 2012, or 13.9% [213]. Of those, more than 100,000, or 55.2% of the global share, involved some funding from the National Natural Science Foundation (NNSF) of China, one of the country's major basic science funding agencies. This administered the equivalent of US$3.1 billion in its 2014 budget.[114] The research output from the Chinese Academy of Sciences (CAS)—which funds and conducts research at more than 100 institutions—is also impressive. CAS scientists published more than 18,000 Science Citation Index[115] articles in 2012 and more than 12,000 articles in Chinese journals [214].

On 15 May 2014, these two principal funders of research in China announced an open access policy for publications. Researchers supported by NNSF or CAS should deposit their papers into online repositories and make them publicly accessible within 12 months of publication. The policies are modelled around those introduced by the NIH in the United States and came into effect the same day they were announced.[116] At this point the open access mandate does not appear to extend to scientific data.

Both CAS and NNSF plan to release more detailed guidelines on implementation. In particular, the NSFC will establish a repository into which researchers can upload papers. This repository is likely to be modelled on PubMed Central developed by the NIH.[117] CAS started developing a network of repositories for its institutes 5 years ago and has a central website [215] for searching them. As of December 2013, more than 400,000 articles had been deposited and had generated 14 million downloads.[118]

3.5.2 Central and Eastern Europe

Many countries in Central and Eastern Europe have well-developed digital infrastructures, and several countries have increased their R&D expenditure in recent years. Estonia and Slovenia now spend more on R&D than the European Union average. The Czech Republic has reached a level that is close to the average, while Hungary, Lithuania, Latvia, Slovakia, and Romania spend significantly less than the average.[119] While these countries do not appear at this stage to have formulated open access policies, the digital agenda promoted by the European Union and the

---

[114] *Ibid.*

[115] Science Citation Index is a bibliometric tool offered by Thomson Reuters. The index provides citation information for articles in included in the Web of Science database.

[116] Xialing Zhang at 72.

[117] *Ibid.*

[118] Xialing Zhang at 72.

[119] R&D expenditure measured as a percentage of Gross Domestic Product. See the OECD Science, Technology and Innovation Indicators [216]; and for non-OECD countries Eurostat [217].

conditions already embedded in European grants are likely to drive the digital sharing of research outcomes originating from these countries in the near future.

3.5.3 African countries

In large parts of Africa, scientific education remains underdeveloped, and funding for science is lacking. At the same time, many African countries have, in recent years, adopted important open access and open government projects and also have committed significant resources to develop relevant infrastructures. The vision for the open access movement in Africa is to spur development and promote the transfer of technologies to the continent.

Kenya recently announced the establishment of a pilot regional data-sharing centre at the Jomo Kenyatta University. The centre aims to accelerate the generation, analysis, management, and archiving of scientific data emanating from Africa. Other significant open data programmes are implemented in Kenya [218], Morocco [219], Tunisia [220], Tanzania [221], Sierra Leone [222], Nigeria [223, 224], and Ghana [225]. In addition, the African Development Bank sponsors the Open Data for Africa Initiative [226] that aims to enhance the statistical capacity of African countries as well as provide the tools necessary to monitor developments, such as progress with implementing the Millennium Development Goals.

It will be interesting to see how open scientific data will be used in innovative ways to promote development across Africa.

Conclusion

The early stages of implementing data stewardship in open science are promising. Key players in the system—research funders, governments, and leading publishers—have made a clear commitment to open scientific data and have developed policies governing it. Such policies are now in place in the developed world and Latin America and are starting to emerge in other countries.

These policies have created a momentum for data curation and are driving the release and sharing of research data globally. Data journals and discipline-specific data repositories have emerged and are becoming more popular. Scientists are increasingly aware of the need to share data and are more readily prepared to work with librarians to develop and implement research data management policies.

Yet challenges remain. The policies for open scientific data explicitly list limitations to data release. This appears to have sent mixed messages to research organisations. Instead of focusing their efforts on finding opportunities for data sharing, many have diverted their resources to ensuring compliance with existing limitations.

In the long term, this stage can be necessary to identify best practices for responsible research data management. In the short term, however, this stage may have delayed data release for other purposes, with major concerns surrounding research data management, particularly the interface between intellectual property and open knowledge, and the sharing of data involving personal information of subjects involved in data collection.

A major shortcoming of the open data policies is the high-level statements of objectives and expectations. They provide little guidance to researchers regarding the preparation of data management plans, the curating, and the sharing of data. One particular concern is the unclear meaning of research data, which leaves many researchers guessing what 'data' they need to make available.

These concerns are examined further in the next chapter, which discusses the meaning of open scientific data.

Chapter 4

The Unclear Meaning of Open Scientific Data

This chapter aims to shed light on the meaning of open scientific data—a term problematic to conceptualise in both policy and practice of open data.

The discussion is structured as follows:

1. What is data?
2. What is scientific data?
3. What falls outside the scope of 'research data'?
4. What is missing in the scope of 'research data'?
5. What makes research data 'open'?
6. The limits of openness

Introduction

The previous chapter found that well-intentioned open data policies do not accommodate the diversity of meanings that can be applied to the term 'data' when used across different scientific disciplines and research projects. Few research funders or publishers define data other than by listing examples of what 'data' might be. The previous chapter also found that such non-exhaustive examples lack the detailed guidance researchers need when depositing data.

This chapter attempts to unpack the notion of 'open scientific data', in all its complexity. It starts by considering the notions of 'data' in the context of scientific enquiry. This is followed by the analysis of the definitions of 'research data' in the open data policies in place. The last part of the analysis centres on the requirements for data 'openness' and 'reuse' and how these terms are evolving as they are adopted by various stakeholders, across different scientific disciplines, and in various contexts. Gaps in the current landscape are identified, along with issues not covered in the definitions and issues falling outside the scope of 'research data' and 'openness'.

Three themes emerge in this chapter—firstly, that the current definitions do not adequately describe open scientific data and the difficulties of conceptualisation, secondly, that the policies create confusion among researchers about the requirements for data deposit and adequate description of the data, and thirdly, that researchers themselves need to be better motivated to take a more active role both in describing the data they produce and in reusing data created by others.

4.1 What is data?

The term 'data' is a plural form of the Latin 'datum'. The term has several meanings in the English language. According to English Oxford Living Dictionaries, 'data' can refer to facts or statistics collected together for reference or analysis, or it can refer to the set of principles accepted as the basis of an argument:

> *... historically and in specialised scientific fields, it is also treated as a plural in English, taking a plural verb, as in the data were collected and classified. In modern non-scientific use, however, it is generally not treated as a plural. Instead, it is treated as a mass noun, similar to a word like information, which takes a singular verb. Sentences such as data was collected over a number of years are now widely accepted in standard English.*[120]

'Data' as a collective noun can refer to a set of known facts or things used as a basis for inference or reckoning.[121]

At the same time, some prominent scholars of digital communications have suggested that data indeed 'are' various 'objects' or 'entities'. Therefore, they continue to treat 'data' as plural.[122]

Another consideration is the very notion of 'scientific data'—which is, as this chapter finds, a term not defined and understood consistently among the key stakeholders. It may therefore be appropriate to approach data as an ever-evolving 'concept' and 'evidence underpinning scientific knowledge' rather than as specific 'objects'. This book adopts the latter approach and, therefore, 'data' is used collectively.

4.2 What is scientific data?

Scholars and researchers tend to interpret 'scientific data' in the context of 'research data' collected in the course of scientific experiments. The terms 'research data' and 'scientific data' are often used interchangeably and irrespectively of the subject collecting the data—whether the subject is a researcher or whether the data collection is semi-automated, such as through online questionnaires, or fully automated, such as data harvested by scientific equipment. 'Research data' may therefore take many forms, come in different formats, and come from various sources.[123] As such, the term 'research data' was meant to be broadly inclusive [230]. Perhaps for this reason, major policies and guidelines define 'research data' by examples.

Some important stakeholders, such as the Research Data Australia Registry developed by the Australian National Data Service, accept data records that their research communities consider to be important, rather than according to an external standard for 'research data' [231]. The reason for this position is simple: there is no established meaning of 'research data'. The analysis below illustrates the diversity of definitions of the term as it has been adopted by key stakeholders.

Among the earliest and most commonly used definitions is that which appeared in 1999 in the National Academies of Science report:

---

[120] Definition of data in the English Oxford Living Dictionaries [227].

[121] Data defined in [228].

[122] For example, Borgman, who consistently uses 'data' to signify plural, has recently defined research data as 'entities used as evidence of phenomena for the purposes of research or scholarship' ([167], p. 29). Borgman cites Rosenberg's historical analysis of the term 'data' who concludes that data remains a rhetorical term, without an essence of its own, neither truth nor reality [229]. However, in the context of scientific communications, and in this book, 'data' is interpreted to be the best possible truth about reality as we know it today.

[123] Borgman [167] at point 3.

> *Data are facts, numbers, letters, and symbols that describe an object, idea, condition, situation, or other factors.*[124]

In 2011, the academies clarified that—in addition to all digital representation of literature (whether text, still or moving images, sound, models, games, or simulations)—the term also applies to:

> *... forms of data and databases that generally require the assistance of computational machinery and software in order to be useful, such as various types of laboratory data including spectrographic, genomic sequencing, and electron microscopy data; observational data, such as remote sensing, geospatial, and socioeconomic data; and other forms of data either generated or compiled, by humans or machines.*[125]

The National Institutes of Health in the United States defines data as:

> *... recorded information, regardless of the form or media on which it may be recorded, and includes writings, films, sound recordings, pictorial reproductions, drawings, designs, or other graphic representations, procedural manuals, forms, diagrams, work flow charts, equipment descriptions, data files, data processing or computer programs (software), statistical records, and other research data [232].*

Such a notion of data spans many fields of science, acknowledging some of the many forms that data can take. In this context, the principles and guidelines developed by the Organisation for Economic Co-operation and Development (OECD) define 'research data' as:

> *... factual records (numerical scores, textual records, images and sounds) used as primary sources for scientific research, and that are commonly accepted in the scientific community as necessary to validate research findings. A research data set constitutes a systematic, partial representation of the subject being investigated ([68], p. 13).*

The Committee on Ensuring the Utility and Integrity of Research Data in a Digital Age, representing three influential research organisations in the United States, defines 'research data' as:

> *... information used in research to generate research conclusions which includes raw data, processed data, published data and archived data and exist in the form of textual, numeric, equation, statistics, images (whether fixed or moving), diagrams or audio recordings.*[126]

From the perspective of researchers, clarity around open scientific data is central to both the conduct of research and preservation of its outputs. As a general guide, the Digital Curation Centre in the United Kingdom recommends that researchers should consider how they will maintain access to any research data that may be necessary for enabling the validation of their research findings [234]. One leading research institution, the University of Glasgow, states:

---

[124] National Research Council (1999), 15.

[125] Uhlir and Cohen (2011) at point 4.

[126] Committee on Ensuring the Utility and Integrity of Research Data in Digital Age ([233], p. 22).

... research data should be interpreted as any material (digital or physical) required to underpin research. For different disciplines this may include raw data captured from instruments, derived data, documents, spreadsheets & databases, lab notebooks, visualisations, models, software, images, measurements and numbers [235].

The Australian Code for the Responsible Conduct of Research provides researchers with the following guidance:

... while it may not be practical to keep all the primary material (such as ore, biological material, questionnaires or recordings), durable records derived from them (such as assays, test results, transcripts, and laboratory and field notes) must be retained and accessible. The researcher must decide which data and materials should be retained, although in some cases this is determined by law, funding agency, publisher or by convention in the discipline. The central aim is that sufficient materials and data are retained to justify the outcomes of the research and to defend them if they are challenged. The potential value of the material for further research should also be considered, particularly where the research would be difficult or impossible to repeat [236].

In line with those guidelines, the Queensland University of Technology defines research data as:

... data in the form of facts, observations, images, computer program results, recordings, measurements or experiences on which an argument, theory, test or hypothesis, or another research output is based. Data may be numerical, descriptive, visual or tactile. It may be raw, cleaned or processed, and may be held in any format or media [237].

In its policy on the management of research data and records, the University of Melbourne identifies 'research data' as:

... facts, observations or experiences on which an argument, theory or test is based. Data may be numerical, descriptive or visual. Data may be raw or analysed, experimental or observational. Data includes: laboratory notebooks; field notebooks; primary research data (including research data in hardcopy or in computer readable form); questionnaires; audiotapes; videotapes; models; photographs; films; test responses. Research collections may include slides; artefacts; specimens; samples. Provenance information about the data might also be included: the how, when, where it was collected and with what (for example, instrument). The software code used to generate, annotate or analyse the data may also be included.

The University of Melbourne makes no functional distinction between physical research products, digital research data and records of research, which can include items such as correspondence, application documents, reports and consent forms [238].

The Monash University Research Data Policy has a similarly encompassing definition:

Research data: the data, records, files or other evidence, irrespective of their content or form (e.g. in print, digital, physical or other forms), that comprise research observations, findings or outcomes, including primary materials and analysed data [239].

In general, all outputs that are accepted in the scientific community as necessary to validate research findings are included among research outputs. However, there is no shared understanding of the term 'research output', and stakeholders interpret the term differently. The key point of differentiation appears to be 'interest to the research community'. In broader terms, whatever 'data' is of interest to researchers should be treated as 'research data'.

For example, laboratory notebooks are often considered 'research data', recognising that they are necessary for reproducing research findings, especially in clinical trials. Even so, some funders exclude laboratory notebooks. The OECD stated that access to laboratory notebooks is subject to considerations that differ from those that deal with open data.[127] These include the commercial objectives, as records in laboratory notebooks are often used to establish the novelty principle of an invention, especially in the United States. Another reason why laboratory notebooks are not treated as 'research data' can be format limitation. Research notebooks still come in paper copies rather than in digital formats.

At the same time, some funding policies, such as that of the Engineering and Physical Sciences Research Council in the United Kingdom, require that:

> *Publicly-funded research data that is not generated in digital format will be stored in a manner to facilitate it being shared in the event of a valid request for access to the data being received (this expectation could be satisfied by implementing a policy to convert and store such data in digital format in a timely manner) [240].*

Indeed, 'research data' can take any format, even though policies mandating open access to research data primarily focus on research data in a digital, computer-readable format. For example, the Horizon 2020 Open Data Pilot is limited to 'digital research data', defined as:

> *'Digital research data' is information in digital form (in particular facts or numbers), collected to be examined and used as a basis for reasoning, discussion or calculation; this includes statistics, results of experiments, measurements, observations resulting from fieldwork, survey results, interview recordings and images [241].*

The digital format has the greatest potential to improve the efficiency of data distribution and its research application, mainly because the cost of transmission through the Internet is negligible. However, open access policies often apply to data that comes in non-digital formats, as documented above, and to data transmitted by means other than the Internet. For example, the OECD Principles could also apply to analogue research data in such instances where the cost of providing access to that data can be held reasonably low.[128]

Another contested area is the division between 'research data' and 'primary materials'. The Australian Code for the Responsible Conduct of Research regards completed questionnaires and recordings as 'primary materials', while transcripts derived from them are 'research data'. Despite this, some researchers have argued that the completed questionnaires and recordings should be treated as research data in terms of the agreed definition [231]. The reasoning used was the questionnaires and recordings qualify as 'factual records, used as primary sources for research'.[129] Consequently, if the research community considers those records as essential for

[127] OECD Principles at Point 10, 14.
[128] OECD Principles at Point 10, 13–14.
[129] *Ibid.*

substantiating research findings, then they also qualify as 'research data' and should be retained for the recommended period.[130]

Data sources also vary widely, as Borgman [167] observed. In the physical and life sciences, researchers gather or produce most data—through observations, experiments, or models. Researchers in the social sciences may gather or produce original data or they may source it from such places such as public records of economic activity. While the concept of 'data' is least well-developed in the humanities, the growth in digital research is leading to the more common usage of the term. Typically, humanities data is taken from cultural records—archives, documents, and artefacts.[131]

4.3 What falls outside the scope of 'research data'?

Some policies define 'research data' by limiting the entities that cannot be treated as research data. For example, in the United States, the Office of Science and Technology Policy states:

> *... [data] does not include laboratory notebooks, preliminary analyses, drafts of scientific papers, plans for future research, peer review reports, communications with colleagues, or physical objects, such as laboratory specimens [242].*

Similarly, the OECD Principles explicitly define what falls outside the scope of research data:

> *... laboratory notebooks, preliminary analyses and drafts of scientific papers, plans for future research, peer review or personal communications with colleagues, or physical objects (e.g. laboratory samples, strains of bacteria, test animals such as mice.*[132]

However, some researchers might argue that laboratory notebooks or preliminary drafts fall under the scope of data because of the importance for their research. The above definitions prove that the notion of 'research data' depends on the context. Those definitions help to explain why 'research data' often depends on interpretation. As Borgman put it, one researcher's signal—or data—may be someone else's noise [243].

4.4 What is missing in the scope of 'research data'?

Only one of the above definitions, namely, the definition of research data developed by the University of Melbourne, explicitly includes metadata as a component of research data. Metadata is structured information associated with an object for purposes of discovery, description, use, management, and preservation.[133] In short, metadata is data about data—information about information. In the context of scientific data, metadata is even more important because it provides the context needed to make sense of what would otherwise be a collection of

---

130 *Ibid.*

131 Borgman [167] at point 3.

132 OECD Principles at point 10, 14.

133 University of Melbourne at point 16.

numbers. Without metadata, any data is unlikely to be reusable and almost certainly would not allow for the research to be reproducible. For this reason, all stakeholders involved in open research data need to explicitly acknowledge that 'research data' includes metadata.

In addition to core research data and metadata, the final component required for reproducibility by research funders is the code or algorithms used to undertake the analyses [244]. In a substantial number of cases, the interpretation and analysis of data are dependent on the availability of software. In some cases, sharing of software code may not be permitted, as the code may be a commercial application or it can be protected by intellectual property such as patents. Yet in all instances where the code *can* be shared, it *should* be shared, and research funders need to include statements in their policies to that effect. The code and the relevant algorithms need to become integral to the term 'research data'.

Furthermore, most definitions of 'research data' do not address the degree of processing of the data that is shared. Research data can refer to 'top-level data' typically underpinning scientific publications or to 'working versions' incorporating different types of analyses, cleaning, and processing steps or to 'raw data' collected in research or harvested by scientific equipment. The various levels of data processing and control are discussed in the context of research data management, in Chapters 5 and 6.

Researchers like to organise their data in a 'dataset', but this is another term subject to dispute. A dataset might consist of a large or small spreadsheet, a text file, a set of files, or all of these. At present, researchers can share open data anything they like, and there are no criteria for assessing the quality of the data being shared other than by checking the parameters for data identification and discoverability. The potential of the data to be reused thus cannot be easily established. Some of the data released under the open access mandate may not be reusable.

4.5 What makes research data 'open'?

A major goal of open scientific data is to increase the sharing of the data by making it available to anyone who seeks it, regardless of location or affiliation, with minimal barriers for access and reuse.

In general, 'data sharing' implies the release of data in a form that others can use [245]. Data sharing thus encompasses many means of releasing data, open data being one such means. Other forms of release include the private exchange between researchers, publication of datasets on websites, the deposit in archives, repositories, domain-specific collections, library collections, or data papers and, finally, attachment as supplementary material in journal articles [246]. The data shared by any of these means would meet the criteria of openness provided that the data:

1. Is freely available on the Internet

2. Permits any user to download, copy, analyse, reprocess, pass to software, or use for any other purposes

3. Is without financial, legal, or technical barriers other than those inseparable from gaining access to the Internet itself [247]

Examples of open data include repositories and archives (including Zenodo, GenBank, Figshare, Dryad), data networks (such as Global Biodiversity Information Facility), virtual observatories (such as Digital Earth), domain repositories (such as PubMed Central), and institutional repositories. The list of major data network is provided at Appendix B.

The Open Knowledge Foundation has developed an extensive definition of 'open works', which also applies to 'open data'. For a work to be open, it must have an open licence, be accessible at a fair reproduction cost, or be freely available on the Internet along with the necessary information on compliance with the work's licence [248].

The aim of these licences is to allow free reuse and redistribution of all, or parts of, the work. The licence must also allow for derivatives of the work to be made and to be subsequently distributed or compiled with any other works. Also, the licence must allow the use, redistribution, modification, and compilation for any purpose. The rights attached to the work must apply to anyone who receives it redistributed, without the need to agree to any additional terms. There may be some clauses that ask for attribution for those who produced the work. There is often a share-alike clause that requires copies or derivatives of a licenced work to remain under a licence that is the same as, or similar to, the original. In general terms, this approach requires a licence to avoid discrimination against any person or group and must ensure that the works are free, so that there are no royalty charges or fee arrangements of any sort.[134]

Nevertheless, levels and standards for openness vary among different repositories and datasets.

For example, some open data repositories permit contributors to maintain their copyright and control over deposited data, which poses challenges to reuse. Furthermore, over half of seemingly 'open' datasets do not include any express licence,[135] which also limits the potential for data reuse. In some instances, data is open but cannot be reused without proprietary software—which, again, limits the potential for reuse and, in that circumstance, the dataset may fall under the protection of copyright law.

Conversely, data generated by open-source software may not be available for reuse in its modified form, if this involves a 'modicum' of creativity and, as discussed in Chapter 7, thus becomes a form of intellectual property. Openness may be tied to funding streams and business models (e.g. charging for value-added data services), as the OECD recently noted ([249], p. 27).

Clearly, there is a discrepancy between 'ideal openness', espoused in policies and in an array of criteria for making data 'open', and 'actual openness', which may only be 'semiopen' or otherwise flawed and may not allow for unfettered data reuse. Or the reuse can still be possible but with questionable legality under copyright law. In some instances, 'open data' is even interpreted as controlled access or restricted access to full datasets.[136]

The OECD specified 13 conditions for open data, yet in any particular situation, only a few are likely to be satisfied.[137]

The *Science as an Open Enterprise* report defines 'intelligent openness' as:

a. **Accessible:** Data must be located in such a manner that it can readily be found. This has implications both for the custodianship of data and the processes by which access is granted to data and information.

[134] *Ibid.*

[135] Initial results from the Global Open Data Index 2016/17 show roughly that only 38% of the eligible datasets were openly licenced. Available at: https://index.okfn.org/ [Accessed: 10 June 2018].

[136] *Ibid.*

[137] OECD Principles [51] at point 10. See also Borgman [167] at point 3.

b. **Intelligible:** Data must provide an account of the results of scientific work that is intelligible to those wishing to understand or scrutinise it. Data communication must therefore be differentiated for different audiences. What is intelligible to a specialist in one field may not be intelligible to one in another field. Effective communication to the wider public is more difficult, necessitating a deeper understanding of what the audience needs in order to understand the data and dialogue about priorities for such communication.

c. **Assessable:** Recipients need to be able to make some judgement or assessment of what is communicated. They will, for example, need to judge the nature of the claims that are made. Are the claims speculations or evidence-based? They should be able to judge the competence and reliability of those making the claims. Assessability also includes the disclosure of attendant factors that might influence trust in the research.

d. **Usable:** Data should be able to be reused, often for different purposes. The usability of data will also depend on the suitability of background material and metadata for those who wish to use the data. They should, at a minimum, be reusable by other scientists ([250], pp. 14–15).

This articulation of the parameters of openness became seminal and was adopted by key stakeholders including the European Commission, which incorporated it and slightly expanded on it the *2014 Guidelines on Data Management in Horizon 2020.* The definition also highlighted the fundamental problem in understanding the differences between data 'use' and 'reuse'.

Pasquetto et al. have clarified the difference.

In the first instance, data is collected by a researcher or a team of researchers, and the first (data) 'use' is by that individual or research team. If the data originator (s) use(s) the same dataset for any later purpose, relating to the original project or not, that too would count as a 'use'. If the data is shared, including as open data, that would be considered a 'reuse'. In other words, 'reuse' implies a subsequent use of the data by someone other than the originator(s).[138]

In practice, it can be difficult to monitor data reuse, mainly because researchers rarely cite the repository [251]. At the same time, data originators themselves inconsistently cite data they deposit for reuse. Encouraging consistent data citation practices might increase dissemination,[139] yet the factors that motivate researchers to reuse data deposited by others are not well understood.

With advances in technology providing better instrumentation and techniques for gathering data, the quantity of data available for reuse is increasing. At the same time, the reuse and sharing of data are becoming prominent in disciplines where these practices were once uncommon [252]. Data reuse is common in geospatial sciences, astronomy, clinical research, social media, and genomic research, among other areas.

Many obstacles to data reuse remain. They arise largely due the fact that 'releasing data and making it usable are quite different matters'.[140] Successful data reuse necessitates detailed documentation of the original data collection and processing steps in the language and in the context that would enable interpretation of the data by any subsequent user. Such data is often referred to as metadata.

---

[138] Pasquetto et al. [245] at point 31, 3.

[139] *Ibid.*

[140] Borgman [167], p. 40.

Yet the requirements for data appear to be far broader than is currently captured by the meaning of metadata. For example, detailed description of the unique methods by which data was collected, processed, cleaned, analysed, grouped, and interpreted in statistically correct ways may all be necessary to enable reuse. Information about the software used, including the software version, may also be required, especially in cases where reproducibility is the desired objective. The software used by the data originator may not be available freely or may require upgrading, which can decrease the possibilities for data reuse.

Similarly, the potential for reuse is decreased unless data is documented in the course of the original research project by those with the expertise of data collection and analysis to describe it [167]. Often, however, researchers are preoccupied with writing publications. They are not rewarded for documenting data. Therefore, questions of responsibilities for data documentation and curation lie at the core of our ability to reuse data.[141]

Many stakeholders in research and academia are exploring the options for overcoming the challenges for data reuse, especially those challenges that can be solved with technology.

In 2014, the deliberations of a workshop in Leiden on fair and safe data stewardship and sharing saw the emergence of the notion that by defining and reaching general agreement on certain principles and practices, then all interested parties would find it easier to access and reuse the data that contemporary science generates [253].

From that meeting came a draft set of principles—that all research objects should be findable, accessible, interoperable, and reusable (FAIR) by both people and machines. Subsequently elaborated, these are the FAIR Guiding Principles, summarised in **Table 1** [31].

The FAIR principles apply to data repositories and incorporate the total 'research object'—code, data, and tools for interpretation [254]. They are the most advanced technical standards for open scientific data to date. In the context of this study, the ideal 'open scientific data' is in repositories or archives that apply the FAIR standards, recognising that some data already in the public domain does not meet the standards. Yet every lesson learnt from imperfect open data brings us one step closer to making open scientific data a reality.

4.6 The limits of openness

While open scientific data is desirable and should be pursued to the maximum extent possible, there are some restrictions. The European Commission Horizon 2020 Model Grant Agreements [255] comprehensively state the legal limitations on the 'openness' of data. The European Union (EU) is a significant funder, distributing over €7 billion for research annually. However, this funder limits, quite substantially, the possibilities for sharing the research data resulting from its projects:

Article 27—Protection of results—Visibility of EU Funding
27.1 Obligation to protect the results

Each beneficiary must examine the possibility of protecting its results and must adequately protect them[142]—for an appropriate period and with appropriate territorial coverage—if:

[141] *Ibid.*

[142] Protection may be sought through patent, trademark, industrial design, trade secret or confidentiality.

To be Findable:

F1. (meta)data are assigned a globally unique and persistent identifier

F2. data are described with rich metadata (defined by R1 below)

F3. metadata clearly and explicitly include the identifier of the data it describes

F4. (meta)data are registered or indexed in a searchable resource

To be Accessible:

A1. (meta)data are retrievable by their identifier using a standardized communications protocol

A1.1 the protocol is open, free, and universally implementable

A1.2 the protocol allows for an authentication and authorization procedure, where necessary

A2. metadata are accessible, even when the data are no longer available

To be Interoperable:

I1. (meta)data use a formal, accessible, shared, and broadly applicable language for knowledge representation.

I2. (meta)data use vocabularies that follow FAIR principles

I3. (meta)data include qualified references to other (meta)data

To be Reusable:

R1. meta(data) are richly described with a plurality of accurate and relevant attributes

R1.1. (meta)data are released with a clear and accessible data usage license

R1.2. (meta)data are associated with detailed provenance

R1.3. (meta)data meet domain-relevant community standards

Table 1.
The FAIR principles for open scientific data.

a. the results can reasonably be expected to be commercially or industrially exploited and

b. protecting them is possible, reasonable and justified (given the circumstances).

When deciding on protection, the beneficiary must consider its own legitimate interests and the legitimate interests (especially commercial) of the other beneficiaries.[143]

Article 36—Confidentiality
36.1 General obligation to maintain confidentiality

During implementation of the action and for 4 years after the period set out in Article 3, the parties must keep confidential any data, documents or other material (in any form) that is identified as confidential at the time it is disclosed ('confidential information').

If a beneficiary requests, the [Commission][Agency] may agree to keep such information confidential for an additional period beyond the initial 4 years.

[143] Ref. [241] at point 51.

If information has been identified as confidential only orally, it will be considered to be confidential only if this is confirmed in writing within 15 days of the oral disclosure.

Unless otherwise agreed between the parties, they may use confidential information only to implement the Agreement.

The beneficiaries may disclose confidential information to their personnel or third parties involved in the action only if they:

a. need to know to implement the agreement and

b. are bound by an obligation of confidentiality.

This does not change the security obligations in Article 37, which still apply.[144]

There are, however, some exceptions to the obligation of confidentiality. The conditions set out in Article 4 of the Rules for Participation Regulation [193] require the Commission to make available information on the results to other European Union institutions, bodies, offices, or agencies and to Member States or associated countries.

Since the Commission is also committed to developing an Open Science Cloud to support open science and innovation [144], perhaps the results might be available to selected European Union users as open data via this means.

Furthermore, the obligations for confidentiality do not apply if:

a. the disclosing party agrees to release the other party;

b. the information was already known by the recipient or is given to him without obligation of confidentiality by a third party that was not bound by any obligation of confidentiality;

c. the recipient proves that the information was developed without the use of confidential information;

d. the information becomes generally and publicly available, without breaching any confidentiality obligation; or

e. the disclosure of the information is required by EU or national law.[145]

Restrictions on open sharing of data proposed by the European Commission are for the protection of security in relation to disclosure and subcontracting.

Article 37—Security related obligations

The beneficiaries [of grants] must comply with the 'security recommendation (s)' set out [by the Commission].

For security recommendations restricting disclosure or dissemination, the beneficiaries must—before disclosure or dissemination to a third party (including linked third parties, such as affiliated entities)—inform the coordinator, which must request written approval from the [Commission][Agency].

144 *Ibid*, 264.

145 Regulation (EU) No 1290/2013 of the European Parliament and of the Council of 11 of December 2013, 81.

Finally, personal data cannot be shared, and this imposes a limit on openness. The restrictions for the processing of personal data as set out in Article 39 of the model grant agreement are canvassed in more detail in Chapters 6 and 7.

The key restrictions to data sharing cited above—the obligation to commercialise and protect the research results with intellectual property and the obligation to maintain confidentiality, the security obligations, and the handling of personal data—are significant impediments to open scientific data. The scope of these restrictions is not yet clearly defined and requires further conceptualisation.

Conclusion

This chapter showed that the terms 'data', 'research data' and 'open data' may hold different meanings for different stakeholders and across different research disciplines, different levels of processing, different data repositories and even in the eyes of individual researchers working on the same project. The only agreement emerging on these definitions is that no single definition will suffice.

Alternatively, no single definition is necessary because the meaning of 'open scientific data' depends both on the context for the use of that data and on the subject using it.

Key stakeholders—research funders, researchers, librarians, and lawyers—may approach the term differently. Funders typically mention 'research data' that underpins research outcomes; researchers talk about databases and spreadsheets, while librarians tend to be preoccupied with metadata and citations. This creates confusion. If researchers are to comply with the policies of funders and publishers, they need to understand what 'data' they should make available. Similarly, if librarians are to provide effective data management services, they need to be certain about what 'data' should be considered and what would make the data 'findable', 'accessible', 'interoperable' and 'reusable' for others.

The diversity of the definitions of 'data' makes any attempts to specify the meaning of 'open scientific data' extremely difficult. Yet this effort is necessary to identify how to best document and curate scientific data to facilitate reuse. The key argument emerging in this chapter is that that even though defining open scientific data is a challenging task, more research effort and resources should be dedicated to this area. Only an improved understanding of the parameters that can make data findable, useful, and reusable can assist in realising the benefits of open scientific data. This chapter finds that the recent FAIR standards are a very helpful contribution to the conceptualisation debate.

Another key point highlighted in this chapter is the necessity of data 'reuse' to realise the benefits of open research. For data to be reusable, it needs to be meticulously documented. In this sense, data documentation is a broader concept than metadata and requires a detailed description of the unique methods by which data was collected, processed, cleaned, analysed, grouped, and interpreted in statistically correct ways. Researchers and data scientists need to tackle this challenge in their research practice, as they are developing improved ways to describe data and are becoming more skilled in reusing data created by others.

The initial focus of the open scientific data movement was on ensuring the release of 'data' into the public domain. Now it is necessary to provide further guidance to research organisations with regard to possible methods of reuse of open research data.

At present, there appears to be a high degree of discrepancy between 'ideal openness' (as espoused in policies and in an array of criteria for making data open) and 'actual openness'. The data available in the public domain may only be 'semiopen' or flawed in some respects and may not allow for unfettered data reuse. Or the reuse in practical terms can still be possible, but the legality of such reuse may be questionable, as further discussed in Chapter 7. Only the practice of open data can help narrow the distance between espoused openness and the way open data is practiced at present. The early experiences with the implementation of open data at CERN and in clinical trials data are discussed in the following two chapters.

Chapter 5

Research Data Management at CERN

This chapter is the first of the two in this book documenting experiences with implementing open data. Specifically, it outlines the practices of research data collection, processing, curation, and release as open data. Some early examples of the use of open data are also provided.

The chapter includes:

1. Organisational approaches to research data management

2. Research data management at CERN

Introduction

The explicit policies mandating open data make it clear that the curation and release of scientific data in electronic formats are no longer an issue. Rather, the discussion has shifted to issues such as what specific data to curate and share, how to do it, in what format, at which time, and according to what conditions. The management of research data is dynamically evolving and presents many challenges to research organisations. While data sharing among peer researchers has been an established practice for many years, the digital curation of data for public release is both very recent and complex. Indeed, making scientific data available and useful to unknown audiences, and for unanticipated purposes, may not be easy to achieve.

This chapter deals with some of the evolving aspects of research data management (RDM). It examines data-driven experiments at the European Organization for Nuclear Research (CERN) and documents some emerging best practice with open data. It is acknowledged that it is not feasible to address, within the purview of a single chapter, all unfolding issues associated with the curation and use of open scientific data. The discussion here starts with a brief overview of the data management approaches taken by research organisations.

This is followed by a detailed discussion of these practices at CERN, including analysis of organisational policies underpinning open data. The chapter concludes by summarising the key lesson learnt from open data practice.

5.1 Organisational approaches to research data management

There are no established definitions of RDM in the context of open scientific data. Rather, data management is defined as a set of organisational practices that lead to specific outcomes. Universities have introduced RDM as a new library service to help researchers to ensure compliance with the mandates recently introduced by funders. The service typically involves assistance with planning, creating, organising, sharing, and looking after research data, whatever form it may take (Cambridge) [256]. Universities acknowledge the key benefits of data sharing for the conduct of science and the benefits for researchers. Some point to successful case studies, and others state that research data represents a significant investment of money, effort, resources, and time (Princeton) [257]. At this stage, most universities tend to view RDM as a short-term function spanning the duration of research projects.

Taken as a whole, most of the reasons (and incentives) for universities now to implement the RDM function appear to be external. This was the case for such well-known universities as Cambridge,[146] Oxford,[147] Harvard [258], Princeton,[148] Stanford [259], Yale,[149] Cornell [260], and Johns Hopkins,[150] as well as the research-intensive Group of Eight universities in Australia.[151] Some less well-known universities—such as Purdue University in the United States and the University of Edinburgh, home to the Digital Curation Centre—seem to have developed more advanced expertise in RDM and so view data preservation as an integral part of their own research processes. Purdue, Yale, and Cornell have also developed data preservation strategies[152] that set out expectations and limit on data preservation and maintenance—including content migration and software and hardware dependency preservation.

Notwithstanding their operating constraints and technological limitations, some of these universities state that preserving the underpinning publications with the data is a high priority, along with any stand-alone data publications and datasets with high research value.[153] However, these policies do not go further to spell out the processes for internal decisions about what is worth preserving.

The experiences with RDM at universities are at early stages. Yet librarians have already positioned themselves as the key players in the RDM process—they link a project's lifecycle to data management because the techniques used by librarians slot nicely into the different parts of the data lifecycle. The six stages of the matrix (**Figure 3**)[154] make up a cycle, with the expectation that data curated by universities will be reused in future research projects. While this data cycle provides a simplified view of RDM, it appears adequate for the purposes of assisting researchers to manage their data, to create a data management plan, and to become aware of the

---

146 The University of Cambridge defines the stages of RDM as creating, organising, accessing and looking after data.

147 RDM at Oxford includes planning how research data will be looked after, how researchers deal with information on a day-to-day basis over the lifetime of a project, and what happens to the data in the longer term (http://researchdata.ox.ac.uk/home/introduction-to-rdm/).

148 The RDM Team at Stanford offers assistance and training that will help researcher create data management plans for grant applications, identify appropriate repositories for research data, understand repository requirements, and deposit data into DataSpace at Princeton University (http://library.princeton.edu/research-data-management).

149 Yale University has also developed the Library's Digital Preservation Policy Framework, which outlines the scope of digital preservation services at Yale University (https://web.archive.org/web/20160329191611; http://wiki.opf-labs.org/display/SP/Home).

150 RDM at Oxford includes planning how research data will be looked after, how researchers deal with information on a day-to-day basis over the lifetime of a project, and what happens to the data in the longer term (http://researchdata.ox.ac.uk/home/introduction-to-rdm/).

151 The University of Adelaide, the Australian National University, the University of Melbourne, Monash University, the University of New South Wales, the University of Queensland, the University of Sydney, and the University of Western Australia.

152 A good repository of published data preservation strategies is available at https://web.archive.org/web/20150224021208/http://wiki.opf-labs.org:80/display/SP/Home.

153 *Ibid.*

154 *Ibid.*

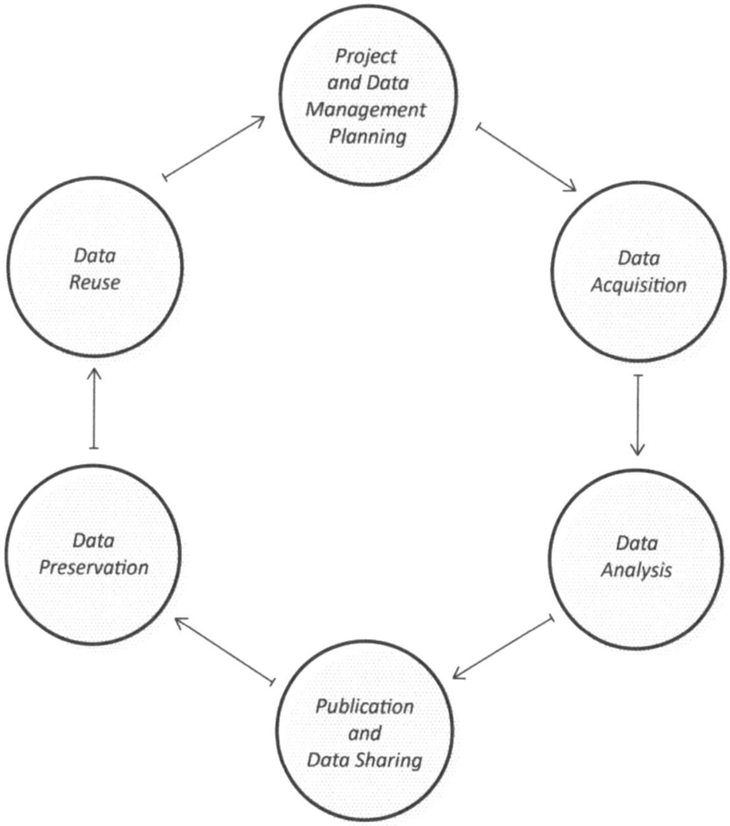

Figure 3.
Research data lifecycle (Source: Briney [261]).

data policies that apply to their work [261]. Although university libraries serve researchers across all scientific disciplines, the curation and preservation of data in the social sciences and humanities are less complex than RDM in other branches of science.

Outside the university sector, RDM in scientific agencies is far better established and forms an integral part of internal research practices. In this context, RDM ensures the long-term preservation of, access to, and the ability to reuse data after research projects have ended. Scientific research organisations and research funders both envisage that preservation should be long term, without defining any specific period.

This flexible approach is also advocated by those institutions that set the standards for data preservation. The leading model in the field, the Open Archival Information System (OAIS), defines 'long-term' as:

> *... long enough to be concerned with the impacts of changing technologies, including support for new media and data formats, or with a changing user community. Long Term may extend indefinitely [93].*

This definition implies that there are two roles in data management—storage (to preserve the data) and curation (to preserve knowledge about the data to facilitate reuse).[155] This definition is user-centric, rather than data producer-centric.

---

[155] Indeed, this duality is widely discussed by archivists as well as by proponents of open access policies. See, for example, Lee and Stvilia [262]; Digital Curation Centre [263]; and Gladney [264].

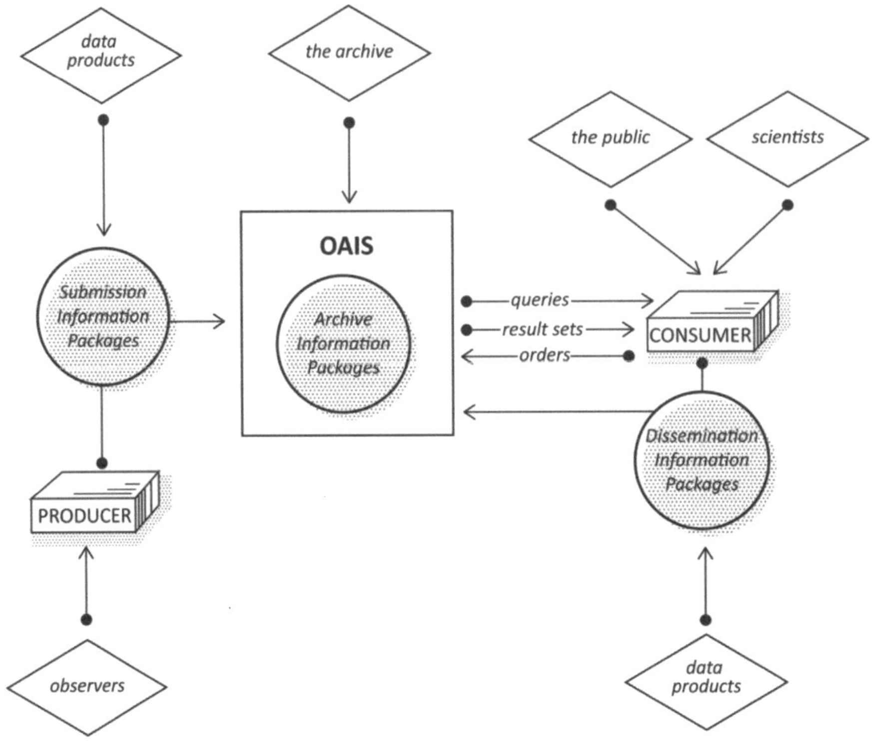

Figure 4.
The highest level structure of an OAIS archive (Source: Reference model for an open archival information system).

Clearly, there is far more to RDM than helping researchers to publish their data so that they comply with the open data mandates. I expect that universities will, over time, both learn from and adopt some of the advanced RDM practices as these evolve and get tested within scientific research organisations. For this reason, the sections below focus on RDM in data-driven scientific research agencies.

So what is required to preserve and maintain access to digital data over the long term? This question is still far from finding a satisfactory answer.

Space agencies have been at the forefront of the debate. The principal model for RDM in large data-driven organisations, including NASA and CERN, is the OAIS reference model. It led to the development of the ISO standard 16363:2012, which has proved useful for research organisations with digital archiving needs. It is the only standard currently endorsed by the Digital Curation Centre[156] for the use in digital preservation planning and management. The structure of the model is illustrated in **Figure 4**, along with the relationships between producers and consumers of data.

In this model,[157] an OAIS archive preserves digital or physical objects for the long term. The archive accepts objects along with metadata and with summaries describing how to interpret the digital objects so as to extract the information within them.

156 The Digital Curation Centre is an internationally recognised centre of expertise in digital curation with a focus on building capability and skills for research data management (http://www.dcc.ac.uk/).

157 See *Reference model for an open archival information system (OAIS)*–CCSDS 650.0-B-1. CCSDS Recommendation, 2002. Identical to ISO 14721:2003. Available at: http://public.ccsds.org/publications/archive/650x0b1.pdf [93] and Bicarregui et al. [265].

That information may need further context. The archive receives the bundle of information in the form agreed in a contract between the data producers and the archive. Once the archive receives the information package, it takes over the responsibility for preservation from the producer. The archive distributes its holdings to the data consumers whom the archive is designed to support. It is the responsibility of the archive to determine, either by itself or by way of consultation, which users should become the designated consumers capable of understanding particular data packages. However, the design of the OAIS archive requires the information to be documented in such a way that allows consumers to interpret the data products without any contact with the data producers—an important consideration for future users.

The fundamental OAIS design has become a standard for major digital archives and repositories, including the Library of Congress in the United States, the British Library, the digital library JSTOR, and many others. Some university libraries are already OAIS-compliant. However, the OAIS design is merely a conceptual model that can only be used as a guide for RDM within research organisations. The OAIS model cannot be likened to the 'gold or green' open access standards[158] that were almost uniformly adopted and implemented by research organisations around the globe. There is no 'standard' for RDM, and developing any standards into the future is a far more complex task than was the case with open publications.

There are some major differences between open publications and open data, and these differences underpin the emergence of unique RDM practices that are, and need to be, researcher-centric. At the same time, librarians and research funders tend to approach RDM with a mindset relentlessly focused on creating and applying 'standards' and 'templates', perhaps because they are influenced by their recent experiences with facilitating open access to publications.

RDM is not simply a standardised technical approach to implementing open data mandates. If open scientific data is to be sustainable, then cultural and organisational issues must first be addressed. In particular, a more advanced understanding is needed of the different natures of open data and open publications. The differences between open data and publications and the tools that may be used to improve the availability and reuse of open data are outlined in Chapter 8.

5.2 Research data management at CERN

CERN is one of the earliest and most influential advocates of open science in the world, committed to collaborative research and the dissemination of results in open access publications and, more recently, as open data. Researchers at CERN invented the World Wide Web in 1989, and the organisation is now using it to revolutionise the ways scientists develop, disseminate, and communicate science and to work and to learn collectively in online spaces.

The mandate for openness is embedded in the CERN charter, which states:

[158] Green open access, also referred to self-archiving, refers to the practice of depositing articles in an open access repository, where it can be accessed freely. The self-publication typically occurs after peer review by a journal, the author posts the same content the journal will be publishing to a web site controlled by the author, the research institution that funded or hosted the work, or which has been set up as a central open access repository.
Gold open access 'makes the final version of an article freely and permanently accessible for everyone, immediately after publication. Copyright for the article is retained by the authors and most of the permission barriers are removed' [266].

> *The Organisation shall provide for collaboration among European States in nuclear research of a pure scientific and fundamental character, and in research essentially related thereto. The Organisation shall have no concern with work for military requirements and the results of its experimental and theoretical work shall be published or otherwise made generally available.*[159]

In 1953, when the CERN Convention was signed, the focus for research in pure physics was to understand atomic structure—hence the name the European Organization for Nuclear Research. Over time, the focus of experiments conducted at CERN has shifted towards particle physics, and organisational practices have also moved towards being more open, inclusive, and capable of forming research teams spanning the entire planet.

There are some 2400 permanent staff and 1300 contractors working on the CERN campus at any time, along with 1000 or so visiting researchers. There are 12,500 scientific users off-campus, in 70 countries and of 105 different nationalities. According to CERN, this number represents more than half of the world's particle physicists.[160] The number of member states has also increased to the current 22, since the opening to non-European members in 2010 when the State of Israel became a full member. The scope of membership possibilities has also expanded. Another seven countries hold associate member status or are in a pre-stage to membership.[161] Countries including the United States, the Russian Federation, and Japan hold 'observer status', and it is envisaged that they may join the organisation in the future. Many other countries, including China, Argentina, Australia, Canada, and South Africa, have signed cooperation agreements with CERN.[162]

The global expansion of CERN in recent years can largely be attributed to its workforce, collaborative spirit and the second-to-none research infrastructure the organisation has developed over the years. It continues to modernise as quickly as technologically possible, with continuing funding and resources received from the CERN member states and other participating institutions. Perhaps even more importantly, CERN has put significant emphasis on publicising its research to the outside world, to both lay and expert audiences.

The experiments conducted at CERN are fascinating, if perhaps largely mysterious to the outsider. They are becoming more and more accessible to the general public—whether through Hollywood movies, particle physics masterclasses

---

[159] Convention for the Establishment of a European Organization for Nuclear Research, signed in Paris on 1 July, 1953 as amended on 17 January 1971, Article II.(1) (https://council.web.cern.ch/en/content/convention-establishment-european-organization-nuclear-research).

[160] CERN estimates there are some 20,000 physicists in the world today. See for example, CERN [267].

[161] Serbia, Cyprus, and Slovenia are associate members in the pre-stage to membership, and Turkey, Pakistan, Ukraine, and India are associate members. Source: CERN [268].

[162] Observer states and organisations currently involved in CERN programmes include the European Commission, Japan, the Russian Federation, UNESCO, and the United States.
Non-member states with cooperation agreements with CERN include Albania, Algeria, Argentina, Armenia, Australia, Azerbaijan, Bangladesh, Belarus, Bolivia, Brazil, Canada, Chile, China, Colombia, Costa Rica, Croatia, Ecuador, Egypt, Estonia, Former Yugoslav Republic of Macedonia (FYROM), Georgia, Iceland, Iran, Jordan, Korea, Lithuania, Malta, Mexico, Mongolia, Montenegro, Morocco, New Zealand, Peru, Saudi Arabia, South Africa, the United Arab Emirates, and Vietnam. Source: CERN [268] at point 23.
CERN also has scientific contacts with Cuba, Ghana, Ireland, Latvia, Lebanon, Madagascar, Malaysia, Mozambique, Palestinian Authority, the Philippines, Qatar, Rwanda, Singapore, Sri Lanka, Taiwan, Thailand, Tunisia, and Uzbekistan.

directed at school children, a strong presence on social media, or popular culture seeking to understand the foundations of the universe. People of all ages and professions are increasingly becoming aware of the experiments and discoveries coming out of CERN and are naturally drawn to them.

Open data forms an intrinsic part of these outreach activities.

5.2.1 Data collection and processing

Most experiments conducted at CERN today concentrate on understanding the data collected in the Large Hadron Collider (LHC)—the largest and most powerful particle accelerator in the world. With a 27 km circumference, the LHC accelerates protons in clockwise and anticlockwise directions at almost the speed of light before colliding them at four points on the LHC ring. The temperatures resulting from collisions in the LHC are over 100,000 times higher than in the Sun's centre [269].

This unique research environment presents unique challenges for data collection and processing. The volume of data generated and collected as part of LHC experiments is staggering. In June 2017, the data centre at CERN reached a new peak of 200 petabytes of data in its tape archives. This is about 100 times the combined capacity of academic research libraries in the United States [270]. Data is gathered from the particle collisions, of which there are around 1 billion per second in the LHC that result in approximately one petabyte of data per second [271]. Existing computing systems cannot record such a data flow; hence it is filtered and then aggregated in the CERN Data Centre.

The centre also performs initial data reconstruction and archives a copy of the resulting data on long-term tape storage. However, even allowing for the vast quantity of data that is discarded following each experiment, the CERN Data Centre processes an average of one petabyte of data per day [272]. This volume is growing and is predicted to continue to grow well into the future, mostly due to the ever-increasing complexity of the experiments and the increasing capacity to process and store data at CERN and other participating institutions.

The demand for data transfer and network capacity is increasing, too. The Worldwide LHC Computing Grid (WLCG) was created to provide the computing resources needed to analyse the data gathered in LHC experiments. Work on the design of the grid began in 1999. At that time, the computing power required to process the LHC data was much lower but still exceeded the funding capacity of CERN. A solution was found involving collaboration with laboratories and universities that have access to national or regional computing facilities. The LHC Grid was created on the basis of a memorandum of understanding signed among these institutions in 2001 [273], and their services were integrated in 2002 into a single computing grid. This facilitates storage and provides the computing power to distribute and to analyse the LHC data nearly in real time and all over the world. Some 10,000 researchers can access the LHC data from almost anywhere [274].

The number of institutions participating in the LHC Grid has grown to over 170, with 13 institutions participating as Tier 1 centres [275] and the remaining organisations as Tier 2 centres [276]. The LHC computing grid consists of two principal grids—the European Grid Infrastructure and the Open Science Grid based in the United States. There are many other participating regional and national grids, such as the EU–India Grid.

The distributed infrastructure has proved to be a highly effective solution for the challenge associated with the LHC data analysis. Not only is the Herculean task of data distribution and storage shared among the participating institutions but the technical advantages of the grid offer unprecedented possibilities for data access, curation, use, and preservation. The advantages are many and are well-summarised on the CERN home page:

> *Multiple copies of data can be kept at different sites, ensuring access for all scientists independent of geographical location. There is no single point of failure; computer centres in multiple time zones ease round-the-clock monitoring and the availability of expert support; and resources are distributed across the world and are co-funded by the participating institutions [277].*

Data processing at the LHC computing grid occurs at four levels, internally known as Tier 0, Tier 1, Tier 2, and Tier 3. Each tier includes several participating institutions with their own computing resources and data storage facilities.

- **Tier 0** is the CERN Data Centre, which is responsible for the collection and initial reconstruction of the raw data collected from the LHC. The centre further distributes the reconstructed data to Tier 1 participating institutions and also reprocesses the data when the LHC is not running. This data centre accounts for less than 20% of the grid's total computing capacity.[163]

- **Tier 1** includes 13 major data storage and processing centres around the world, connected by optical fibre links working at 10 gigabits per second [278]. This high-bandwidth network is generally restricted to data traffic between the CERN Data Centre and Tier 1 sites and among the Tier 1 sites themselves. These institutions provide a round-the-clock support to the grid and take responsibility for storing their share of the raw and reconstructed data, as well as for reprocessing and storing the resulting output. Each Tier 1 site has connections to a number of Tier 2 sites, usually in the same geographical region.

- **Tier 2** involves over 150 universities and scientific organisations that originally were intended as centres for performing specific data analyses. As time went on, Tier 2 centres also became involved in data reprocessing and data offloading, particularly during a peak grid load that arose without warning due to higher-than-expected data collection that was beyond the capacity of the Tier 0 and Tier 1 centres. Each tier centre has at least one staff member dedicated to maintaining the LHC Grid.

- **Tier 3** nodes, apart from contributing processing capacity as required, enable individual scientists to access the grid though local computing resources. These may be part of a university department or simply the laptops of researchers.

There is no formal connection between the grid and the final users, as the agreements are with hosting institutions. However, the end users can choose from a broad range of services—including data storage and processing, analysis software, and visualisation tools. The computing grid verifies user identity and credentials and then searches for availability on sites that can provide the resources requested.[164] As required, users can access the grid's computing power and storage. They may not even be aware of the hosts of the resources.

---

[163] *Ibid.*

[164] CERN [277] at point 33.

Essential for the smooth functioning of the grid was the commitment of all participating organisations to use open-source software to power the grid. The CERN legal department played a central role in driving the early discussion among the participating institutions. In line with its commitment to an open Internet, CERN is also committed to open software, open hardware, and open source. As a leading software developer at CERN recently puts it:

> *We are a pure Linux shop from the point of view of real computing and real software development. That enables us to work fast and cut some corners [279].*

Crucially, the use of Linux, FLOSS, and other open platforms allows the grid centres to contain costs by deploying entirely generic components in processing and storage networks.[165]

Accordingly, CERN relinquishes all intellectual property rights to the software code, both in the source and binary forms. Permission is granted for anyone to use, duplicate, modify, and redistribute it. Similarly, all participating institutions warrant and ensure that any software that they contribute to the grid can be integrated, redistributed, modified, and enhanced by other members ([273], Article 10.1). Several participating institutions in the United Kingdom reported that the choice of Linux also made it easy for more centres to offer resources [279]. In using open software to power the grid, CERN is leading the development of open standards for distributed computing. Maarten Litmaath recently suggested that this CERN infrastructure can be used as a model for cost-effective collaborative computing in other fields of scientific research. The model can also be easily implemented in developing countries, which often do not have the resources to invest in data processing and storage [280].

5.2.2 Open data policies governing access to research data

Access to the LHC data stored in the grid centres occurs at various levels and combines multiple phases of data processing, access, use, and control. The LHC experiments generate large datasets, and before these enter the analysis phase, they undergo intricate quality assurance processes. The result is a trail of research outputs with varied stages of refinement and usage [281]. Direct access to the grid and raw data is enabled for some 10,000 physicists engaged in specific projects grouped around one of the four primary LHC data collecting detectors (particle collision points), internally referred to as 'four LHC experiments' (see **Figure 5**).

Each of these detectors has a separate team of researchers accessing and analysing the data collected. The largest are the ATLAS and CMS experiments, with some 6000 researchers working in one of the two collaborations. These are some of the largest scientific teams ever formed, as evidenced in the list of thousands of authors included at the end of their publications.[166]

The LHC data powers these mega collaborations. Access to the initial LHC data is restricted for several years, to the members of a specific experiment, as explained below. In fact, the principal motivation for building and operating the experiments is access to and a shared understanding of that data, along with the right to author publications subsequently.[167]

---

[165] *Ibid.*

[166] A recent physics paper from CERN has listed 5154 authors and has, as far as anyone knows, broken the record for the largest number of contributors to single research article. See Aad et al. [282].

[167] Bicarregui [265] at point 19.

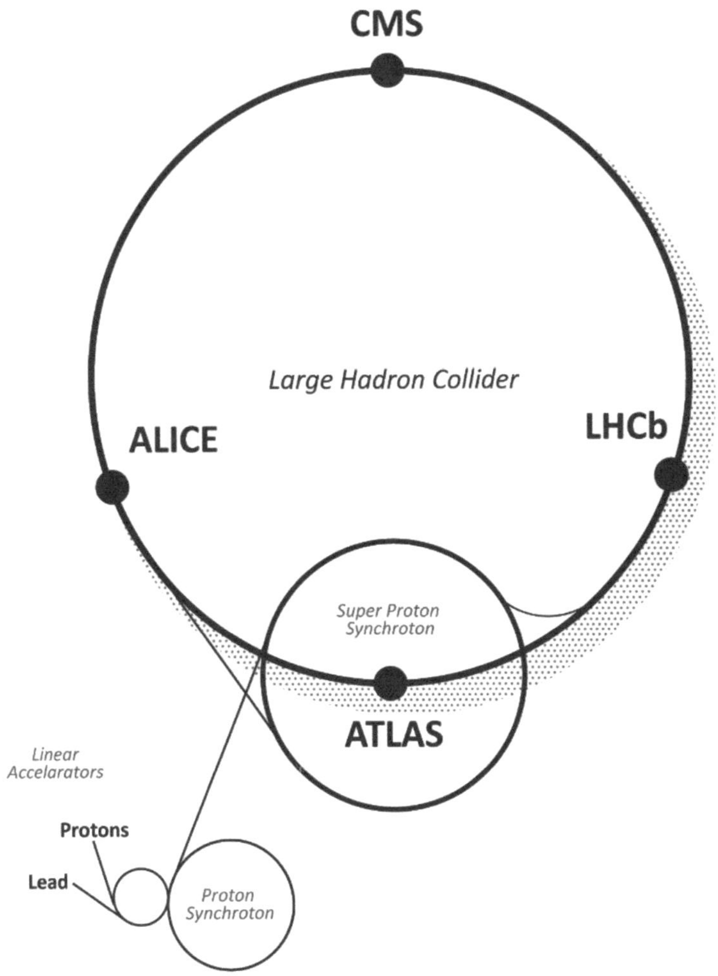

Figure 5.
Data harvesting points at the large hadron collider (Source: Wikimedia Commons).

The ATLAS and CMS experiments use detectors designed for general purposes to investigate the broadest ranges of particles possible. The two teams compete, rather than collaborate, with each other. Such competition is an effective way to cross-validate the outcomes of analyses produced by either of the two teams. As such, members of the ATLAS collaborations do not have access to the CMS data and research methods and vice versa. However, cross-migration of researchers between the two collaborations can occur, and such transfer also facilitates access to the data of the competing experiment. A level of secrecy about data processing and research methods remains essential due to the nature of scientific research performed by the two teams. The fact that the two detectors were independently designed is vital to the cross-validation of any discoveries [283]. For these reasons, it is unlikely that the first analyses of ATLAS and CMS real and raw data—representing the lowest and most guarded level of access—will ever be available as open access.

The two remaining experiments at CERN are known as ALICE and LHCb. They focus on research-specific phenomena. Instead of using an enclosed detector at the collision point, as is the case in ATLAS and CMS, the LHCb experiment uses a series of subdetectors to collect data concerning particles thrown forwards in one direction by the collision.[168] One subdetector is mounted close to the collision point, with the others lined up over 20 m. The positioning of detectors enables examination of the slight differences between matter and antimatter by monitoring the movements of a particle called the 'beauty quark' [284].

Finally, the ALICE experiment is a heavy-ion detector designed to study the physics of strongly interacting matter at extreme energy densities. The conditions simulated at ALICE are thought to resemble those that occurred in the universe just after the big bang. The ALICE collaboration studies a phase of matter called 'quark-gluon' plasma, observing as it expands and cools and progressively gives rise to the particles that constitute the matter of the universe today.[169]

Each of the four LHC experiments produces unique data of interest to both the scientific and non-scientific communities around the world. Because of the open and collaborative nature of research at CERN, and the increasing awareness of the LHC experiments involving data, it is often thought that all data collected at the LHC is available as open data. This is incorrect. The data made available in the public domain represents only a tiny fraction of the data collected in the LHC. What becomes available is data requiring a higher level of analysis that directly underpins publications or carefully selected research experiments—the outcomes of which are peer-reviewed and cross-validated by other CERN researchers.

Access to the LHC data is governed by policies for the access and preservation of the data collected and processed by any of the four experiments. Each collaboration team has developed its own data preservation and access policy [285] that share some common characteristics and recognise four different data user groups:

1. Original collaboration members requiring access long after data harvesting is completed

2. The wider high-energy physics community and researchers from relating scientific disciplines

3. Those in education and outreach

4. Members of the public with an interest in science.

Each of these user groups has different data needs and requires the LHC data and supporting analyses at different levels of processing. Therefore, the open data policies of all four experiments have adopted a uniform classification of the LHC data developed by the Study Group for Data Preservation and Long-Term Analysis in High Energy Physics in 2009 [286], as follows (**Table 2**).

While CERN has already shared Level 1 data for a number of years, it needed a central point of access for Level 2 and Level 3 data, noting that Level 3 data can already be accessed through the grid by researchers directly associated with one of the four collaborations.

Level 4 data (raw data) collected at the LHC is not yet available as open data. Given the complexity and costs of data collection and calibration, as well as the technical expertise required, CERN has no intentions to make Level 4 data available in the public domain any time soon. Such data requires a large software, discovery,

[168] *Ibid.*

[169] CERN [269] at point 25.

	Data type	Data access point	Primary users
level 1	Data directly related to publications that provide documentation for the published results.	High-Energy Physics Literature Database: Inspire (http://inspirehep.net/); and HEP Data (https://hepdata.net/)	Interested scientific members or the general public (= any internet user).
level 2	Simplified data formats.	The Open Data Portal: http://opendata.cern.ch/	Outreach and education providers and users.
level 3	Reconstructed data, simulation data, and the analysis software needed to allow a full scientific analysis.	The Open Data Portal (selected datasets are available after an embargo period spanning 3 to 10 years). The WLHC Grid (scientists working in one of the four CERN collaborations and approved scientific members). No embargo period.	High energy physicists.
level 4	Raw data and access to the full potential of the experimental data.	The CERN data centre.	Restricted CERN users (data constructors and data-takers) working in one of the four collaboratons.

Table 2.
Levels of data access at CERN.

processing, and database infrastructure for meaningful use and interpretation of it. Even the members of the four LHC experiments generally cannot access Level 4 data. The data is uncalibrated and meaningless for direct analyses. However, CERN is open to the possibility of making subsets of data available for external use.

Therefore, CERN does not propose to devote resources to providing open access to the full raw dataset, although it might consider providing access to representative smaller samples of the Level 4 data.[170] Furthermore, physicists associated with CERN can access Level 3 data directly through the grid. At the same time, Level 2 data and some subsets of Level 3 data are, after the expiration of the embargo period, increasingly becoming available as open data on a dedicated server [288].

The parameters determining the level of access to the LHC data are based on the credentials of the potential user. CERN strictly differentiates between internal and external users and then between the varying levels of access permitted to individual users within the two main user groups—with Level 3 being the most guarded data and Level 4 being the most restricted data. Level 1 data is available by default—that is, immediately with publications that the data underpins. Level 2 data is carefully selected and tested before the release for educational purposes. The key access decision points are depicted in **Figure 6**.

5.2.3 The Open Data Portal

The CERN data portal is the key enabling platform for Level 2 data and selected subsets of Level 3 data after the expiration of the initial exclusivity period spanning 5–10 years. As shown in **Figure 7**, the home page offers users two profiles—education, consisting principally of visualisation tools and learning resources and research, providing direct access to the working environment along with tools for starting research projects at high school and other outreach institutions.

The portal, launched in November 2014, currently includes public data releases from the CMS, ALICE, ATLAS and LHCb experiments. This data comes with the software and supporting documents required to understand and to analyse it,

[170] CERN [287], ATLAS Data Access Policy released on 21 May 2014, 4.

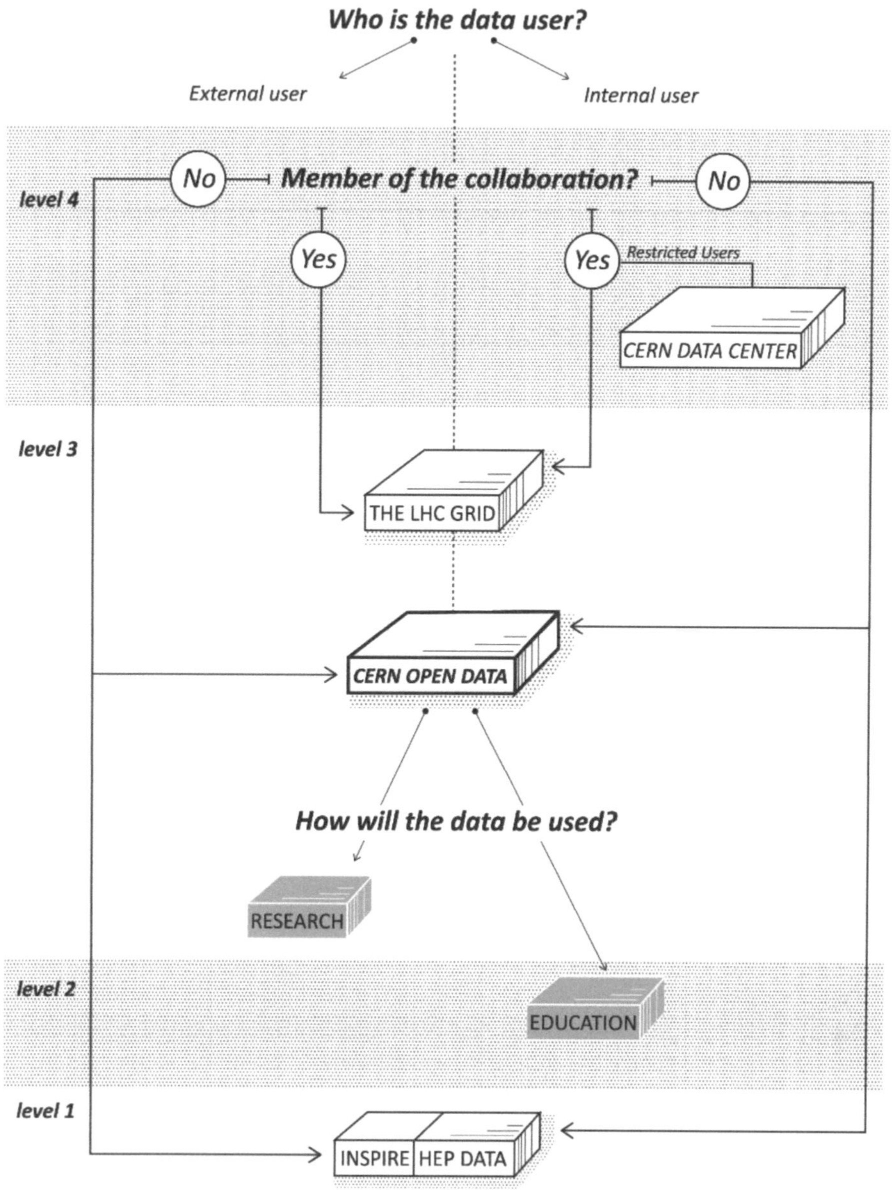

Figure 6.
Key data decision points at CERN.

supplemented with examples illustrating how a user, even from the general public, could write code to analyse the data [289]. There are several high-level tools for working with the data, and it is possible to download virtual machine images to enable external researchers to create tailored work environments.

These datasets are released in batches managed by one of the four CERN experiments. The releases are widely publicised in the media, and early experiences confirm that the publicity has assisted in attracting a large number of first-time visitors to the open data website.

CMS data forms the core of the current open data holdings. The CMS collaboration was the first committed to open data and has, to date, released more than 300 terabytes (TB) of high-quality open data. Included in that figure is over 100 TB collected by the CMS detector in 2011 and around 27 TB collected in 2010 [290].

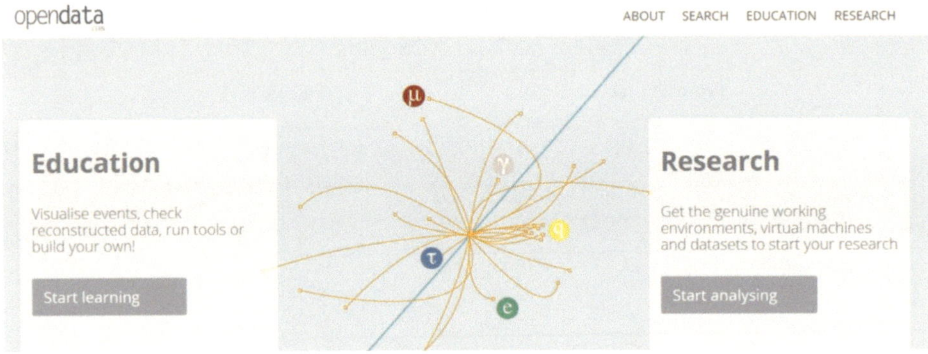

Figure 7.
The landing page of the Open Data Portal at CERN.

With rich metadata and comprehensive documentation, the data and the tools are released under the Creative Commons CC0 waiver, further discussed in Section 7.3 of this book. The data and software are presented in the MARC 21 format for bibliographic data [291], adjusted to accommodate fields for technical metadata or contextualisation. For consistency and to permit easier referencing, each record in the portal is created with a Digital Object Identifier (DOI) 'used for the identification of an object of any material form (digital or physical) or an abstraction (such as a textual work)' [292]. There is the expectation that users will cite the open data and software by the way of these identifiers, permitting tracking of reuse and thus contributing to assessment of the impact of the LHC programme [293]. CERN has adopted the FORCE 11 Joint Declaration of Data Citation Principles [294] and intends to include links to a published result of the (re)use cases in the future [295].

The two entry points on the CERN Open Data Portal, research and education, were adopted with a view to making it easier for users to identify relevant materials. After extensive testing and refinement of both entry points, students from the Lapland University of Applied Sciences in Finland and groups of researchers at CERN reviewed the portal's content, tested the tools, and confirmed that examples were reproducible.[171]

In the education portal, users can find simplified data formats for analysis as training exercises. Each has a comprehensive set of supporting material providing easy use by, for example, high-school students and their teachers in CERN's masterclasses. Students can use datasets, reconstructed data, processing tools, and learning resources to further explore and to improve their knowledge of particle physics.

The research portal presents datasets for research. It also offers reconstructed data, essential software, and guides for virtual machines. The available datasets are explained in detail, including the methodologies for validation and examples for how they could be used.[172]

One of the most popular datasets frequently accessed by users is the data produced as part of the experiments that led to confirmation of the existence of the Higgs boson elementary particle[173] at CERN in 2012. That discovery, made jointly by the ATLAS and CMS collaborations, was acknowledged by the Royal Swedish

---

171 *Ibid.*

172 CERN Open Data Portal at point 52.

173 The Higgs boson is an elementary particle in the Standard Model of particle physics. First suspected to exist in the 1960s, confirmation of the Higgs boson was formally announced by CERN at the end of 2012.

Academy of Sciences in its announcement of the awarding of the 2013 Nobel Prize in Physics to François Englert and Peter Higgs for their theoretical work on the same subject half a century earlier [296].

CERN has promoted the use of the open dataset through the 'Higgs boson machine learning challenge'. This competition was created with a view of encouraging machine learning techniques using the Higgs boson data. The challenge ran over 6 months in 2014 on the Kaggle platform [297] and was highly successful, with 1785 teams participating and over 35,000 submissions posted on the web. Several of the machine learning methods proposed by the participants have been applied to real data at CERN, and the winners of the competition were invited to CERN to discuss the results with the CERN physicists. This outstanding example of joint work between expert and non-expert teams illustrates in a powerful way the potential that access to open data has to motivate both collaboration and new research.

5.2.4 Data and analysis preservation

CERN is a self-funded organisation, and the open data mandates recently introduced by research funders have not directly impacted the CERN researchers. The mandates have, however, raised the profile of open data and have given a fresh impetus to thinking about data preservation and sharing within the organisation.

When I first visited CERN in 2009, the general view was that data could mean anything and that there were many risks associated with sharing of the LHC data. At that time, the CMS collaboration was experimenting with open data, and the ATLAS collaboration was opposing it. The other two collaborations were closely watching the experiences at CMS. Over time, all four collaborations embraced the sharing of selected subsets of their data, supporting metadata, analyses, and software.

The key incentive for harnessing support for open data across the organisation was the long-established need for data preservation within the high-energy physics community. This discipline is known for its well-developed preprint and data-sharing culture—a practice that also assisted the organisation in rolling out gold open access[174] to all its publications as early as in 2002 [298]. CERN is recognised as a leader in the open access movement and has developed the Invenio digital library software[175] covering articles, books, journals, photos, videos, and other publishing outputs.

The LHC data is unique and forms an important element of the scientific legacy of the organisation. The end of any CERN experiment or scientific project does not usually mean shelving the data. On the contrary, physicists often continue to use the data or they refer to it when cross-validating later results. This can lead to new findings long after the initial experiments are published—for example, when the earlier data is analysed by means of improved methods or software. An outstanding example of this practice is research undertaken by the joint 2004 Nobel Prize in Physics laureates (Davis J. Gross, H. Davis Politzer, and Frank Wilczek), who researched asymptotic freedom in the theory of the strong interaction between nuclear forces. Their work incorporated retrospectively evaluated data from the JADE experiment completed back in 1986 [300].

The need to make Level 3 data openly available to wider audiences presented new challenges in data preservation with a view to achieving reusability, reproducibility, and discoverability of the data. In particular, there was the need to

[174] See definitions of gold and green open access at point 20.

[175] Invenio was originally developed to run the CERN document server, administering over 1000,000 bibliographic records in high-energy physics [299].

thoroughly document and preserve metadata, along with the need for data format and software version control that had already been well-identified before the development of the Open Data Portal. These processes are internally known as the CERN Analysis Preservation Framework, and they have involved prototyping a central platform for all four LHC collaborations to preserve the supporting information about their analyses and about the tools used for them.

The library team, supported by the four collaborations and the IT team, conducted a number of pilot studies and collected information about how researchers record their research workflows [301]. This was followed by an extensive consultation process and testing that eventually resulted in the new CERN analysis preservation (CAP) library service, hosted by the Invenio digital library platform. The service was designed with a unique disciplinary research workflow, which captures each step and the resulting digital objects [302].

To facilitate the future reuse of multiple research objects, researchers need to plan, from an early stage of their experiments, how they will preserve data. They also need to provide sufficient contextual information around the analysis. A standard analysis (i.e. a record) stored in the CAP server contains detailed information about the processing steps, the datasets that are used, and the software (and version) used. In addition, detailed information about the physics involved is included, along with detailed notes on the scientific measurements.

The ATLAS collaboration made an important contribution to the process. Some of the researchers felt extremely uneasy about the possibility of someone else independently reproducing their Level 3 data experiments without the same knowledge as the members of the collaboration of the intricate internal processes. Members of the collaboration have studied the concept of data reproducibility intensely and, in order to facilitate (in their own words) 'preservation of the recipe, not the pizza' [303], they have developed a useful internal distinction and vocabulary for describing the subtle differences between what they framed as 'data reproducibility' and 'data replicability'.

Reproducibility, analogous with the 'pizza', describes the concept of archiving existing software, tools, and documentation used in the analysis procedures. The proof that an analysis is reproducible is the ability to redo the steps, in close detail, as they were undertaken by the original analysis team. To succeed, all the 'ingredients' that produced the original outcomes need to be preserved as they were at the time of publication. Those ingredients include computer configuration (e.g. operating system and architecture), the software releases used at the time, and the datasets as then reconstructed. These requirements are mostly useful for short- and medium-term preservation. Reproducibility, they concluded, has the most application in the confirmation and clarification of the published result.[176]

Replicability, analogous to the 'recipe', refers to the process of ensuring that the original analyses are repeatable using the most recent version of software tools and data formats. Since the amounts of data involved are enormous, storing indefinitely those datasets reconstructed with old software releases will not be possible. There is an imperative, therefore, to ensure the old data remains readable by newer versions of the software.[177] Those working on the ATLAS experiment are investigating options to ensure replicability in this sense. The ATLAS collaborators believe replicability might be achievable via code migration and regression testing as well as detailed human-readable information about how the analyses were performed. This information will be invaluable for newer members of the collaboration who would

---

[176] *Ibid.*

[177] *Ibid.*

not be familiar with the older software and analysis procedures. For this reason, the ATLAS team argues, relying solely on reproducibility is not sufficient for preserving data for future access.

In the meantime, the other collaborations continue to 'preserve the pizza' wherever this is deemed necessary and achievable within the resources available. For example, the current ALICE data access policy states that:

> *... while formats can change with time, the collaboration provides software releases suitable to read and process any format, or alternatively to migrate data from one format to another. Since processed data can exist in several versions, only the version used for the final publication of the results is considered as a candidate for data preservation [304].*

Like ATLAS, the CMS experiment is committed to preserving Level 3 data by 'forward-porting'—that is, by keeping a copy of the data reconstructed with the best available knowledge of the detector performance and conditions. This data includes simulations and is capable of analysis by the central CMS analysis software. While at this time it is not possible to reconstruct the CMS data [293], the analysis procedures, workflows, and code are preserved in the CMS code repository.

The pilot CAP testing revealed that, while there were many similarities in the data workflows and processes among the four collaborations, these practices do not allow for the later reproduction of the analysis in a uniform way across the four experiments. The key challenge, therefore, was to establish, firstly, interoperability with a variety of data and information sources and, secondly, connectors between the various tools used by each collaboration. The CAP is not an effort to enforce a standard across experiments, which is the push in other scientific disciplines. Rather, the CAP aims to flexibly accommodate the requirements of the four data collaborations.[178]

The data preservation processes included in the four open data policies have been embedded in the internal research workflows and have become part of daily practice. This is an unintended, yet probably the most tangible, benefit accrued from the internal work on open data at CERN so far. The CERN Library reported that the new CAP service helps researchers to better manage their research workflows by making internal work practices and data more accessible and discoverable.[179] It is believed that the CAP practices will, eventually, also save researchers time and effort as they will be able to utilise the work of others more readily.

Following the CAP pilot, the ATLAS collaboration reported that the key learning outcome was the planning for data preservation from an early stage of any experiment. The ATLAS event data model took this into consideration, among other matters [305]. Also resulting from the CAP implementation is improved access to past corporate knowledge for new members of the collaboration.

Finally, and perhaps most importantly, the improved data curation at CERN has confirmed the organisation's potential to conduct open science and has provided physicists with new means for looking at ongoing and past data analyses. As well, the data enables physicists at CERN to look at novel ways for engaging colleagues outside their individual collaborations. For example, the ATLAS collaboration is exploring the potential of the recasting of analyses. This might result in providing a robust mechanism for the testing, by those outside the collaboration, of new physics models against well-validated analysis chains [306].

---

[178] Chen et al. [302], at point 70, 354.

[179] *Ibid*, 349.

Despite the tangible outcomes achieved through experiments with open data at CERN, there remain researchers at CERN who are yet to be convinced about the utility and value of making lower-level data available to external users as open data. Their concern is a possible lack of interest from non-experts outside physics to meaningfully interrogate the datasets ([89], p. 111). As mentioned earlier, processing CERN lower-level data requires access to high computing power, and it is unlikely that many external users would have such access. Knowledge of physics and data practice in the field is also required to understand the data and the experiments—even in cases where data is meticulously described and when all necessary software and algorithms are made available to the users. The sceptics have a point here, and only future developments in technology and the uses of CERN open data will tell whether their concerns can be overcome.

5.2.5 The use of open data

5.2.5.1 Research

Research activity on the open data website seems to respond to new data releases. Following the release in 2014 of the CMS data compiled in 2010, some 82,000 users visited the site. Of these, 21,000 viewed the data in more detail. The portal had almost 20,000 visitors who used at least one of the tools (event display or histogramming). On average, the web page was used by 1000 people a day. Of these, 40% looked at the detailed data records and 1% downloaded a Level 3 dataset.[180] Just over a year later, in April 2016, the CMS data compiled in 2011 was released, totalling some 300 TB of data. This release saw 210,000 users visiting the site, of whom 37,000 viewed the data in more detail and 66,000 used the event display facility.

When a new batch of open data is released, it is accompanied by extensive press and social media coverage, followed by a peak of interest from the public. In these periods, CERN sees some 70,000 distinct users visiting the site a day. After several weeks, the interest drops to a normal level, which is around 2000 distinct users per day. CERN also sees smaller peaks in the non-release periods due to social media events, such as a recent Reddit 'Ask Me Anything' session that attracted some 10,000 users to the site.[181]

In October 2017, the CMS open data team was excited to see the publication of the first independent study produced reusing CMS open data. The CMS team had put extensive effort into describing the datasets, supporting tools, configuration parameters, workflows, other auxiliary information, and all the 'insider' knowledge that went into constructing the dataset. It was therefore rewarding for the team to see Jesse Thaler's group from MIT succeed in understanding and studying the data independently from the CMS team. The MIT study revealed a universal feature within jets of subatomic particles, which are produced when high-energy protons collide [307]. This research would not have been possible without access to the CMS data.

5.2.5.2 Education

To identify the technical tools and instructions necessary to bring the CMS open data to a wider audience, CERN ran a number of pilot projects in Finnish high

[180] Cowton et al. [295] at point 59, 4.

[181] I am very grateful to Tibor Simko, Sunje Dallmeir-Tiessen, and Achim Geiser for collating the statistics.

schools [308]. The International Particle Physics Outreach Group began in 2005 and runs masterclasses in high schools in over 40 countries. Currently, these masterclasses utilise Level 2 data from all four data detection centres at CERN. For instance, 10% of the ATLAS data is available for students to search for a Higgs boson. This masterclass is extremely popular and has reached locations other than schools, such as science centres and museums.

The largest national masterclass programme is offered in Germany. Every year more than 100 young facilitators, mostly masters and PhD students, take CERN data to German high schools. Around 4000 students are invited to further their qualifications as part of the masterclass network, often choosing for themselves the topics of their research theses.

Elsewhere, masterclasses offered in Greek schools are combined with virtual LHC visits in which students link with a CERN physicist working on the ATLAS or CMS experiments.[182]

Due to the rising demand for LHC masterclasses, CERN is investing more resources into developing this resource further. In fact, all four collaborations concur that the benefits arising from Level 2 data are clear and represent a good return on the organisation's investment of resources and staff time.

5.2.6 Data embargo period

CERN researchers are of the view that data exclusivity is required before their data can be shared with external parties. Generally, the data embargo period spans from 3 to 10 years from when the data was taken.

There are several reasons for this long embargo period. Firstly, the lead times for the LHC experiments are substantial. For example, the ATLAS collaboration formally commenced operations in 1994, following 10 years of planning. The first ATLAS data was taken in 2009, and its expected lifetime is more than 20 years. What is more, data curation and processing require a huge and ongoing commitment of research effort. The ATLAS collaboration estimated that each ATLAS member spends, on average, 100 days a year on 'data authorship'. The clear majority of researchers regards this as time spent on 'non-publishable work' and describes it as unrewarded effort. For this reason, most physicists view the incentives associated with data curation largely in terms of exclusive access [309].

The data release period varies across the four collaborations. The CMS experiment is most prone to data sharing and has the shortest embargo period of 3 years. On the other hand, the ATLAS experiment requires the longest embargo period—this is defined as a 'reasonable embargo period' ([287], p. 2). In general, data will be retained for the sole use of the collaboration for a period argued to be commensurate with the large investment in effort needed to record, reconstruct, and analyse it. After this period some portion of the data will be made available externally, with the proportion rising over time. The LHCb collaboration will normally publish 50% of its research as open data after 5 years, rising to 100% after 10 years [310]. The ALICE experiment has committed to make 10% of its data available in 5 years, rising to 100% after 10 years [304].

The CMS collaboration has opted to release Level 3 data publicly on an annual basis. Additionally, releases will be made during long LHC machine shutdowns and on the basis of best efforts during running periods. During the lifetime of CMS, the upper limit on the amount of publicly available data, compared with that available only to the collaboration, will correspond to 50% of the integrated luminosity

[182] *Ibid.*

collected by CMS. Usually, data will be released 3 years after collection, even though the collaboration can decide to release particular datasets either earlier or later [293].

5.2.7 The value of CERN open data

The four open data preservation and sharing policies at CERN result from delicate negotiations and robust internal discussions about the needs and principles for data sharing and preservation. The policies have created a shared understanding of open data at CERN, forging a consensus between many divergent attitudes and views. By codifying the key principles, defining the various components of data at various stages of their processing, developing the criteria (incorporating the levels of processing, preservation, and access), and developing supporting documentation for data preservation, the organisation has greatly improved its internal data management flow. The resulting policies are high level, yet the discussion driving the development of these policies has transformed the way data and supporting analyses are preserved, documented, and used.

The processes underlying these developments were thoroughly workshopped and tested as pilots and only then were they embedded in the internal data flow and research conduct. These processes were driven bottom-up, by the CERN physicists who see the benefits to their work—including further analysis and discovery and validation of their efforts. The library and IT teams have provided hands-on support and facilitated the development of data documentation, citation, linking, and discoverability tools, as well as suitable platforms. Open data at CERN facilitated the emergence of a collaborative and open-ended conversation across the entire organisation. At CERN, open data is not the result of mandates imposed on researchers by external funders, even though external mandates initially prompted the CERN researchers to think about open data.

The greatest value of open data at CERN stems from the benefits that the robust experimentation with, and the sustained thinking about, open data has engendered within the organisation. The value lies in the continuous learning and constant improvement of data quality as a result of improved preservation, curation, accessibility and increased potential for reuse. These processes are transforming not only the minds of researchers and their research conduct, but they are also likely to lead to improved research outcomes.

The value accruing from the use and reuse of CERN open data by external parties is yet to be seen. However, the initial experiences with the outreach programmes have been immensely encouraging.

Conclusion

The World Wide Web was invented at CERN, and the organisation is now using it to conduct big data experiments to extend our understanding of data-driven science.

CERN does not have the computing and financial resources to crunch all the data it collects as part of the Large Hadron Collider experiments in Geneva. Instead, it relies on grid computing powered by computer centres in many parts of the world. The Worldwide LHC Computing Grid gives a community of over 10,000 physicists near real-time access to LHC data. In using open hardware, open software, and open standards to power the grid, CERN is leading the way in developing cost-effective solutions for 'big data' tasks. And portions of that data are increasingly becoming available in the public domain as open data.

The four open data preservation and sharing policies at CERN are the result of a mix of delicate negotiations and robust internal discussions about the needs and principles for data sharing and preservation—both for internal organisational purposes and for sharing the LHC data with external parties. The policies have created a shared understanding of open data at CERN, forging a consensus between many divergent attitudes and views. The organisation has greatly improved its internal data management flow by codifying the key principles, defining the various components of data at various stages of their processing, developing criteria, and providing the supporting documentation for data and analysis preservation.

At CERN, open data is not the result of mandates imposed on researchers by external funders, even though external mandates initially prompted the CERN researchers to think about open data. The resulting policies are high-level, yet the discussion driving the development of these policies has primarily occurred among researchers and research teams. In this process, the library and IT teams have provided hands-on support and facilitated the development of data documentation, citation, linking, discoverability tools, as well as suitable platforms. Open data at CERN facilitated the emergence of a collaborative and open-ended conversation across the entire organisation. This combined effort and cumulative thinking has transformed the way the LHC data and supporting analyses are preserved, documented, and used.

Not all data produced at CERN is available as open data at this stage. CERN recognises four distinct groups of prospective data users—from collaboration members, to the wider high-energy physics community, to those in education and outreach, and members of the public with interest in science. Corresponding with the needs of these users is the classification of the LHC data into four distinct levels with different access rights. While open data can serve all of these users, lower-level LHC data—that is, Level 3 and Level 4 data—are only available to expert users. Restricting access to lower-level data to expert users is necessary at this stage, as significant computing power and knowledge of particle physics are required to understand and reuse the data. However, portions of low-level data are increasingly becoming available as open data for research.

CERN has become a leader in the open data field because its management and senior researchers appreciated early that a good data management practice will not only satisfy research requirements in the short term but also serve as an organisational blueprint driving continuous improvement in scientific research and scholarly communications for many years to come.

The greatest value of open data at CERN stems from the benefits that the robust experimentation with, and the sustained thinking about, open data has engendered within the organisation. The value lies in the continuous learning and constant improvement of data quality as a result of improved preservation, curation, accessibility and increased potential for reuse.

The value accruing from the use and reuse of CERN open data by external parties is yet to be seen. However, the initial experiences with the outreach programmes have been encouraging, as evidenced by the high demand for the open datasets that committed and enthusiastic outside users are busily downloading and reusing.

Chapter 6

Open Sharing of Clinical Trial Data

This chapter summarises the experience with the digital sharing of clinical trial data, focusing on the methods and stages of data sharing and the issues that act as barriers to data sharing.

The discussion is structured in four key sections:

1. The value of open clinical trial data

2. Stakeholders in the sharing of clinical trial data

3. The stages of data sharing

4. The challenges of open data sharing

Introduction

The previous chapter examined the practices and methods for sharing particle physics data and identified the key challenges and lessons learnt in the process. This chapter turns to consider the practice of the digital sharing of clinical trial data. Clinical testing of new pharmaceuticals is governed by rigorous ethics and research protocols.

In this chapter, I examine how these protocols are being applied to shared data resulting from clinical trials. The examination starts by identifying the drivers for the open sharing of clinical trial data. This is followed by discussion of the role of various stakeholders in driving the data release, focusing especially on pharmaceutical regulatory agencies. I then describe the stages of data release as they have emerged in recent years and compare these stages to those at CERN. The final section discusses the challenges arising in open sharing of clinical trial data. I pay particular attention to privacy concerns—to managing the risks of data misinterpretation and to the motivations for researchers to curate and to share data and collaborate with colleagues.

6.1 The value of open clinical trial data

Clinical trials are crucial in determining the safety and efficacy of pharmaceuticals and for ensuring appropriate and effective treatment. Clinical trials represent the largest portion of the estimated US$1.3 billion total cost of developing a new drug and bringing it to the market [311]. In the digital era, doctors and patients increasingly require access to clinical trial data as they use the Internet and online resources to learn about diseases, treatment and side effects. Patients also share knowledge and experiences and participate in online communities, many of which are disease-specific. Such active involvement by patients can be helpful in determining the course of their treatment and care. According to the President of the Institute for Clinical Systems Improvement:

> *An important component of patient contribution is to balance what evidence-based medicine and conventional medical wisdom recommends with what is possible, desirable and most acceptable for the individual patient.*[183]

In this emergent field of consumer-driven research, patients are no longer just passive recipients of care. They are becoming more aware and more active—becoming members of the care and research team, engaged in decision-making regarding their treatment plans.[184] At this time, such participation remains limited to highly educated patients and social groups [313–317], even though with increasing education levels around the world, the prospects for patient-driven medical research are increasing, too. Some online communities of patients have already made a difference to the quality of life of those suffering from rare cancers and other diseases [318, 319]. In some cases, patient participation in medical research has resulted in the ability to recruit participants for clinical trials in rare diseases and to get them actively involved in community engagement activities, as reported in the inaugural issue of the *Journal of Participatory Medicine*.[185]

As medical research is becoming more patient-driven, calls for broader access to clinical trial data intensify. The established system of data sharing is being tested. Access to clinical trial data has traditionally been made available only to researchers following the requests made to investigators, research sponsors or journal editors [320]. These traditional methods used for clinical trial data dissemination are far more advanced than in other scientific fields. For example, the descriptors for clinical datasets are more advanced than in other disciplines [321]. However, the sharing of clinical trial data still occurs in closed professional circles through direct sharing rather than online, via public repositories.

There are several reasons for such restricted data sharing. Firstly, many clinical trials are not reported [322]. Secondly, only positive results usually get published in journals [323, 324]. Thirdly, of those published results, only a small portion of clinical trial data gets deposited along with articles in peer-reviewed journals [325, 326]. Finally, the data that is supposed to get published under open data mandates may not be readily available to other users.

For example, a 2009 study of data-sharing requests made to investigators listed in *PLOS Medicine* and *PLOS Clinical Trials*—two authoritative journals committed to data sharing—found that there was a very limited compliance with the PLOS data-sharing policy. The policy explicitly stated that:

> *... data should be provided as supporting information with the published paper. If this is not practical, data should be made freely available upon reasonable requests.*[186]

Upon lodging 10 such requests, the authors of the study were able to obtain only one dataset. Two email addresses of the investigators listed as contacts for data sharing were no longer valid. Four investigators were unwilling to share their data either because they were too busy or that it would take too much work to organise

---

[183] Comments made by Dr. Kent Bottles, President of The Institute for Clinical Systems Improvement. See Frydman [312].

[184] *Ibid.*

[185] Frydman [312] at point 2.

[186] *PLoS Medicine Editorial and Publishing Policies* as valid at 4 March, (2009). Cited in Savage and Vickers [327].

and to annotate the datasets or that data sharing was not yet possible because further analyses were needed with the data. Two investigators did not respond to the data requests and numerous follow-up emails. The authors of the study concluded that policies set by journals that require the sharing of data do not facilitate availability of datasets to independent investigators.[187]

A similar study published in 2006 summarised the results of data requests made directly to authors of articles published in psychology journals. Their success in obtaining data was slightly higher, even though only a handful of the journals had in place a data-sharing policy. Out of 141 requests, the authors received data in 26% of cases over the 6 months of their efforts to contact the authors [328].

The most recent and comprehensive study was published in 2013. That study, employing several research methods, examined the potential for sharing genomic data published under open data mandates. In one approach they directly contacted the authors of eligible papers from two journals committed to data publication. Specifically, they contacted 19 authors and achieved a 59% return rate within 7.7 days [329]. This result is markedly better than those reported in earlier studies. The authors surmised that the attitudes to data sharing have improved in recent years. However, they also noted that recent studies based on human data still had low success rates, perhaps due to privacy issues that present a barrier to data sharing in these scientific disciplines.[188]

The same study also examined the elements of open data policies that positively correlate with data publication. Based on extensive statistical analyses, the authors concluded that mandatory data-sharing policies can effectively drive data release, provided two additional conditions are met.

Firstly, the mandates should require the archiving of data in repositories and, secondly, that a data accessibility statement must be included in the manuscript. Mandatory data archiving does not itself stimulate availability of open data if the data accessibility statement in the manuscript is missing—all three requirements must be met. In other words, the most stringent policies comprising the three elements lead to significantly more data release and by some distance.[189]

A similar conclusion was reached by a 2011 study in the field of gene expression data (microarray datasets). Piwowar and Chapman examine d whether correlation exists between the strength of open data mandates and the probability of data release. The authors found that only 17 out of 70 relevant scientific journals had in place 'strong' (meaning mandatory) data archiving policies. And those with strong open data mandates were more likely to achieve publication of research data, with a success rate of more than 50%. Journals with 'recommended archiving' achieved a deposit rate of just over 30%, while a journal with no policy had only about 20% availability [330].

Another interesting finding was that journals with a higher impact factor were more likely to have the data published online than journals with substantially lower impact factor. Accordingly, a positive correlation exists between high-quality research and the availability of data.[190] A similar finding resulted from the 2013 study by Vines et al. [329].[191]

---

[187] *Ibid.*

[188] *Ibid.*

[189] *Ibid*, 36. In 'mandate archiving' into those journals for which a data accessibility statement was required in the manuscript, the chances of finding the data online were 974 times higher for those with no such policy.

[190] *Ibid.* Specifically, Piwowar found that a 244 journal with 244 an impact factor (IF) of 15 was 4.5 times more likely to have the microarray data online than a 245 journal with an IF of 5.

[191] See Vines et al. [329] at point 15.

From the studies discussed above, it is apparent that online sharing of clinical data is a desirable practice to enshrine in open data policies, even though compliance with those policies remains limited. The funders' and publishers' policies that merely encourage the deposit of research data generally achieve lower deposit rates than those with more prescriptive policies. In all cases, however, the deposit rates remain low and rarely exceed 50%. The lack of implementation suggests there are cultural and other factors that act as barriers to data release and open sharing.

Factors contributing to limited data sharing are discussed further in the following sections. The first section outlines the various stakeholders involved in the sharing of clinical trial data. This is followed by an explanation of the various forms and stages of data sharing and factors that have been identified as limiting or inhibiting researchers and their organisations from sharing research data.

6.2 Stakeholders in the sharing of clinical trial data

Several stakeholders are involved in the process of clinical trial data collection, processing, analysing, and subsequent sharing with other parties. These include the patients or other people participating in clinical trials, funders and other sponsors of trials, pharmaceutical regulatory agencies, medical research institutes and universities, external research investigators, journal publishers, and learned societies. The stakeholders play different roles in the process leading to data sharing.

6.2.1 Patients or other research subjects participating in trials

The role of human subjects participating in clinical trials has traditionally been limited to providing the necessary data. Patients involved in clinical trials were seen merely as data providers. In light of the calls for patient-centred health care, patient advocacy groups focus on the greater engagement of patients—not just in clinical trials, but also in the decisions made around the process of the design and conduct of clinical studies, including the process of data sharing [331–333]. Patient engagement increases study enrolment rates, improves credibility of the results, and assists researchers to secure funding and to design study protocols [334].

Patient involvement comes at increased costs, especially logistic costs. Yet, since much of the cost is borne by the patients themselves, the argument that the role of patients should be limited to just data provision is no longer plausible. At the same time, there are cultural barriers to greater patient involvement in the healthcare system. This is because both the established research method and societal expectation are to perform research *on* patients, and not *with* patients [335]. Accordingly, patients still continue to be regarded as a source of clinical trial data, rather than as active participants in the clinical research process [336].

With the emergence of online platforms promoting the engagement of patients in clinical trials, as summarised in **Table 3**,[192] this practice may be changing. The impact of these platforms on the practice of clinical trials is yet to be seen.

The process of recruiting participants for clinical trials is governed by established ethical norms and protocols. Out of these, the moral right of people participating in a trial to make their own choices to participate is the most important. Informed consent is a critical aspect of the research ethic. The basic principle behind informed consent is to protect the autonomy of human subjects and, in particular, to ensure that the welfare and interest of the person are always put above

[192] Based on Domecq et al. [334], at point 22.

Area of engagement	*Platform*
Identifying research priorities	James Lind Alliance (http://www.jla.nihr.ac.uk/) PCORI (www.pcori.org)
Designing and undertaking research	PatientsLikeMe (www.patientslikeme.com) 23andME (www.23andMe.com) OMERACT (www.omeract.org) Reg4All (https://www.reg4all.org/) Sage Bridge Platform (http://sagebionetworks.org/platforms/)
Improving access to clinical trial data	European Union (www.clinicaltrialsregister.eu) Trials 4 Me (http://trials4me.lillycoi.com/) NIH (https://clinicaltrials.gov/)

Table 3.
Selected online initiatives designed to engage patients in clinical trials.

society's interest. In practical terms, that means society's betterment can never be built on sacrificing the rights and health of research participants [337]. Strict internal procedures are in place to review all clinical trial proposals and to ensure that adequate informed consent procedures are followed. The ethical principles governing informed consent have important repercussions for data sharing.

The procedure for obtaining informed consent includes obtaining participants' approval for data sharing and/or data archiving. It is a lengthy procedure and before enrolling, each prospective participant in a clinical trial must, among other things, be provided with a statement describing:

- The management of confidentiality of the collected information
- How records (data) that identify the participant will be kept
- The possibility that regulatory agencies may inspect the records.[193]

Since potential future uses of clinical data cannot always be known in advance, the patients' consent for data sharing can create a tension for ethical research practice.[194] At the same time, data archiving can also be seen as ethical practice, because it ensures that data is collected in line with rigorous methods and that the data is utilised to the maximum extent possible. This can help to develop new treatments and avoid unnecessary wasting of time and resources, including the time of research participants.

What is more, clinical research practitioners are well-versed in the potential risks resulting from the unauthorised sharing of data. Mechanisms have been developed to anonymise data so as to protect the privacy of research subjects and prevent data matching.[195] The emphases on privacy controls and patient consent are unique to research using clinical trial data and pose challenges in other forms of data

---

[193] See, for example, the requirements of the US Federal Food and Drug Administration [338].

[194] The institutional review board or independent ethics committee reviews a research proposal to ensure that adequate informed consent procedures are determined and implemented in an ethical way without jeopardising the rights, safety, and well-being of the human subjects.

[195] Data matching involves bringing together data from different sources, comparing it, and possibly combining it.

sharing. At this point, research ethics committees in the United States tend not to approve informed consent documents that require sharing of patient-level data. The reasons put forward for this practice are the ethical considerations for protecting participants and efforts to minimise any risks arising from data sharing ([339], p. 54).

In the past, patients participating in trials were required to sign broad consent forms, which left them little control over data and its future use. With the increasing focus on patient-centred health care, there has been a shift towards allowing patients to decide how their information and clinical data is used and to manage these permissions online. Initiatives such as Reg4All and Sage Bionetwork Bridge have developed digital forms for obtaining informed consent. These forms enable patients to decide who can use their data and how they use it. Reg4All also allows patients to track the uses of their data [340].

The early indications from these experiments are positive. Over 70% of patients sharing their data via Sage Bionetwork Bridge have opted to share data broadly and not to limit user access [341]. This finding also suggests that the universal adoption of electronic data sharing in clinical trials as envisaged by John Wilbanks, the founder of Sage Bionetwork, may indeed be feasible. His particular objective is to collect medical data from health-tracking and health-monitoring devices and applications installed on the smartphones of trial participants.

One limitation to this development is that the process of granting informed consent electronically is quite cumbersome, due to the considerable scope of informed consent. Sage Bionetwork enables the consent form to be processed on a mobile device, but that involves over 20 consent steps.[196] The points the potential data providers are asked to consider with regard to data sharing include:

- What exactly is being shared?
- What purpose or purposes are being served by sharing?
- Who 'owns' the data? Can it be sold?
- Who is responsible for the security and privacy of the data?
- Where will the data be warehoused?
- Who will have access to the data?
- What happens if I change my mind?
- How am I protected if my data is disclosed?[197]

These new approaches to obtaining digital consent allow participants to choose whether to share data but also to participate in the clinical trials, irrespectively of their responses to the question on sharing.

However, in a clinical research setting, there is an ongoing debate surrounding the issue referred to as 'compound consent' [342].

The primary argument for *not allowing* patients to participate in the trial if they elect not to share their data is that this would lead to discrepancies between the

[196] *Ibid.*

[197] *Ibid.*

findings produced by the original research team and any subsequent uses of the data. Specifically, it would be impossible to conduct any secondary analyses of the dataset collected during the trial and to verify the original findings.

The primary argument for *allowing* patients to participate in a clinical trial if they elect not to share some or all of their data is to build trust among trial participants, especially those from vulnerable social groups or those with sensitive diseases. Participation by these people in clinical trials is crucial to the development of new medicines targeting such specific conditions. In these cases, it has been argued that compound consent might be an appropriate way to achieve greater enrolment in clinical trials.[198]

The conditions of informed consent may need to be adjusted to specific clinical trials and to specific patients group, allowing patients to have greater control over their data. This appears to be the latest best practice, but it poses some limitations on future data sharing and on the replication of outcomes achieved in earlier clinical trials.

6.2.2 Regulatory agencies

The ultimate objective of commercial clinical trials is to gain regulatory agency approval of pharmaceuticals for human use. Sponsors of clinical trials seeking regulatory approval from agencies such as the European Medicines Agency (EMA) or the U.S. Food and Drug Administration (FDA) must provide detailed clinical study reports (CSRs) with data on individual participants in their marketing applications for new products. Regulatory agencies are therefore in a strong position to influence the conduct of clinical trials, including data-sharing principles. Up until very recently, the practice of gaining marketing and regulatory approvals for pharmaceuticals has been well-defined and rigorous, yet it is not particularly transparent in terms of enabling public access to the materials submitted by companies as part of the approval process. The landscape has changed completely in recent years, with the EMA leading the way in facilitating open sharing of clinical trial data globally.

In the past, the agency was criticised for not releasing sufficient information after receiving external requests [343]. It is possible for any European Union citizen to request information from any European Union institution, including the EMA.[199] Nonetheless, the EMA was not releasing a sufficient degree of information in response to such requests.

In early 2010, the European Ombudsman considered that the agency's repeated refusals to disclose public documents constituted acts of maladministration [344]. The agency's reasoning had been that the documents requested fell under the exceptions contained in the Rules for the Implementation of Regulation of the European Commission on access to EMA documents [345]. In its decisions to refuse access, the EMA had invoked Article 3(2)(a) of the rules, which refers to the protection of 'commercial interests of a natural or legal person, including intellectual property'.[200]

However, the Ombudsman held that the EMA reasoning was unconvincing, given that the study reports and protocols requested did not appear to involve any commercial interest. The Ombudsman ordered that the complainants be granted access to the clinical study reports and corresponding trial protocols.

---

[198] Institute of Medicine [339], at point 29, 51.

[199] See Article 255 of the treaty establishing the European Community.

[200] See EMA/MB/203359/2006 Rev. 1 Adopted.

In response, the EMA later that year published a new policy governing access to the documents it holds [346]. This was a significant step towards greater transparency. In under 5 years since then, the EMA has released more than 1.9 million pages in response to such requests [343].

Another milestone was the announcement by the EMA Director in November 2012 to the effect that the agency was committed to broader data sharing in order to 'rebuild trust and confidence in the whole system'.[201] This was followed, in July 2013, with the release of a draft policy on the publication of and access to clinical trial data—defined as both clinical study reports and de-identified individual participant data—immediately after the regulatory decision by the EMA is made [347]. In the draft policy, the EMA stated that CSRs do not contain commercially confidential information and therefore could be released with no redactions.

In response to the draft policy, the EMA received over 150 submissions focusing on three areas—firstly, protection of patient privacy, secondly, whether information contained in CSRs could be considered commercially confidential and be used by competitors for commercial advantage, and, thirdly, the legality and enforceability of the data-sharing agreement between the EMA and data users [348].

Following extensive consultations, the final policy was released at the end of 2014 and came into effect on 1 January 2015, with the first reports made available in late 2016 [349]. The policy applies to clinical data—composed of clinical reports and individual patient data and statistical methods submitted under the centralised marketing authorisation procedure (covering the whole of the European Union).

Under the policy, the EMA will make available CSRs with commercially confidential information redacted, after making a regulatory decision on whether to grant or to refuse marketing authorisation.[202] Any member of the public may view this information on the EMA website or download it after registering and agreeing to the terms of use.

The key aspects of data use include:

- The user may not seek to reidentify the trial subjects or other individuals from the clinical reports in breach of applicable privacy laws.
- The clinical reports may not be used to support an application to obtain a marketing authorisation and any extensions or variations thereof for a product anywhere in the world.
- The clinical reports may be used solely for academic and non-commercial research purposes.[203]

Individual participant data is not yet available onlinc. The EMA plans to make this available in late 2019–2020, depending on the completion and testing of an online portal that needs to be consistent with the European Union regulations protecting individual privacy.

The recent EMA policy has already faced multiple legal challenges from pharmaceutical companies. The issue of commercial confidentiality was also recently adjudicated in the General Court of the European Union. The court recently delivered three well-considered judgements in cases brought by companies objecting to the disclosure of their documents and data submitted to the EMA. The court

[201] *Ibid*, 8.

[202] *Ibid*.

[203] *Ibid*, Annex 2.

dismissed all three cases and considered the companies had failed to provide any concrete evidence of how the disclosure of the contested documents would undermine their commercial interests. Those cases are analysed in Section 7.3.

The developments in Europe have stimulated expert discussion around data sharing in other parts of the world. In the United States, the Institute of Medicine released a report on the sharing of clinical trial data, which is the most authoritative study on the subject to date. The study was released in 2015, following extensive consultations.[204] Nevertheless, the FDA does not currently support the open sharing of clinical reports or data submitted as per the marketing approval process, referring to the strict trade secret and personal data protection laws in the United States.

Data submitted to the FDA is governed by two statutes—the *Freedom of Information Act*[205] that deals with disclosure in response to citizen requests and the *Trade Secrets Act*[206] that limits affirmative disclosure by the government. A relevant regulation defining the constraints is 21 CFR 20.61(c), which provides that:

> *... data and information submitted or divulged to the Food and Drug Administration which fall within the definitions of a trade secret or confidential commercial or financial information are not available for public disclosure [350].*

Moreover, the authors of the 2015 study concluded that these statutes, together with case law interpreting them, generally prohibit regulatory agencies such as the FDA from releasing information that is likely to cause substantial harm to the competitive position of the person from whom the information was obtained. However, unlike EMA, the FDA has not yet tested whether the release of CSRs and other data provided as part of the approval process may be eligible for release since it rarely includes patient-level data.

One important issue raised in the 2015 report is whether the FDA has the authority to issue regulations that could override the constraints of the *Trade Secrets Act*, which does allow federal government agencies in the United States to disclose trade secrets and confidential information unless such disclosure is authorised by the law.[207]

Scholars have put forward two scenarios under which the FDA might be able to do so. Firstly, the FDA potentially has the authority to disclose trade secrets for public health reasons, resulting from the provision in the *Hatch-Waxman Act* stating that the FDA is supposed to release clinical trial data after the data exclusivity period expires [351]. Secondly, the FDA has expansive authority to impose on regulated parties 'other conditions' that 'relate to the protection of public health'.[208]

In the past, the FDA has relied on this authority to propose disclosure rules for clinical data concerning human gene therapy.[209] In 2001, the FDA argued that several significant public health goals would be served through greater disclosure of data.[210] However, following publication of these analyses, the FDA withdrew the

---

204 Institute of Medicine [339], at point 29.

205 5 USC § 552.

206 18 USC § 1905 (1982).

207 18 USC § 1905 (1982).

208 Under Section 501(i) of the *Food, Drug and Cosmetic Act*.

209 See FDA 'Proposed Rule on Availability for Public Disclosure and Submission to FDA for Public Disclosure of Certain Data and Information Related to Human Gene Therapy or Xenotransplantation', 66 Fed. Reg. 4692 (2001).

210 *Ibid.*

Rule on Availability for Public Disclosure that it had issued in 2001 when making the human gene therapy decision on data publication [352]. The decision thus closed the second possible option for releasing clinical trial data submitted as part of the FDA approval process.

In early 2018, the FDA announced plans to conduct a series of pilots to release portions of CSRs redacted by the FDA to exclude confidential commercial information, trade secrets, and personal data that can fall subject to privacy laws [353]. Patient-level data is not included in the pilots.

One final comment on the role of regulatory agencies in setting the standards for data sharing is that only a small proportion of all clinical trial data is submitted to regulatory authorities. Most academic and publicly funded trials are not designed with the objective to seek regulatory approvals. Therefore, the data presented to regulatory agencies represents only a small subset of the clinical trial data available globally.

At the same time, the data is of high commercial value and therefore has the significant potential to influence future practice and study—which highlights the importance of regulatory agencies in the open data debate.

6.2.3 Industry partners

Another important stakeholder group consists of the industry partners who spent significant resources on clinical trials with the sole objective to develop and market new products. For these reasons, the information produced in clinical trials is regarded as confidential, and the culture of data sharing is not favoured by industry.

The reasons this group puts forward for confidentiality include:

- The documents from clinical trials may hold considerations based on confidential interactions with regulatory authorities.[211]
- The documents may contain data that is subject to personal protection and informed consent.
- The data may disclose internal business or internal scientific expertise and business development strategies.
- Access to data might lead to conflicting or incorrect secondary uses by non-qualified users.
- Participating researchers and investigators wish to be able use the data in articles about the trials, which is important to career progression and is an important incentive for researchers to participate in industry-led clinical trials.

A further factor put forward in the argument against data disclosure was that industry partners like to use previous clinical data in the development of subsequent products and access to such information could give competitors an advantage —thus shortening the lead time between the marketing of the first product and when similar products begin to appear based on the original.[212]

[211] Institute of Health at point 29, 62.

[212] *Ibid.*

Scholars and industry partners alike have argued that the lead time from 'research to market' is the key factor facilitating return on investment in research and development [354]. That lead time has already decreased substantially in recent years and further decreases through data disclosures might discourage further investments in drug development.[213] This issue is of particular importance to the development and marketing of biosimilars and is further discussed in Section 7.3.

To date, most data sharing by pharmaceutical companies is based on internal policies that require researchers to submit detailed proposals, which are subject to strict internal reviews by the company and often limit the release to highly redacted data. In some cases, external investigators have obtained access to industry-sponsored clinical trials and have conducted independent secondary analyses that identified significant issues in the underreporting of negative results and serious side effects.

These studies also have reported industry failure to publish the results of negative trials for widely prescribed therapies [355]. While industry groups have denied such claims, the subsequent sparring has, in several cases, initiated further clinical trials to test the contested issues and led to billion-dollar settlements of legal disputes.[214] In some other cases, changes in the labelling of pharmaceuticals or restrictions to prescribing certain drugs to risk-prone patients were required.[215]

Such grave instances of professional misconduct and manipulation of clinical trial data further support the case for releasing clinical trial data.

It the meantime, complaints from researchers and investigators on repeated denial of access to clinical trial data have initiated discussions among industry partners to introduce more transparent approaches to data release and expert sharing.[216] The open-sharing polices released by the EMA also played a major role in changing industry approaches to data sharing. Major pharmaceutical industry associations in Europe and the United States have committed to the sharing of clinical trial data and have agreed to develop a process for data sharing [357].

One issue in urgent need of addressing is the cost of sharing clinical trial data. There are several cost components to open clinical data, and additional human resources are required to redact confidential information and personal data from reports and data.

Other costs are associated with preparing and reviewing the reports and data for publication—including due diligence and payments to external reviewers and auditing panels to ensure compliance. Additional work is required to prepare templates for informed consent that would enable greater data sharing and to provide lay summaries of the data.[217] Almost half of the applications submitted for FDA approval are filed by small businesses [358], and the submitters may not have the resources for preparing clinical trial data for publication.

6.2.4 Other stakeholders

There are many other stakeholders with the leverage to set standards and to encourage the sharing of data arising from clinical trials. In addition to those

---

[213] *Ibid.*

[214] See Table 3.1 'Examples of Effects of Independent Analyses Carried Out on Clinical Trial Data', in Institutes of Health (2015) at point 29.

[215] *Ibid.*

[216] For a good summary, see Krumholz et al. [356].

[217] The costs detailed by industry are itemised in Institute of Medicine [339] at point 29, 68.

mentioned already, research funders and publishers are significant stakeholders. Their role in data publication and release is outlined in Chapter 3.[218]

Other important stakeholders include researchers and investigators involved in clinical trial design, collection, processing, and analysis of data. Research investigators are not involved in the data collection but typically use it for secondary analyses and reanalysis of the results, which are typically published in scientific publications. The work of clinical researchers and investigators is largely directed by industry partners. Again, this raises the issue of funding for data sharing. In the 2015 study, researchers raised grave concerns that if data sharing becomes an unfunded mandate, the costs of sharing will reduce the funding available for new grants. This would, in turn, result in fewer new trials.[219] The study further noted that this concern is particularly cogent for researchers working in low-resource settings such as those affected by neglected global diseases.[220]

Medical research institutes and universities also have an important stake in the sharing of clinical trial data. They can influence data sharing through infrastructure support, providing incentives and training to researchers and by conducting scientific reviews. Universities employ many investigators involved in clinical trials, and they often provide the infrastructure for the design and execution of clinical trials.

Public research organisations and universities currently provide relatively little support for data curation, documentation, and sharing. While they may have created a research data management function in libraries, these are not, at this point, staffed by expert data analysts who could assist researchers with the documentation and preparation of the data for publication. What is more, there is currently little or no training provided to researchers in the procedures, documentation methods, and structures needed to share data. Even if such training modules were available, they would have to compete for the researchers' time. Given that the incentives for data sharing are minimal, data preparation is generally not a priority for researchers. These issues are examined in the section dealing with incentives below.

Other stakeholder clusters with an increasing role in clinical trials are the patient advocacy groups and associations dealing with rare diseases. These are not-for-profit organisations, foundations, or even loose networks that aim to raise funds for research and study and to provide patient education and support for clinical care. Patient advocacy groups are active in the recruitment of patients for clinical trials. In recent years, these groups have become more active, such as creating online platforms for patient engagement (see **Table 3**). In the United States, patient advocacy groups have become more active providers of the data collected directly by their members—such as from their smartphones or medical measurement devices [359]. With increasing demands for participatory medicine, patient advocacy groups will likely play a more important role in clinical trials into the future.

6.3 The stages of data sharing

From the discussion above, it is apparent that the sharing of clinical trial data occurs through various networks and platforms—from sharing data underpinning publications, through providing extensive clinical summary reports and individual data to regulatory agencies as part of the marketing approval process, to sharing clinical data directly between industry partners and research investigators and to depositing data online in discipline or research-specific repositories.

---

[218] Especially Sections 3.2 and 3.4.

[219] Institute of Health at point 29, 72.

[220] *Ibid*, 73.

Similar to the stages of processing and release of particle physics data, described in the previous chapter, clinical trial data is also being shared along different stages of processing, granularity, and control. Such data can also be shared openly, by depositing it online or upon request. Given these similarities, and for the purposes of consistency, the sharing of clinical trial data is described below along four levels, with Levels 1, 3, and 4 roughly corresponding to data-sharing levels at CERN. Level 1 is the data underpinning publications, Level 3 consists of analysable datasets that enable full reproducibility of analyses, and Level 4 represents raw data (or experimental data) collected in the course of research studies.

6.3.1 Data Level 1: data underpinning publications

Given that changes to policies on releasing clinical trial data by regulatory agencies are very recent and are not yet fully implemented in practice, publication in peer-reviewed scientific journals remains the primary method for sharing clinical trial data with the scientific and medical communities, as well as with the public. Typically, several publications are written in the course of a clinical trial.

The first publication usually covers the key objectives of the trial and reports the key outcomes and baseline measures. Subsequent publications focus on a specific aspect of the primary analyses and report outcomes for a particular subgroup of patients.[221]

The deadline for the release of data underpinning publications varies among publishers and research funders. The study by the Institute of Medicine recommended depositing data within 6 months from publication.[222] The WHO Joint Statement on public disclosure of results from clinical trials includes an 'indicative timeframe' of 24 months from study completion, to allow for peer review [360]. Funders and publishers generally tend not to include a specific deadline in their policies, as discussed in Chapter 3.[223] Instead, research funders tend to use wording such as 'within a reasonable timeframe'.[224] The reason for this is that researchers have argued that they require time to write publications resulting from their research and that their careers may be jeopardised if others use their data before the publications are finalised. This study summarises recommendations in this regard in Sections 8.3.4 and 8.3.5.

Differences also exist among funders, publishers, and researchers as to what they consider 'data underpinning publications'. While funders generally tend to suggest that 'data' refers to any corresponding dataset, which includes data supporting the claims made in the publication, the Institute of Medicine has further clarified the meaning of Level 1 data. Its study refers to this data as the 'post-publication package'—which, in the view of the review committee, should consist of the 'analytic dataset and metadata, including the protocol, statistical analysis plan,[225] and analytic code, supporting published results'.[226]

---

[221] Institute of Medicine at point 29.

[222] *Ibid.*

[223] See Section 3.4.

[224] National Science Foundation (2010).

[225] Statistical analysis plan describes the analyses to be conducted and the statistical methods to be used in a clinical trial. It typically includes plans for analysis of baseline descriptive data and adherence to the intervention, prespecified primary and secondary outcomes, and definitions of adverse and serious events and comparison of these outcomes across interventions for prespecified subgroups.

[226] Institute of Medicine at point 29, 108.

However, it is unclear whether the recommended post-publication dataset should include everything required to reproduce the published results, as published, or whether it should simply include enough evidence to support the findings. The committee further shared the view of the National Research Council, which in 2003 stated that:

> *Community standards for sharing publication-related data and materials should flow from the general principle that the publication of scientific information is intended to move science forward. More specifically, the act of publishing is a quid pro quo in which authors receive credit and acknowledgment in exchange for disclosure of their scientific findings. An author's obligation is not only to release data and materials to enable others to verify or replicate published findings (as journals already implicitly or explicitly require) but also to provide them in a form on which other scientists can build with further research [361].*

As such, the review committee stated that publication data should ideally be shared immediately after publication.

6.3.2 Data Level 2: summary data

Level 2 data in clinical trials is represented data, which can include any of the following—lay summaries of results to be published in prescribed registries (such as ClinicalTrials.gov), clinical study reports, either full or extracts from these reports, or summaries of clinical trials aimed at the general public.

All clinical trials are subject to requirements to report the results in registries, usually multiple registries, depending on the sources of funding and the approvals sought following completion of the trials. These summary reports are typically available on the registry website and generally are limited to major outcomes and adverse events.[227]

The approaches taken to the publication of summary reports differ sharply between Europe and the United States.

In the United States, the *Food and Drug Administration Amendments Act* (FDAAA) requires results of trials of FDA-regulated products to be reported to ClinicalTrials.gov within 12 months of study completion.[228] In 2016, the policy was extended to apply to *all* clinical trials funded in whole or in part by the National Institutes of Health—regardless of study phase, type of intervention, or whether the trial is covered under the FDAAA [362]. The reasoning put forward for such extended reporting was that:

> *... when research involves human volunteers who agree to participate in clinical trials to test new drugs, devices, or other interventions, this principle of data sharing properly assumes the role of an ethical mandate [363].*

The data elements to be provided under the legislation include participant flow, demographic and baseline characteristics, outcomes and statistical analyses,

---

[227] Adverse events are 'unfavourable changes in health, including abnormal laboratory findings that occur in trial participants during the clinical trial or within a specified period following the trial' (ClinicalTrials.gov, 2014). See also Institute of Medicine [339], p. 107.

[228] Under Section 402(j) of the *Public Health Service Act*, as amended by Title VIII of the *Food and Drug Administration (FDA) Amendments Act* of 2007 (FDAAA), and the regulation Clinical Trial Registration and Results Information Submission, at 42 CFR part 11.

adverse events, the protocol and statistical analysis plan, and administrative information.

The revised mandate accommodates delays of data submissions for up to an additional 2 years for trials of unapproved products for which initial FDA marketing approval or clearance is being sought.[229] Despite the fact that the law provides for hefty fines for missing data submissions, compliance with the prescribed timeframe was lagging.

In Europe, the release of summary data is driven by the EMA. Under the 2015 EMA data sharing policy outlined earlier in this chapter, the EMA is fully committed to publishing clinical reports submitted to the agency as part of the marketing approval process. The EMA defines clinical reports as comprising these documents:

Clinical overview—a critical analysis of the clinical data submitted. This should present the risks and limitations of the medicine development programme and the study results, analyse the benefits and risks of the medicinal product in its intended use, and describe how the study results support critical parts of the prescribing information.

Clinical summary—a detailed factual summary of the clinical information. This should include information provided in clinical study reports from any meta-analyses or other cross-study analyses for which full reports have been provided in the submission, as well as post-marketing data for products that have been marketed outside of the European Union.

Clinical study report—a detailed document about the method and results of a clinical trial. It will be a scientific document addressing safety and efficacy and its content. This should include several appendices, of which three should be published online, as follows:

1. **Protocol and protocol amendments,** describing the objectives, design, methods, statistical considerations and organisation of a clinical trial.

2. **Sample case report form,** a questionnaire used by the sponsor of the clinical trial to collect data from each participating site.

3. **Documentation of statistical methods,** providing a description of the methods used for collection, analysis, interpretation, presentation, and organisation of the data [364].

The EMA is the first regulatory agency to require full publication of CSRs, and given the breadth of the information required for online publication, the data is likely to be meaningful to diverse audiences for further study and analysis. The required data is to be published within 60 days after the European Commission decision on marketing authorisation or within 150 days after the receipt of the withdrawal letter, as stated in **Table 4**.[230]

The summary data under the EMA data-sharing policy is currently published on the EMA clinical data portal [365], which will be, in the near future, substituted for a new portal to enable publication of individual patient data (Level 4 data) in accordance with strict privacy laws in the European Union. The new portal is expected to be operational in 2019.

---

[229] NIH at point 86.

[230] *Ibid.*

	Data type	Data limitations	Data availability
level 1	**Data underpinning journal publications** (underlying data) typically report the main outcomes of clinical trials.	Lack of detailed data and information about study design, efficacy and safety analysis.	Based on individual policies of research funders and publishers. Compliance with the policies is currently lagging.
level 2	**Summary data** **EMA: Clinical reports** including clinical overviews, clinical summaries, and clinical study reports (CSR), together with appendixes to the CSRs. **FDA: Lay-language trial summary** **FDA: PILOT:** Portions from CSR that contain complete summaries of the study results, the protocol and protocol amendments, and the statistical plan.	Data redacted to exclude commercial confidential information detailed in Annex 3 of the EMA policy. Only high-level results, without supporting data PILOT: Data redacted by FDA to exclude confidential commercial information, trade secrets, and personal information.	**EMA:** 60 days after the EC decision on marketing authorisation or within 150 days after receiving the opinion of the Committee for Medicinal Products for Human Use. **FDA:** High-level summaries to posted on www.clinicaltrials.gov within 12 months of study completion. No mandate to release CSR at this stage.
level 3	**Analysable datasets** – pre-processed data prepared to address specific research questions. **Include individual patient data.** Related software and algorithms need to form part of the dataset.	Resource intensive: require detailed documentation of all the steps and assumptions taken to collect and process the data, including statistical methods, algorithms, tools and protocols. Require protection of privacy of research subjects.	**EMA:** expects to publish patient level data from 2019/2020. Questionable whether covered by open data mandates of research funders and publishers.
level 4	**Raw data, including individual patient data**	Full potential for research reproducibility. Require protection of privacy of research subjects.	Not routinely shared with the broader scientific community or the public, but portions of the data can be released under the Freedom of Information legislation.

Table 4.
Levels of access to clinical trial data.

6.3.3 Data Level 3: analysable datasets

Level 3 data refers to pre-processed data prepared to address specific research questions. Such data may be a subset of the original dataset collected in clinical trials, or it can be a full dataset after application of defined cleaning and processing steps and after performing statistical analyses. Related software, metadata, and algorithms need to form part of the dataset.

Level 3 data, or subsets thereof, are required to reproduce the results published in CSRs or in publications. However, research organisations, in general, and industry partners, in particular, are generally reluctant to share Level 3 data with external parties.[231] This data represents the full potential for secondary data analyses, and the risks associated with data sharing and reuse are greater than those with lower level data.

Of particular importance to regulatory agencies are the tasks of developing mechanisms to mitigate the risks associated with the protection of the privacy of research subjects and to avoid potential errors of misinterpretation of secondary

[231] The reasons put forward by industry for not sharing data are discussed in Section 6.3.3 of this book. The reasons put forward by researchers for not sharing data are discussed in Section 6.4.4.

analyses. The EMA is the most advanced in developing such mechanisms and expects to publicly release patient-level data in late 2019.

At this point, however, the sharing of Level 3 data is limited to expert users and is usually delayed for several years after the initial study date, especially if secondary trials are still under way. For these reasons, the policy developed by the EMA may present a momentum in driving the release of reusable clinical data globally.

6.3.4 Level 4 data: raw data, including individual patient records

The lowest level data in clinical trials is the data collected directly from patients or obtained through other means, such as by sourcing the data from medical equipment or from health applications of patients. This data may or not be cleaned, preprocessed, or packaged. It is, however, usually structured, due to the prescribed design of clinical trials. Access to raw-level data and patient records would be highly beneficial for designing new clinical trials based on previous data. While Level 3 data can also offer such functionality, the reuse of Level 3 data may be limited to the cleaning and statistical techniques taken by the original research team. By contrast, Level 4 data enables the design of new data cleaning and processing protocols.

Level 4 data is generally not shared with external audiences, except in expert settings. Portions of Level 3 and/or Level 4 data may be obtained under freedom of information legislation. In the United States and Europe, the regulatory agencies generally disclose non-summary safety and efficacy data from a specific application only in response to such requests. The potential for sharing this type of data as open data will increase when experiences with sharing and reusing higher-level data emerge. Of particular interest will be efforts to allow the reusability of Level 3 data while protecting the privacy of research subjects.

The issues of privacy are covered in detail in Chapter 7, Section 7.5, of this study. Other challenges associated with the sharing of clinical trial data are discussed below.

6.4 The challenges of open sharing of clinical trial data

6.4.1 Demands on researchers and changing attitudes towards data sharing

Curating and sharing research data, in general, and clinical trial data, in particular, pose several challenges to researchers. Many of these are interconnected with the challenges of data management described above.

The key challenge is that preparing and maintaining usable data repositories require a great deal of effort and resources, especially the time of researchers who collected the data and need to describe it in meaningful ways to make the data legible to prospective users while ensuring simultaneous compliance with the open data mandates and any confidentiality, privacy, and internal policies that may apply. This is a time- and labour-intensive process, especially in organisations implementing controlled access to data. Receiving and processing applications for data release, developing agreements and contracts, producing and transferring data, and responding to subsequent requests for clarification involve a broad range of people across the data-sharing organisation [366]. In this sense, open data more resembles new data products than readily available outputs from previous experiments. Research organisations typically have limited resources to handle these requests, which can result in conflict with other demands on staff time, such as ongoing research. In the absence of support from research funders to prepare the datasets, some research units may require applicants to provide funding to cover the necessary staff time, which in effect means spending research money on curation.[232] In the absence of funding specifically to curate and release data as open data, researchers continue to share their data with others in different ways.

Recent surveys of researchers across many disciplines also confirm this finding. For example, in a 2016 survey conducted by Wiley, over 4600 researchers reported the three most common ways of sharing data as via conference (the box ticked by 48% of respondents), as supplementary material in a journal (40%), or, informally, upon request received from other colleagues (33%). Only 20% of researchers ticked the box stating they had shared data formally via an open access repository, whether via institutional, discipline-specific, or journal repositories.[233] The authors of the study concluded that:

> *... these results demonstrate that researchers continue to be unclear on what [open] 'sharing' data means in the sense of providing unlimited, appropriately licenced and permanent access to their data.*[234]

At the same time, data sharing among researchers has markedly increased in recent years. The same survey found that 69% of researchers said they had shared data from their research in some way. This represents an increase of 17% from the same survey conducted by Wiley 2 years earlier, in 2014.[235] A similar result was reported in a survey of over 1200 researchers by Elsevier and the Centre for Science and Technology Studies. Specifically, 65% of respondents said they had previously shared their data with others [369]. At the same time, over one-third of researchers did not share their data from their last projects.[236] The attitudes of researchers to data sharing are summarised in **Figure 8.**[237]

Another interesting finding of the two studies is the reasons why researchers prefer to share (or not to share) their data. Both surveys confirm that researchers share data because it is an established practice in their field of science, such as genomic research, or that the mandates of publishers or funders require data sharing. Other primary reasons for data sharing include an ethical and moral responsibility to share data and the public benefits likely to accrue from data sharing. The Elsevier survey also established that when researchers share their data directly, the vast majority—over 80% of researchers—choose to share data with direct collaborators. This suggests that trust is an important aspect of sharing data and that credit and increased visibility are not major motivators for data sharing, as discussed below.

6.4.2 Incentives for researchers

The greatest challenge to data sharing is, arguably, the lack of incentives for researchers to share data. What is even worse, many researchers do not see value in data sharing, as documented by survey results and many authoritative studies. For example, a recent survey of researchers who received grants from the Wellcome Trust showed that the potential loss of publication opportunities, along with the

---

[232] *Ibid.*

[233] The results of the survey are reported here: Wiley Open Science Researcher Survey [367]; and Wiley Network [368].

[234] *Ibid.*

[235] *Ibid.*

[236] *Ibid*, 20.

[237] Source: Elsevier and the Centre for Science and Technology Studies [369] at point 98.

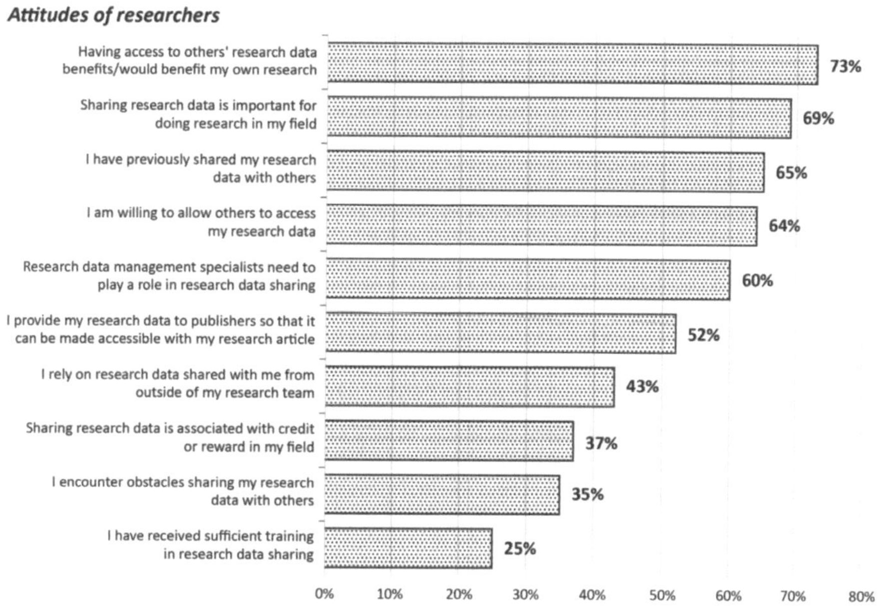

Figure 8.
Attitudes of researchers to data sharing (measured as % of respondents who agree with the statement).

belief that publishing is the only criterion for successful grant funding and academic advancement, was the major factor in the inhibition of data sharing [370].

Much effort has gone into the development of data citation practices and into measuring impact through data citation [371–376]. Yet researchers have little reason to value data metrics (including citations), because increased data impact is not the incentive for data collection and sharing in the first place. Rather, data collection is necessary to conduct research and write publications for which research grants are provided, for which researchers are rewarded, and upon which the careers of researchers depend. As noted by the Institute of Medicine [339]:

> *In the eyes of performance review and promotion committees, the primary criteria for academic success rest on publications, funding, leadership, and teaching. Data sharing is not an activity that receives attention from promotion committees, and there is insufficient recognition of the intellectual effort involved in designing, accruing, curating, and completing a clinical trial data set. In this way, the lack of incentives for sharing clinical trial data is analogous to the recognised dearth of incentives for team science within university settings.*[238]

Furthermore, researchers need reasonable time and exclusivity to work with the data they collect and to achieve the outcomes of their original research before they can share that data with others.

For these reasons, data and impact citation practices are unlikely to promote the curation and release of open scientific data and to promote collaboration among researchers, as further explained in Chapter 8, Section 8.3. Subsequently, this study argues that acknowledging the original data collectors as co-authors of any subsequent publications arising from the data reuse might be a more effective way to promote the release of research data as open data.

---

[238] Institute of Medicine at point 29, 76.

6.4.3 The limits of research reproducibility

Achieving research reproducibility is one of the objectives put forward in support of open scientific data.[239] In clinical trials there is a huge interest in replicating results, initiated by some contested evidence that the results of clinical trials for new medicines presented in marketing approvals may be wrong, or at least misleading, as discussed earlier. If a scientific result can be confirmed or disproved by sharing the underlying data, then disputes could be resolved faster, some have argued [377].

However, efforts to reproduce results often reveal research and data processing disagreements on which these disputes are based. Interrogating data may not be the answer to this. In fact, the early experiences with data reproducibility suggest that this may not be the golden key in verifying research results, despite the fact that some researchers have proclaimed reproducibility as the gold standard for future science [378, 379].

The nub of the problem with research reproducibility is the lack of agreement across scientific disciplines on how to document research data so as to ensure its reuse by independent users. The parameters for data reuse are far broader than just sharing metadata and supporting documentation, as discussed further in Section 8.3 of this book.

Other experts in the field, such as Borgman, have pointed out the problematic nature of reproducibility noting that very fine distinctions are made between validation, utility, replication, repeatability, and reproducibility, with each of these terms having a distinct meaning within individual scientific disciplines ([167], p. 209). The sharing of data resulting from clinical trials and genomic research is particularly challenging, due to a very large amount of data analysis that lead to meaningful discoveries [380]. On some occasions, the objective might be to replicate the original research undertaken, using the same techniques, while other approaches may aim to achieve comparable results using similar inputs and methods. The first approach would verify the published results, while the latter would confirm the hypotheses being tested, as Borgman also observed.[240]

Clinical trials are very much concerned with replication, yet the necessary resources and the costs of reproducing research trials might be prohibitive. Raw-level data is typically required to achieve reproducibility, and such data is expensive to document and curate and may not even be available for sharing. The Institute of Medicine reported that biomedical companies often attempt to replicate the results reported in a journal article as a first step in determining whether a line of research is likely to be productive.[241] Such companies may spend millions of dollars, but the investments may well not yield any success.[242]

In some ways, the calls for research reproducibility can also be seen as 'reinventing the wheel' rather than focusing on future research. By challenging the authority of previous research, trust among researchers that is the basis for sharing data may be undermined. In many circumstances, reproducibility has severe limitations and should not be the stated objective for open scientific data.

---

239 See Chapter 2, Section 2.3.4.

240 Borgman at point 106.

241 Institute of Medicine at point 29.

242 *Ibid.*

6.4.4 Managing ethical uses of open data

One of the risks raised by researchers as an impediment to data sharing is the possibility of data misuse or even wilful misinterpretation of the data. In the situation where there is a lack of agreement on what constitutes data reuse and reusability, these concerns are justified. In the absence of robust data descriptors, the data may be analysed incorrectly, and incorrect conclusions may be drawn. Another concern is that the purpose for which data is later reused may be incompatible with the original purpose for which the data was collected. Such purposes may include causes with which the original data creator disagrees or does not wish to be aligned. Researchers also raised concerns that future data users may not give proper credit to the original creators. A further concern is that data may be used to harm future business activities of research organisations, such as allowing others to commercially exploit the data.

At present, research organisations employ various methods to manage the risks. One approach for managing forms of permitted use can be the selection of appropriate licencing mechanisms, as discussed in Chapter 7, Section 7.3. While the Creative Commons Zero Waiver places a few limits on how the data can be reused, the broader suite of the Creative Commons 4.0 licences allows organisations to limit commercial uses of the data or the creation of derivative works. While such licences may limit the definition of open data, the sharing of research data for limited (non-commercial) purposes is still a better option than not sharing it.

Another alternative, recommended by the Open Data Institute in the United Kingdom [381], is to share data under CC-BY-SA 4.0 licence, which requires that any derivative works created from the research data be published under the same licence. This approach may help research organisations to manage undesired reuses of the data—for example, to use the data in commercial reports and to do so without attributing the original data creator.

In the field of clinical trials, data use agreements (sometimes also called data-sharing agreements) are often used to guard against the risks of data misuse. While these agreements go against the free sharing of open data, they do allow sharing for limited purposes. The key terms of such agreements in clinical trials include:

- Prohibition of any attempts to reidentify or to contact research subjects.
- No further sharing of the data.
- No commercial use.
- Requirements to attribute the original authors.
- No permission to brand any subsequent works as originating from the data producer.
- Non-endorsement of any future uses of the data by its originator.
- Secure handling and processing of the data.
- Assignment of intellectual property rights for discoveries made from the shared data.
- Limited warranties—no guarantees that data is fit for secondary uses, so reusers cannot claim damages if data is misapplied.

The last, and most effective, tool for managing the risks of data misuses and misinterpretation is through professional and ethical conducts supported by mandatory training. The complaints about data misuse can be resolved by appropriate disciplinary committees. After all, data sharing and reuse are a collective responsibility, and researchers have a key role in ensuring that data is reused ethically and in accordance with established norms and protocols.

Conclusion

Open data policies have renewed the focus on the sharing of clinical trial data, especially following the release of the EMA open data policy in 2014, with deep implications for clinical practice and research. The sharing of clinical trial data is now a more established practice within the discipline, as recent surveys confirm. The stages of data sharing and the responsibilities when sharing are clearly established across the entire research discipline, and there is a high degree of similarity in the data-sharing levels and practices among both public and private sector organisations.

At the same time, the sharing of research data in publications and directly with peers is still the method preferred over depositing clinical trial data in public repositories, especially at the level of patient data. The reasons for limited open data sharing identified in this chapter include:

i. Safeguarding the privacy of research subjects

ii. Ensuring compliance with confidentiality requirements of private research funders

iii. Fear of potential unethical use and even the wilful misuse of the data by others

iv. Lack of incentives for researchers to curate and share data

v. Lack of funding allocated to open data curation and release

vi. Lack of compliance with the open data mandates

The legal and privacy issues of data sharing are discussed further in the next chapter (Chapter 7), while Chapter 8 offers further insights into the issue of misinterpreted incentives and provides recommendations to address those issues.

Another finding of this chapter is that sharing clinical trial data does not necessarily lead to research reproducibility, as is often assumed by policymakers. Only data reusability can facilitate research reproducibility. However, low-level data is typically necessary to achieve reproducibility. Such data may not be readily available for sharing as open data or can be costly to curate. Therefore, reproducibility should only be the desired and stated objective in carefully selected research areas.

This chapter has further argued that the research profession has in place rigorous procedures for managing the privacy and confidentiality issues arising in the sharing of clinical trial data. Soft mechanisms such as codes of ethics and professional and research conduct, combined with data use agreements, have been found to be highly effective tools for managing the possible risks associated with the sharing of patient-level data. The new portal currently being tested by the EMA will showcase the world's best practice in enabling the safe and secure sharing of patient-level data as open data.

The successful sharing of clinical data as open data requires a combination of both approaches—professional and ethical data use, accompanied by robust technologies. Researchers are therefore the best positioned to control data sharing into the future.

Chapter 7

Legal Issues Arising in Open Scientific Data

This chapter aims to answer the question: what are the legal impediments to providing open access to, and the reuse of, research data that is publicly funded?

More specifically, this chapter aims to ascertain the boundaries for the release and reuse of data and/or databases, considering the current and recently proposed legal and policy frameworks and exceptions to copyright infringement.

The chapter consists of the following parts:

1. Copyright in research data
2. Ownership of research data
3. Licencing models for open scientific data
4. Different types of data reuse
5. Privacy and confidentiality issues in research data reuse

Introduction

The preceding chapters examined the many barriers to open data—with the lack of understanding of the concept of data, change of research practices and culture, attendant change management, research data management and funding issues being identified as the most prominent barriers to facilitating open access. There are, however, several legal issues associated with open research data in general and databases in particular. This chapter discusses these issues arising at two critical stages—namely, data release and data reuse. These issues are investigated in two parts.

The first part examines the legal issues arising in data release. The focus is on intellectual property rights, especially copyright in data and databases. There is also the uncertainty around data ownership, which is identified as the root cause of subsequent problems affecting data licencing, the lack of interoperability and clarity around the conditions governing data reuse. The chapter goes on to examine some relevant licencing models.

The second part concentrates on practical matters around data reuse—the need to regard intellectual property rights, where relevant, and the need of governments to facilitate text and data mining. It examines different types of data reuses and whether these can infringe different kinds of rights. Finally, the second part considers the specific issue of the privacy of research subjects and the tensions researchers face between the duty of confidentiality and the requirements to share data.

7.1 Copyright in research data

Data and databases play central roles in facilitating open access to scientific results. Legal protection of them does, therefore, strongly affect how scientists and researchers use data. The question of whether research data falls under intellectual property protection is a complex subject that is dependent on the nature of the data and the conditions under which the data is created, structured, and used. The legal basis for the protection is the existence of international legal frameworks, especially copyright frameworks, which also cover data and collections of data.[243] The international copyright framework is explored in the following sections. This is followed by an analysis of copyright law as it applies to data and data collections in several jurisdictions—Australia, the United States, and the European Union.

7.1.1 The international copyright framework

The scope of copyright protection and associated rights and the extent of the exclusive rights enjoyed by copyright owners are governed by several international treaties. Out of these, the Berne Convention, signed in 1886, is the oldest.[244] The Convention had the objective of providing a solution to the absence of international recognition for the copyright protection regimes of individual countries.

Over time, the Convention has evolved to establish the standards for the minimum level of copyright protection that all parties to it should implement. Those standards have been modified periodically as the notion of property has become more prominent. The Agreement on Trade-Related Aspects of Intellectual Property Rights (TRIPS) of 1994 [382] and the WIPO Copyright Treaty (WCT) of 1996 [383] have built on the Berne framework to accommodate advances in technology[245]—including software, databases, and the protection measures that new technologies both enable and require. Consequently, all parties to the Berne Convention—including Australia, the United States, and all member states of the European Union[246]—have used the framework set by the above-mentioned international treaties to develop national copyright law.

The scope of copyright protection in the Berne Convention is defined in Article 2, which includes quite a detailed listing of protected works, including:

> *The expression of 'literary and artistic works' shall include every production in the literary, scientific and artistic domain, whatever may be the mode or form of its expression, such as books, pamphlets and other writings; lectures, addresses, sermons and other works of the same nature; ... photographic works to which are assimilated works expressed by a process analogous to photography; ... illustrations, maps, plans ...*[247]

[243] This distinction between data and collections of data corresponds with the separation in copyright law between ideas that cannot seek protection and the expression of those ideas that can.

[244] See the Berne Convention for the Protection of Literary and Artistic Works of 9 September 1886, last amended in the Paris Act of the Berne Convention on 28 September 1979 (http://www.wipo.int/treaties/en/ip/berne/). In 2017, the Convention had 175 signatory states, according to the World Intellectual Property Organisation (WIPO), the UN agency which administers it.

[245] Other relevant treaties, also administered by WIPO, include the Rome Convention for the Protection of Performers, Producers of Phonograms and Broadcasting Organisations (1961), which secures the rights for the performers of artistic and literary works in phonogram and broadcast recordings and the rights of the producers and broadcasters of those recordings (See http://www.wipo.int/treaties/en/ip/rome/), and the WIPO Performances and Phonograms Treaty (1996), http://www.wipo.int/treaties/en/ip/wppt/, which covers, among other matters, sound recordings, broadcasts, and performers' rights. Although these are not the classical form of data, these may represent data in some scientific disciplines.

[246] In the case of the WIPO Copyright Treaty and TRIPs, the EU is a signatory member in its own right.

[247] Article 2(1) of the *Paris Act (1971)* of the Berne Convention (http://www.wipo.int/treaties/en/ip/berne/pdf/trtdocs_wo001.pdf).

Applying this definition to scientific outputs, it follows that scientific publications, regardless of their formats, are subject to copyright protection. However, the situation is not straightforward when it comes to research data that is often just a collection of facts, typically collated using automated or semiautomated instruments or scientific equipment. But, in addition, seemingly uncreative collections of data, such as phone directories, have in recent years sparked litigation and have stimulated policy debates about the extent to which copyright applies (or should apply) to the data.

There are two reasons behind the lack of clarity around the existence of copyright in research data.

The first is that the scope of 'research data' is extremely broad—data can be anything that researchers consider to be the evidence supporting their findings, as discussed in Chapter 4. It can be unstructured data, or it can be a vast dataset, or it can be a figure, a table, or a photograph embedded in these objects. Some of these data elements may be subject to copyright, while others are not.

The second reason is that the application of copyright to data and compilations of data raises many issues. This is largely because the concept of 'data' is a new concept, created in the computer age, while copyright law emerged at the time of printed publications.

At first sight, it may appear that copyright regimes do not apply to data and datasets. Simple facts and ideas do not qualify for copyright protection, whereas the original expression of ideas, classified as 'works', may qualify [384]. Research data in its own right is unlikely to meet the originality standards and, therefore, is unlikely to qualify as a protectable subject matter.

However, copyright can apply to original compilations of data and thus to databases. As discussed in more detail below, courts have confirmed this distinction. Different jurisdictions have assessed the way in which the balance between the 'works' and ideas has been achieved (in the selection and/or arrangement of data) as the test of originality that applies to collections of data, tables, and compilations. The test varies from country to country, as summarised in **Table 5**.[248]

7.1.2 Australia

The position in Australia on the copyright in compilations and databases was settled by the High Court in *IceTV Pty Ltd v Nine Network Australia Pty Ltd* [385] and subsequently by the Full Federal Court in *Telstra Corporation Limited v Phone Directories Company Pty Ltd* [386].

Historically, the common law measure was that originality could be demonstrated by the application of 'skill', 'effort' or 'judgement' (the doctrine of 'sweat of the brow'), as Sackville summarised:

> *The course of authority in the United Kingdom and Australia recognises that originality in a factual compilation may lie in the labour and expense involved in collecting the information recorded in the work, as distinct from the 'creative' exercise of skill or judgement, or the application of intellectual effort [387].*

Earlier Australian cases were considered in *Desktop Marketing Systems Pty Ltd v Telstra Corporation Ltd*.[249] This centred on Telstra's White Pages and Yellow Pages

---

[248] **Table 5** was prepared by Vera Lipton (the author), and the definitions are based on the references (latest cases) discussed in this section.

[249] *Ibid.*

Australia	United States	The European Union
Database will be protected by copyright under Australian law if it a) is a literary work b) is expressed in material form c) meets the originality test and d) has a relevant connection with Australia (for example, published in Australia or produced by an Australian resident). Originality involves a triple requirement: 1. the data compilation must not be copied, 2. a human author was involved in reducing or converting the database to a material form, and 3. there be some independent intellectual effort directed to expressing the work in the material form.	A compilation independently created by the author… that possesses at least some minimal degree of creativity (modicum of creativity). Presumably, the vast majority of compilations WILL past this test. The absence of creativity is manifested in an 'entirely typical' or 'garden-variety' end product constructed by processes which correspond to 'an automatic mechanical procedure' or to a so … 'routine process'.	A broad, dual protection under copyright law and sui generis database rights. Originality defined as the 'author's own intellectual creation'. Originality expressed through the 'choice, sequence and combination of those words that the author may express his creativity in an original manner and achieve a result which is an intellectual creation.' A small selection of word was found to constitute an intellectual creation. The sui generis database right of protection applies if the creators have invested sufficient time, money, and skill into developing their database. Investment refers to resources used to seek out existing independent materials and collect them in the database.

Table 5.
The criteria determining the existence of copyright in databases.

—compilations of names, addresses, and telephone numbers—and the 'headings book', produced by Telstra for use in classifying listings, and whether they constituted original literary works. In its judgement, the court found that this was indeed the case. Specifically, the court found that compilations of facts could qualify as original literary works if skill, judgement, and knowledge were exercised in compiling or arranging the facts or if substantial effort and expense were incurred during that process [388]. Therefore, it was recognised that the originality test was satisfied by this limited form of intellectual input.

In *IceTV*, the High Court considered copyright in programming guides, the *Weekly Schedules*, produced by the television broadcaster Nine Network Australia. The question of originality was considered in terms of whether taking the time and title data was taking a substantial part of the copyright work.

At first instance, Bennett held that the 'slivers' of information taken were not of a sufficiently substantial quality to be considered a substantial part. Specifically, she held that only the labour and skill involved in putting together the guide (the expression of the information) were relevant, and not the labour and skill involved in the programming decisions (the creation of the information). However, the Full Federal Court took a wider view—it found that data with the time and title was the 'centrepiece' of the guides, and so it concluded that the taking of time and title data amounted to taking a substantial part of the copyright work [385].

In the High Court [389], Gummow, Hayne, and Heydon found that the originality of the weekly programming schedules was in the selection and presentation of the information on times and titles and then packaged with additional program information and program synopses to make up a composite whole. However, the preparatory work involved in producing the time and title information was not relevant to substantiality, and there was left only 'the extremely modest skill and labour'. They also cautioned against reliance on the *Desktop Marketing* emphasis on appropriation of skill and labour, suggesting that the reasoning was out of line with the understanding of copyright law over many years [385].

One year later, in 2010, the Full Federal Court applied these principles in *Telstra Corporation Ltd v Phone Directories Co Pty Ltd* [390, 391]. In this case, Telstra claimed copyright in the content, form, and arrangement for each listing and enhancement in the White Pages and the Yellow Pages; in the overall structure of the listings in both directories; and in the headings, the presentation of the listings under headings, and the cross-referencing in the Yellow Pages. Both the Federal Court at first instance and the Full Federal Court on appeal found that the directories were not original works. A unanimous Full Federal Court affirmed that copyright did not apply to the White Pages and Yellow Pages as compilations because the works lacked 'human authors' who exercised 'independent intellectual effort' to create the form of the directories.[250]

Justice Keane and Justice Perram agreed that it was not necessary to name each author; the only requirement was to demonstrate that authors existed. If individuals had reduced the directories to material form through manual effort or had controlled a computer program in fashioning the form of the work, then the directories would have been original works. On this occasion, however, the task of transforming the information into a form ready for publication was carried out by software alone. Perram held that although humans were ultimately in control of the software, their control was over an automated process, and they did not directly form the material themselves. Therefore, there was no author of the directories and copyright did not exist in them [391].[251]

To summarise, as the consequence of the *IceTV* and *Phone Directories* cases, for a database to be eligible for copyright protection, it must meet the triple requirement that:

1. The data compilation must not be copied.

2. A human author must be involved in reducing or converting the database to a material form.

3. There must be some independent intellectual effort directed to expressing the work in the material form.[252]

Based on these criteria, it appears unlikely that research data created and arranged in databases in Australia would fall under the scope of copyright protection.[253]

Furthermore, copyright owners in Australia also have certain related rights, specifically moral rights—the right of integrity of authorship, the right of attribution of authorship, and the right against false attribution of ownership where copyright exceptions allow certain uses of copyrighted material without the authorisation of rights holders. Australia's copyright system includes an exception for 'fair dealing' for research or study ([392], p. 484). However, since it is unlikely that 'data' and 'databases' produced in Australia are subject to copyright, there is no need to apply the exemption to research data.

7.1.3 The United States

A database is protected by the United States *Copyright Act of 1976* [393] as a compilation, defined as:

---

[250] Fitzgerald and Dwyer [388] at point 13.

[251] per Perram at 101.

[252] See Fitzgerald at point 13.

[253] See Ricketson et al. [384] at point 8.

> *... a work formed by the collection and assembling of pre-existing materials or of data that are selected, coordinated, or arranged in such a way that the resulting work as a whole constitutes an original work of authorship.*[254]

The concept of originality was further defined by the Supreme Court in *Feist Publications, Inc. v. Rural Telephone Service Company, Inc.* The Supreme Court held that:

> *Although a compilation of facts may possess the requisite originality because the author typically chooses which facts to include, in what order to place them, and how to arrange the data so that readers may use them effectively, copyright protection extends only to those components of the work that are original to the author, not to the facts themselves... As a constitutional matter, copyright protects only those elements of a work that possess more than de minimis quantum of creativity. Rural's white pages, limited to basic subscriber information and arranged alphabetically, fall short of the mark. As a statutory matter, 17 U.S.C. Section 101 does not afford protection from copying to a collection of facts that are selected, coordinated, and arranged in a way that utterly lacks originality [394].*

The Copyright Act is specific in stating that the copyright in a compilation applies only to the compilation itself, and not to the source data ([393], Par. 103 (b)). The decision in *Feist* confirmed that 'raw facts' have no protection under copyright law. Compilations of those facts require the application of a 'modicum' of creativity to be protected by copyright.

The originality requirement does not appear to be particularly stringent:

> *Original requires only that the author make the selection or arrangement independently ... and that it display some minimal level of creativity. Presumably, the vast majority of compilations will pass the test.*[255]

However, the selection in the rural telephone directory did not pass the test, for lack of the 'modicum' of creativity.

The criteria for 'modicum' are established as 'those constituent elements of a work that possess more than a de minimis quantum of creativity'.[256] Even a slight amount of creativity will suffice—'some creative spark, no matter how crude, humble, or obvious it might be'.[257] Furthermore, the modicum of creativity must be 'independently created by the author'.[258] The absence of creativity is manifested in an 'entirely typical' or 'garden-variety' end product constructed by processes which correspond to 'an automatic mechanical procedure'[259] or to a so ... routine process.[260]

Based on this reasoning, copyright law in the United States does not, in theory, appear to prevent the extraction of unprotected data from an otherwise protectable database. However, 'original' compilations of research data are likely to be subject to copyright protection which has repercussions for data licencing and may limit the possibilities for the sharing and reuse of data structured in databases. Only

---

254 *Ibid*, Par. 101.

255 Feist at point 25, at 358–359.

256 *Ibid.*, at 363.

257 Feist at 345.

258 *Ibid.*

259 Feist at 362.

260 *Ibid.*

copyright holders can licence the data, and, in some cases, there would be multiple owners of copyright in one dataset resulting in copyright co-authorship of the work. That can create problems with data licencing unless all authors agree to the same licence conditions or waive their copyright. Furthermore, the distinction between raw facts (not covered by the protection) and a compilation of raw facts (to which copyright protection extends) is also not clearly delineated, especially in the cases of subsequent copies and derivatives of databases involving the original raw facts.

7.1.4 The European Union

Copyright law in the European Union has developed using the framework established by international treaties, such as the Berne Convention signed by all European Union member states, or by treaties to which the European Union is a signatory member in its own right, such as the WCT and TRIPS. These treaties are implemented through several European Union Directives—namely, the Directive on the legal protection of computer programs (Software Directive) [395], the Directive on rental and lending rights [396], the Directive on satellite broadcasting and cable retransmission [397], the Directive on the term of protection [398], the Directive on the legal protection of databases (Database Directive) [399], the Directive on the harmonisation of copyright and related rights in the information society [400], the Directive on the resale right [401], the Directive on certain permitted uses of orphan works [402], and the recently adopted Directive on collective rights management [403].

The European Union provides the strongest, double layer of protection of databases facilitated by the copyright laws and the Database Directive, which introduced a sui generis database right. As such, databases are, in the first instance, protected by copyright when the selection or the arrangement of the database represents its author's own intellectual creation. This layer of protection covers only the database structure, not its content, as is the position in the United States. The second layer of protection is the sui generis database right, which protects the content of the database—in the cases where there has been a substantial investment in the obtaining, presentation, or verification of the data—from acts of extraction (copying) and reutilisation (redistribution, communication to the public, etc.) of the whole or a substantial part of the contents of the database [404]. If the database meets the requirements for protection under both copyright law and the sui generis database rights, then the two types of protection are cumulative.[261]

With reference to the first layer, the test for originality has been harmonised across the European Union with regard to software[262] and databases[263] and photographic works[264] in the two relevant Directives mentioned previously. The European Court of Justice in *Infopaq International A/S v Danske Dagblades Forening* clarified the requirement of originality as the 'author's own intellectual creation' and established that the originality of a work must be assessed through its 'elements':

> *Regarding the elements of such works covered by the protection, it should be observed that they consist of words which, considered in isolation, are not as such an intellectual creation of the author who employs them. It is only through the choice, sequence*

---

[261] Article 7(4) Database Directive.

[262] Article 1(3) Directive 2009/24/EC.

[263] Article 3(1) Database Directive.

[264] Article 6, Directive 2006/116/EC of 12 December 2006 on the term of protection of copyright and certain related rights.

> *and combination of those words that the author may express his creativity in an original manner and achieve a result which is an intellectual creation.*[265]

In *Football Dataco Ltd et al. v Yahoo! UK Ltd,* the European Court clarified the position with regard to the threshold of originality in databases as follows:

> *... the fact that the setting up of the database required, irrespective of the creation of the data which it contains, significant labour and skill of its author ... cannot as such justify the protection of it by copyright under Directive 96/9, if that labour and that skill do not express any originality in the selection or arrangement of that data [405].*

Furthermore, the Directive does not provide for database right protection to apply to every aggregation of data. For example, databases that arise as a by-product of doing business do not attract database right protection. The sui generis database right of protection applies only if the creators have invested sufficient time, money, and skill into developing their database. The substantial investment must be either in the obtaining, verification, or presentation of the database contents.[266] This requirement was first tested in the *British Horseracing Board Ltd v William Hill Organisation Ltd* [406], in which the European Court of Justice found that 'obtaining' excludes the costs incurred in the creation of new data from being considered relevant to satisfy the requirement of the substantial investment:

> *... the expression investment in ... the obtaining ... of the contents of a database must ... be understood to refer to the resources used to seek out existing independent materials and collect them in the database, and not to the resources used for the creation as such of independent materials. The purpose of the protection by the sui generis right provided for by the directive is to promote the establishment of storage and processing systems for existing information and not the creation of materials capable of being collected subsequently in a database.*[267]

As such, the costs incurred in creating data for a database cannot be considered 'substantial investment'. However, the costs necessary for the verification of the accuracy of the data and for the presentation of such data to third parties do count in the assessment of whether the investment was substantial. This differentiation can also be used to extend the term of the protection granted under the sui generis right. The moment the database is completed or disclosed to the public, this right arises automatically, without any formal requirement. Protection under the database right is limited to 15 years, in theory. However, in practice, it has the potential to be perpetual. If the database is periodically updated, and such updating includes a substantial investment in reconfirming the accuracy of the information contained in it, then the period of protection can be continually renewed.[268] This is because the creator will have a new right to the altered database or its substantial part.

---

[265] *Ibid*, 45.

[266] Article 7, Database Directive.

[267] *Ibid*, 31.

[268] Article 10, Database Directive. Furthermore, Article 24 provides that 'a substantial new investment involving a new term of protection may include a substantial verification of the contents of the database'. See also Davison [407].

From the above, it is apparent that the scope of the sui generis database right goes well beyond the scope of copyright protection. The owner of the protected database has the exclusive right to prevent the extraction and/or reutilisation of the whole or of a substantial part, whether evaluated qualitatively and/or quantitatively, of the contents of that database.[269] Yet enforcing those rights and demonstrating that database rights apply has been a high bar to satisfy before the courts. The above-mentioned *Football Dataco* case to enforce database rights failed. So did the *British Horseracing Board* case.

However, the situation may be changing in the wake of the 2013 decision by the Court of Justice in *Innoweb BV v Wegener ICT Media BV and Wegener Mediaventions BV* [408]. In this case the court held that, in the European Union, the operators of aggregator websites that allow users to search for content on external databases, and provide the same search functionality as those source sites, and then display the found content on the aggregator sites may breach the database rights of the owners of the original content. In other words, in this situation the reutilisation of dataset content offends the protection for sui generis rights of the database creator that is provided under Article 7(1) and (5) [409].

This case is interesting in that it further prevents copying and reusing database content, even though it is questionable whether the original database at issue would have met the substantial investment criteria. The above judgement strengthens the position of database right owners. At the same time, it signals that others, for example, researchers or public libraries, must take care when designing their own search technologies that interrogate the databases created by other parties and then present that information within their own websites.

The broad scope of the sui generis database right and its interpretation by the courts are not a welcome development for open data. In many respects, the sui generis database right in Europe provides database rights holders more protection than the creators of original works can enjoy under copyright law.

Therefore, using somebody else's data produced in the European Union carries an inherent risk of IP infringement, especially as the exceptions to the sui generis database right are extremely limited. The main exception provided by the Database Directive is for the material extracted to illustrate teaching or for scientific research, with due acknowledgement of the source and a limit to the extent that extraction is justified by the non-commercial purpose.[270] Furthermore, there is no right of reutilisation for these purposes—it cannot be redistributed. An additional complication is the uncertainty of its reference to scientific research and whether this signifies 'illustration for scientific research', rather than simply 'scientific research'. Finally, the meaning of 'non-commercial purpose' in a teaching or research environment is also complicated. Finally, this exception is not mandatory, and some European Union countries—including Ireland, France, and Italy—do not have it in national legislation [407].

---

[269] Article 7 offers protection against acts of extraction or reutilisation of the whole or a substantial part of the database, evaluated qualitatively or quantitatively. The same article, in its fifth section, clarifies that the repeated and systematic extraction and/or reutilisation of insubstantial parts of the contents of the database, implying acts which conflict with a normal exploitation of that database or which unreasonably prejudice the legitimate interests of the maker of the database, shall not be permitted. Extraction of insubstantial parts of the database does not infringe the database right. The sense of this norm is to avoid repeated extraction of insubstantial parts, which leads to the reconstitution of the database as a whole or as a substantial part thereof.

[270] Database Directive, at 26.

Therefore, the data created by European research organisations may need different treatment from data produced in other parts of the world. The strong protection of databases in the European Union appears to be at odds with the commitment to develop a Digital Single Market and data-driven economy—of which open scientific data, particularly via the Open Science Data Cloud, is an important component. Some committees of the European Parliament have called on the European Commission to abolish the Database Directive.[271] The committees have said they believed the Directive was 'an impediment to the development of a European data-driven economy'.[272] The European Commission appears to be aware of the limitations presented by the sui generis database right and has recently reaffirmed its commitment to develop the right environment and conditions for digital networks and services to flourish by providing, among other things, the right regulatory conditions [410]. Over 3 months in 2017, the Commission held public consultations on the application and impact of the Database Directive with the report following in 2018 [411].

As the discussion above shows, all three jurisdictions considered in this study have now adopted a test that requires a level of creativity to determine the existence of copyright in selecting the contents for or arranging a database. With such a test, data produced by researchers, at least in its unstructured or semi-structured form, will most likely fail to qualify for copyright protection. The one difference is in the European Union, where most databases are likely to fall under the provision for sui generis database protection, provided substantial investments in the databases are made. In early stages of the open data process, some international funders have suggested that where research data is protected by copyright law, it is not a proper subject for open access ([412], p. 18). Over time, however, legal mechanisms have evolved that enable the IP issues to be appropriately managed.

So how does the existence of copyright affect open scientific data and how can these issues be managed?

In broad terms, research organisations are familiar with copyright and related rights as they apply to publications, and they are making open research data available on the assumption that copyright also applies to open scientific data. The adopted approach is that the IP issues can be managed through appropriate licencing mechanisms, which would allow research organisations to waive their rights in data and enable others to reuse the content without any restrictions. However, there are issues with this approach.

The first is that the clearance of data rights is far more complex than clearing copyright and related rights in publications. There are two key reasons for this. One is that data owners must be identified in order to waive the rights and, unlike the initial rights in publications, the owners of research data may not be obvious. The second reason is that open data may include embedded objects and composite copyright that may be governed by multiple IP rights and multiple legal regimes. These concerns need to be managed and need to be managed early in the process.

I canvas these matters in the following sections—firstly, discussing data ownership, and then looking evolving licencing mechanisms for open scientific data.

[271] See in December 2015, the Committee on Industry, Research and Energy and the Committee on the Internal Market and Consumer Protection have called on the Commission to reconsider the sui generis database right (http://www.europarl.europa.eu/sides/getDoc.do?type=REPORT&reference=A8-2015-0371&format=XML&language=EN).

[272] *Ibid.*

7.2 Ownership of research data

Anecdotal evidence says that researchers, academics, students, and even academic researchers often believe that they own the data they collect in the course of their research. This position stems from their understanding that data and databases can be subject to copyright and, therefore, researchers are the legitimate owners because they have 'created' it. This view is incorrect. While they are employed to perform research, the data that researchers produce typically belongs to other parties. In most cases of researchers who are employees of a university or a research organisation, the rights to the data they produce is owned by their employers, pursuant to the operation of law[273] or contractual assignment. In sponsored research, the research organisation typically owns the data but leaves the role of data steward to the principal investigator. In industry-funded research, the data typically belongs to the sponsor; however, the right to publish it can also be extended to the investigator. The position with regard to the ownership of research data in the three jurisdictions under investigation is detailed below.

7.2.1 Australia

The ownership of research data in Australia is primarily determined by the organisation where the researchers work. It is currently the policy of the Australian Government to assert its ownership over intellectual property developed with public funding [392, 413]. This extends to apparently copyrighted data. The ownership of intellectual property in publicly funded research organisations is legislated, while most universities in Australia have in place internal procedures and employment contracts with their staff. Such contracts explicitly address the ownership of intellectual property, which also includes data.

Many universities have revised their internal IP ownership arrangements after the landmark decision in *University of Western Australia vs Gray* [414]. In this case, the university initiated legal proceedings against an employee to argue that the intellectual property, namely, patents, developed in the course of his employment belonged to the university. Dr. Bruce Gray was appointed as Professor of Surgery at the university in 1985. He carried out research, both before joining the university and after, on the use of microspheres to deliver anticancer agents to the sites of tumours. Dr. Gray filed various patent applications in relation to this work on behalf of a company, Sirtex Medical Ltd., of which he was a director. Subsequently, the company acquired the intellectual property from Dr. Gray. However, the university considered it had some rights to the intellectual property as a consequence of its employment of Dr. Gray to carry out research.

A decision by Justice French was delivered on 17 April 2008. The judgement effectively held that Dr. Gray's employment contract, which included a duty to carry out research, did not include a duty to invent, and accordingly the IP in the inventions Dr. Gray developed was not owned by the university. Justice French also found that the IP regulations of the university, which purported to invest the intellectual property rights of academic staff in the university, were invalid.[274] The university filed an appeal to the Full Bench of the Federal Court, which in its judgement on 3 September 2009 dismissed the appeal and confirmed the earlier decision of Justice French.

---

[273] For example, s 35 (6) Australian Copyright Act (http://www8.austlii.edu.au/cgi-bin/viewdoc/au/legis/cth/consol_act/ca1968133/s35.html).
[274] *Ibid*, FCA 49.

Several issues highlighted in the case can, by extrapolation, also be applied to the ownership of research data. Universities in Australia do not routinely rely on the operation of common law to assert their rights to academic IP. Instead, they make express provision for university ownership, typically by incorporating into academic employment contracts the terms of a university statute or policy to that effect. In the case of *UWA*, French J held that the IP regulations had not been validly passed or incorporated, and therefore the common law applied [415]. Since the decision, universities have amended their policies, and it is therefore unlikely that the common law further applies.

The judgement highlighted the public function of universities. It specifically acknowledged that universities serve the public purpose by offering education, by supporting research facilities, and by awarding degrees. It found, also, that commercial activities performed by universities had not displaced its traditional functions to the extent that it became 'limited to that of engaging academic staff for its own commercial purposes' ([416], p. 184). French further held that academics are to set and pursue research priorities and to publish or share research results. He also said that these freedoms collide fatally with a duty to maintain the secrecy that employer patent ownership inevitably requires. As such, an implied term favouring university ownership would be 'unsupported by a duty of confidence',[275] as in that case it would oddly mean that the academic 'would have been free to destroy the potential patentability of an invention by progressively putting research results into the public domain' ([416], p. 192). Alternatively, this view would be supported by an obligation of confidentiality, which is something so manifestly in opposition with traditional academic freedoms and practices that it cannot be maintained.[276] This judgement explicitly states that the public function of universities comes first and any commercial considerations follow. As such, this position supports the case for open research data.

With regard to the ownership of data produced in publicly funded research organisations, such as the Commonwealth Scientific and Industrial Research Organisation (CSIRO), Section 54 of the *Science and Industry Research Act 1954*[277] provides that 'discoveries, inventions, or improvements' made by CSIRO officers in the course of their 'official duties' are owned by CSIRO, an Australian Government identity. The organisation also takes express assignments of IP in its employment agreements. As a result of the statutory provisions and these assignments, CSIRO controls, under Commonwealth executive approval, all research outputs created in the organisation—whether as data, publications, inventions, or other types of intellectual creations.

However, the CSIRO has not been at the forefront of research data sharing. Some of the data it produces is made publicly available by the organisation on its website, or in other publications, or via researchers (with CSIRO approval). However, only a few data sharing initiatives have emerged from the organisation—with the Atlas of Living, a free, online national biodiversity database being perhaps the best known.[278]

At the same time, the organisation is strongly committed to research commercialisation. In recent years it has had a strict internal policy of confidentiality, and it appears that many researchers fear being criticised for giving away data that could potentially be used to generate revenue for the organisation. The position

---

[275] *Ibid*, 191.

[276] *Ibid*, 192.

[277] This Act established CSIRO and regulates its governance.

[278] https://www.ala.org.au.

for confidentiality was supported by reasoning that the industry funds around 30% of CSIRO research. However, the remaining part is publicly funded, and the Australian Government increasingly expects greater returns from its investments in research.[279]

In March 2017, the Productivity Commission, in its report on an inquiry into data availability, proposed that 'the research community to put its house in order when it comes to data sharing' [392]. It specifically recommended that the data of publicly funded research be available beyond the initial researchers.[280] CSIRO is the largest and the most significant Australian publicly funded research organisation. Its organisational approaches to open research data therefore may need to change as the result of such recent reviews.

Rather than focusing on data ownership, the Productivity Commission preferred to stress the need for greater access. The default position in Australia is that all data created with public money should be publicly accessible within a reasonable time unless there is a compelling reason not to make it available.[281] The Australian Government announced in August 2017 that national, state, and territory governments should provide free and open access arrangements for all publicly funded research within 12 months of publication. This widens the Australian Government policy that presently governs grants from both the Australian Research Council and National Health and Medical Research Council.[282] The Productivity Commission report covers some of this territory, even though the examination is not specific. The report offers innovative approaches to releasing medical data and addresses the issue of the privacy of research subjects, discussed in Section 7 of this chapter.

7.2.2 The United States

The ownership of research data in the United States is typically determined by the employer of the researcher, similar to the position in Australia. As employees, researchers are hired by the university—which, in most cases, retains the rights to the data and other forms of expression. This principle is not open to debate as a legal matter [417]. A natural extension of this principle is that all the data created in the course of employment or with institutional support belongs to the employer. In federally sponsored research governed by the Bayh-Dole Act,[283] the research organisation also owns the data but permits the principal investigator on the grant to control the data [418]. However, the investigator is just a caretaker, not the owner of the collected data. He/she has charge of the collection, recording, storage, retention, and disposal of data.[284] More recently, the wording of research grants and contracts, and of the informed consent forms signed by participants in clinical trials, is also likely to delineate data ownership or disposition. The National Institutes of Health and the National Academies of Science include the requirements for data sharing among the terms and conditions of research grants, as discussed in Chapter 3.

---

[279] I gratefully acknowledge all the generous support, counsel, information, and insights I have received from Mr. Brett Walker, a former CSIRO counsel.

[280] *Ibid.*

[281] *Ibid.*

[282] See Recommendation 16.1, Productivity Commission [392].

[283] The Bayh-Dole Act or Patent and Trademark Law Amendments Act deals with intellectual property arising from federal government-funded research. The Act was adopted in 1980, is codified at 94 Stat. 3015, and in 35 U.S.C. § 200–212, and is implemented by 37 C.F.R. 401.

[284] *Ibid.*

Unlike the established practice in which academic institutions have often waived copyright in the literary and scholarly works of their researchers, universities and research organisations generally do not have an established tradition of abandoning ownership rights to data generated in the course of research by their employees. When faculty members leave an institution, they often negotiate with it to keep their grants and data. In industry-funded research, data typically belong to the sponsor, although in some instances the right to publish the data may be extended to the investigator.[285]

The key focus in the United States has been on consideration of who may access the data developed in the course of scientific research. This was partially driven by the United States patent law, which, until 2014, was based on the 'first to invent' principle. Laboratory notebooks and other evidence developed in the course of academic research were often used as evidence of the inventiveness principle, and academic researchers often appeared as expert witnesses in courts.

The focus on data access is still more dominant than discussion around data ownership. It is generally assumed that research organisations own the data of their researchers. However, the owner of the data does not always have control over it, as is the case in other types of intellectual property to which IP protection can apply. When it comes to research data, other parties may have legal access to it under prescribed conditions and for prescribed purposes. Moreover, data may be taken for public use without the need to seek the consent of the owner—subject to constitutional requirements for due process and fair compensation [419]. Ultimately, in the United States, the question of who owns the data appears to be less of a concern than the matter of the rights and responsibilities of data holders.

Recent years have seen increased calls from patients in the United States to claim rights in data they produce in the course of clinical trials, as previously outlined in Chapter 5. One controversial issue concerning data ownership concerns cell lines and DNA sequences, which can represent 'data' in clinical trials. Controversies have arisen concerning whether research subjects and patients actually own their own tissue or DNA.

Such challenges are not new. A case brought by John Moore against the University of California in the late 1980s raised issues about whether a patient has ownership of his tissue that was used in research to develop a cell line that had commercial interests. In 1976 Moore had gone to the UCLA Medical Center seeking treatment for hairy cell leukaemia. The research performed on cells from his spleen led to the development of a patent 6 years later. Moore sued the University of California Regent as well as the company where his doctor was working, stating that the altered tissue was his own property and that he wanted to recover damages. The claimant also said that he had not been informed about the potential use of his tissue by the researcher. The California Supreme Court held that Moore had a right to sue the doctor for failing to inform Moore of what he intended to do with his cells [420]. However, Moore did not win the right of ownership of his cells nor any entitlement to the data and subsequent financial proceeds that might be generated from the research done using the cells. The court said that if all subjects had the right to their own tissue, it could hinder biomedical research.

The court reasoned that before a body part is removed, it is the patient who possesses the right to determine the use of that part.[286] However, the court construed that the removal of a body part with informed consent was an 'abandonment' of that part.[287]

[285] Fishbein [417] at point 80, 129.

[286] *Ibid*, 500.

[287] *Ibid*, 501.

The judge did not say what rights (if any) others may have in the abandoned body part or whether such 'data' can be used for research purposes and shared subsequently. This issue is of utmost importance and has been brought back to the spotlight in relation to collecting newborn blood samples by some state governments, especially California. While collecting the samples to screen babies for genetic diseases requires the informed consent of the parents,[288] the established practice was to store de-identified samples in a state database and to use them for federal research. In 2017, the Department of Health and Human Services and 15 other federal agencies jointly issued a 'final rule' that:

> *strengthens protections for people who volunteer to participate in research, while ensuring that the oversight system does not add inappropriate administrative burdens [422].*

The effect of this rule is that researchers do not need consent to use de-identified blood spots and, in some cases, can even use identified blood spots without consent.[289] Parents can, however, opt to destroy the blood samples after the newborn test is performed.

7.2.3 European Union

Draft legislation currently being considered by the European Union would specifically regulate ownership in data in general and research data in particular. In the context of the European Commission free flow of data initiative, the agency stated that:

> *... the barriers to the free flow of data are caused by the legal uncertainty surrounding the emerging issues on 'data ownership' or control, (re)usability and access to/ transfer of data and liability arising from the use of data [423].*

Data ownership in the European Union was recently considered by a private law firm [424], which found that European Union case law does not explicitly recognise an ownership right in data. However, the European Court of Justice opened the door for a discussion on ownership in intangible assets in its *UsedSoft* judgement issued on 3 July 2012 [425]. In this ruling, the court held that the commercial distribution of software via a download on the Internet involves the transfer of ownership [426]. Specifically, the CJEU held that the copyright holder's exclusive distribution right in a computer program is exhausted upon the first sale of the program, including in a program downloaded over the Internet under a user licence agreement. The court held that such licencing involves the transfer of ownership. Therefore, the owner of copyright in software is unable to prevent a perpetual 'licensee' from reselling the 'used software licences'.

7.3 Licencing models for open scientific data

For data to be released in the public domain as open access, it must meet certain conditions. The Berlin Declaration defines such conditions as:

---

[288] Blood spots are defined as 'human subjects' and require informed consent for federal research. See H. R.1281—Newborn Screening Saves Lives Reauthorization [421].
[289] *Ibid.*

The author(s) and right holder(s) of the data grant(s) to all users a free, irrevocable, worldwide, right of access to, and a license to copy, use, distribute, transmit and display the work publicly and to make and distribute derivative works, in any digital medium for any responsible purpose, subject to proper attribution of authorship (community standards will continue to provide the mechanism for enforcement of proper attribution and responsible use of the published work, as they do now), as well as the right to make small numbers of printed copies for their personal use [63].

For research data to be open, specifically where exclusive ownership rights exist, it needs to be released (published) in the public domain under an open licence. Several licences have evolved over time to meet the specified conditions for 'open scientific data'.

7.3.1 Creative Commons Zero public domain dedication (CC Zero)

Unlike the other six licences developed by the Creative Commons, CC Zero (sometimes presented as CC0) is not a licence but rather a waiver, to the fullest extent permitted by law, of copyright and the full scope of related (or neighbouring) rights. The waiver was developed with an intention to facilitate the sharing of research data. Specifically, the person waiving their rights (the affirmer):

... overtly, fully, permanently, irrevocably and unconditionally waives, abandons, and surrenders all of Affirmer's Copyright and Related Rights and associated claims and causes of action, whether now known or unknown (including existing as well as future claims and causes of action), in the Work (i) in all territories worldwide, (ii) for the maximum duration provided by applicable law or treaty (including future time extensions), (iii) in any current or future medium and for any number of copies, and (iv) for any purpose whatsoever, including without limitation commercial, advertising or promotional purposes [427].

Consequently, the waiver enables users of the data to copy, modify, distribute, and perform the work, even for commercial purposes and to do so without asking permission.

An important point to mention is that, unlike the first three versions of the Creative Commons licences, the waiver covers both copyright and sui generis database rights. Further, CC Zero avoids problems with attribution stacking[290] by removing the legal requirement to give attribution while acknowledging that the scientific community has a well-established culture and norms that encourage the recognition of sources. As such, CC Zero is the recommended tool for releasing research data into the public domain.

7.3.2 Creative Commons 4.0 suite of licences

Creative Commons 4.0 is a suite of standard, globally applicable terms that allow anyone to openly licence all forms of creative works and datasets. These public licences are exceptionally user-friendly and enable copyright owners to licence their works on the Internet and elsewhere. Unless directed otherwise (by research funders, scientific organisations, or other owners of copyright in research data), owners can choose the conditions for the future reuse of the works. These may include Attribution (BY), Non-Commercial Use (NC), No-Derivatives (ND), and

290 The accumulation of attributions that occurs as each reuse of data incorporates acknowledgements of all prior users.

Share Alike (SA). A tool on the Creative Commons website can generate text, taking into account the conditions selected, by which the copyright owner may grant a worldwide, non-exclusive, perpetual licence to any user to reproduce, display, perform, communicate, and distribute copies of that work.[291] The same licence permits any future reuse of the work according to the stipulated conditions and without the need to contact the copyright owner. The licence applies to all media and formats, whether known now or subsequently devised. All Creative Commons 4.0 licences are irrevocable, meaning that once the licenced work is distributed on the Internet, the author can no longer change the type of licence or withdraw it.

The Creative Commons 4.0 licences are widely used in the context of scholarly publication and the dissemination of research results. The current (fourth) iteration of the licences is recommended, as it also provides for the sui generis rights in the European Union and includes mechanisms to avoid attribution stacking (in the case attribution is selected).[292]

The development of the Creative Commons 4.0 licences has eliminated the need to apply other licences to scientific contents. One such example is the Public Domain Dedication and Licence previously developed by the Open Knowledge Foundation and used in some European Union countries. This strongly resembled the CC Zero waiver; however, it was designed to enable licencing of databases and its contents in the European Union, paying particular attention to the European sui generis database right. With the adoption of the fourth iteration of the Creative Commons licences, many European organisations now recommend solely one suite of licences, namely, the CC Zero waiver and 4.0 licences.

7.3.3 Other licencing issues

Given that copyright is unlikely to apply to data itself, but instead applies to original compilations of the data, it follows that much data is arguably not subject to copyright protection. This is, for example, the current position in Australia with regard to computer-generated data. Another example that would seem to be exempted from copyright protection is unstructured data developed in the course of a research project or harnessed by other means from scientific equipment. The lack of copyright protection in data is the general position with regard to data generated in the United States.

This raises interesting questions about whether any property rights can be claimed in such 'data without author' and what the legal basis for such a claim might be. Arguably, data that is not subject to copyright protection can still constitute 'confidential information' or other forms of 'intellectual property' especially if the data is governed by contractual arrangements with industry or other research collaborations. In these cases, any property rights in such 'data without author' would be most likely determined in the contracts. However, since the data is not subject to copyright protection, and thus does not have an author, issues arise with regard to how to release the data in the public domain. In such cases, when no rights are attached to research data, then there is no ground for licencing the data. Standard copyright licences, such as the Creative Commons licences, are not appropriate.[293]

---

[291] www.creativecommons.org.

[292] Note: Attribution is not a selectable option in CC 4.0.

[293] In the absence of copyright, companies sometimes license data under 'know-how' agreements, and in these cases the ownership of the data is usually vested in the company, or a subcontractor to the company. Adopting this approach may not be appropriate for research data, due to public nature of academic research.

There are two ways institutions have chosen to release research data to which copyright does not apply. Some organisations in the United States release their data in the public domain without a licence. This was the early approach taken by the Harvard-MIT Data Center. Secondly, some organisations in the United States release data under the CC Zero waiver, and this seems to be the recommended practice for sharing research data and databases [180]. Such an approach is preferred because it signals to future data users that the data is without any legal restrictions on reuse.

Creative Commons has also developed the Public Domain Mark (PDM) with a view to enabling marking of materials, including data, which belong to the public domain. Unlike the CC Zero waiver, which can only be used by copyright holders, PDM can be used by anyone.

PDM is not a legal tool in any respect. It was developed with a view to acting as a label, marking material that is free of known copyright restrictions [428]. However, Creative Commons currently does not recommend the PDM for materials for which the copyright status differs from jurisdiction to jurisdiction, even though the tools for marking and tagging such works are currently under development. In the absence of these marking tools, there is a concern that the PDM tool might be used to overwrite the rights of lawful copyright owners. Therefore, using PDM to release research data is not recommended, and the CC Zero waiver has become an established norm around the world.

7.4 Different types of data reuse

The previous section described the challenges associated with data release. I now move to describe the challenges arising in data reuse.

This study has identified three such issues: firstly, the inability of data users to perform automated analysis and mining of digital data; secondly, ensuring the ethical use of data and limiting the risks of inaccurate interpretation; and lastly, ensuring the privacy and confidentiality of research subjects involved in clinical trials. These challenges are examined below.

7.4.1 Text and data mining

Legal uncertainty remains with regard to certain data uses and reuses in the digital environment. Typically, linking and mining of data and text are necessary to extract value and insights from datasets or other forms of data. However, such uses may constitute copyright infringement.

This uncertainty stems from several factors. Firstly, databases and some forms of data may be protected by copyright, as discussed above. Secondly, such data may be available in the public domain, but is not open, meaning that a prospective user can access the data but may not be able to reuse it or is unaware of the terms under which the data may be reused. Thirdly, new types of data uses, such as linking and mining, may cover several data sources and span several jurisdictions. Making temporary copies of the data is usually necessary to perform large-scale data analyses. Yet the act of copying is not clearly covered in the scope of exceptions and limitations to copyright infringement. Moreover, the scope of these exceptions varies from jurisdiction to jurisdiction, and this may hinder data interoperability and reusability.

Text and data mining generally involves automatically collecting information and extracting data and insights from digital data by means of software. Citing various legal and literature sources, the European Parliament has defined the process of text and data mining in these terms:

TDM works by:

1. *Identifying input materials to be analysed, such as works, or data individually collected or organised in a pre-existing database*

2. *Copying substantial quantities of materials which encompasses:*

    a. *Pre-processing materials by turning them into a machine-readable format compatible with the technology to be deployed for the TDM so that structured data can be extracted*

    b. *Possibly, but not necessarily, uploading the pre-processed materials on a platform, depending on the TDM technique to be deployed*

3. *Extracting the data*

4. *Recombining it to identify patterns into the final output ([429], p. 5)*

The nub of the problem with text and data mining is the requirement to create a temporary copy of the data. While data itself is not protected by copyright and/or the sui generis right, a database might be, especially if substantial parts of the original database are extracted for purposes other than research or learning.

Publishers have typically taken a sceptical approach to allowing text mining, even for research purposes, and instead have promoted obtaining a licence on a case-by-case basis. This is time-consuming and involves high transaction costs. Some academic journal publishers, such as Elsevier and Oxford University Press, allow text and data mining for non-commercial use [430]. This permission overrides the need to seek permission from the publishers to reuse the content. However, permissions that specifically address data mining are uncommon at this time.

There are two principal ways to ensure that text and data mining does not infringe copyright law. The first is the fair use doctrine enshrined in the United States copyright law; the second is the system of exceptions and limitations embedded in Australian and European Union law. The United States system is considered more favourable to text and data mining due to its inherent flexibility. Many scholars and policymakers have argued that Europe lags behind the United States in unlocking the value of data because of its inflexible copyright laws.[294]

7.4.2 The fair use system in the United States

The fair use doctrine is stipulated in Paragraph 107 of the United States Copyright Act [393]. The application of the doctrine requires consideration of several factors to determine whether a certain use of copyrighted works indeed constitutes 'fair use'. These include factors such as:

> *... the purpose and character of the use, including whether such use is of a commercial nature or is for non-profit educational purposes; the nature of the copyrighted work; the amount and substantiality of the portion used in relation to the copyrighted work as a whole; and the effect of the use upon the potential market for or value of the copyrighted work [431].*

[294] See, for example, the discussion of the text and data mining exemption in the European Parliament here.

The factors are weighed as a whole, and so the claimant need not win on every factor for a court to rule in favour of fair use.

More recently, the use of text and data mining was considered in the cases involving the Google Books Library Project, especially in the *Authors Guild, Inc. et al. v. HathiTrust* [432]. In this matter, Google had created digital copies of books held in university libraries and then provided digital copies to HathiTrust Inc., which developed a searchable database for use by researchers and scholars. The search results included 'snippets' of text. Judge Chin held that the digitisation of books by Google was 'highly transformative' as it adds value, serves several important educational purposes, and may enhance the sale of books to the benefit of copyright owners. In this reasoning, the judge explicitly referred to 'text and data mining' as a new area and method of research.[295] A similar judgement by the district court for the Southern District of New York explicitly referenced the benefit of Google Books to TDM, noting that it 'transformed the book text into data for the purpose of substantive research, including data mining and text mining in new areas' [433]. While the consideration of fair use varies from case to case, the previous judgements indicate that text and data mining is likely to be considered 'fair use', especially if undertaken in the course of research.

7.4.3 Australia

As it stands, Australian copyright law does not currently allow text and data mining of large datasets. Australia does not have a text and data mining exemption but has, on several occasions,[296] considered introducing a fair use system similar to that of the United States in place of the current 'fair dealing' system. However, the response of the Australian Government to these reviews is lacking. The current 'fair dealing' system allows certain limited exceptions for use of copyrighted works for criticism and review, research and study, reporting the news, use in judicial proceedings, and parody and satire.

The 2014 review by the Australian Law Reform Commission specifically considered the effects of text and data mining in the context of copyright law. In that review, it was concluded that where the text or data mining involves the copying, digitisation, or reformatting of copyright material without permission of the copyright owners, it may give rise to copyright infringement [434], especially if the whole dataset needs to be copied and converted into a suitable format (such as XML format). In such cases, the copying would exceed a 'reasonable portion' of the work and so fall under the scope of infringement. The inquiry also said that it 'seemed unlikely' that text and data mining might fall under the temporary reproduction of work exception. The recommendation was to introduce the 'fair use' system based on the United States system. However, this recommendation has not been adopted by the government, which—in the words of the then Attorney General—'was still to be persuaded that the adoption of fair use was the best direction for Australia law'.[297] This position has not changed under the current Australian Government, and, as a result, copyright law poses challenges to data reuse. The recommendation of this study in this regard is provided in Chapter 8.

---

[295] *Ibid.*

[296] In between 1998 and 2018, eight reviews considered introducing fair use, and six reviews explicitly recommended it.

[297] Senator the Hon. George Brandis QC, Attorney General and Minister for the Arts (2014). Address at the opening of the *Australian Digital Alliance fair use for the future. A practical look at copyright reform forum.* Canberra, 14 February.

7.4.4 The European Union

The threshold for copyright protection in data, even raw data, is relatively low in the European Union. In *Infopaq*,[298] the Court of Justice held that even a short sequence of 11 words may be subject to copyright if it reflects a sufficient level of creative choices leading to an 'own intellectual creation'.[299] Multiple extractions of text from the same source, such as the systematic mining of a blog, further increase the risk of infringement. It seems clear that, as a general principle, relatively small takings of data can raise copyright issues.

However, the European Union is currently considering broad and ambitious reform to the European Copyright Directive that was adopted in 2001 and is now considered outdated. The current package of proposals[300] has been developed over several years and includes a new copyright exception for text and data mining. Such an exception is necessary to ensure harmonisation of laws across the European Union. Some member states have, however, recently proceeded to introduce national text and data mining exemptions.

The first country to do so was the United Kingdom, following the recommendations of the Hargreaves Review ([435], p. 47) and so adopting a text and data mining exemption on 19 May 2014.[301] The exception only applies to non-commercial research. According to the amended legislation ([436], Par. 29A):

> *... the making of a copy of a work by a person who has lawful access to that work does not infringe copyright if it is made so that that person can carry out a computational analysis of anything included in that work for non-commercial research purposes.*[302]

France, Estonia and Germany have also introduced text and data mining exceptions. The French exemption is extremely narrow and covers only reproduction from 'lawful sources' made available with the consent of the rights holders, as well as the storage and communication of files created in the course of performing text and data mining activities.[303] The scope of the exemption adopted in Estonia is similar to the United Kingdom's law and is limited to text and data mining performed by any person but only for non-commercial purposes.[304] Germany is the latest European country to introduce the text and data mining exception, in March 2018. It covers the act of reproduction necessary to undertake text and data mining for non-commercial purposes.[305]

The package proposed for the entire European Union is currently being considered by the European Parliament and includes various changes to the scope of the proposed exception. Of particular interest is the enabling of researchers and

---

298 CJEU, 16 July 2009, case C-5/08, *Infopaq*.

299 *Ibid*, 48.

300 See Proposal for a Directive of the European Parliament and of the Council on Copyright in the Digital Single Market (https://eur-lex.europa.eu/legal-content/EN/TXT/PDF/?uri=CELEX:52016PC0593&from=EN).

301 Regulation 3 of the Copyright and Rights in Performances (Research, Education, Libraries, and Archives), Regulations 2014, No. 1372, adding Article 29A to the Copyright, Designs and Patents Act 1988. The regulations came into force on 1 June 2014.

302 *Ibid*, Par. 29.1.

303 See European Parliament at point 2, 17.

304 *Ibid*, 18.

305 *Ibid*.

businesses to harness the benefits of data mining. A specific case was put forward for including start-ups in the scope of the exemption. It was argued that the exception would allow start-ups to increase the European Union competitiveness and knowledge leadership in the field of big data analytics, as desired by the Commission [437]. Another reason put forward for including non-commercial use in the exemption was reasoning that nearly all research today includes multi-parties—public, private, and not-for-profit, among others. As such, limiting the scope of the exemption to non-commercial research may not cover any data uses by parties other than researchers working in publicly funded research organisations.[306]

7.5 Privacy of research subjects

Protecting data, including research data, is an increasingly important topic for research and regulatory agencies, especially those involved in clinical trials. People participating in clinical trials have a right to expect that their personal data and the information shared with their doctors will remain confidential. Health services depend on trust, and trust depends on confidentiality [438].

At the same time, sharing patient information for research purposes is an important prerequisite for advancing public science and the well-being of all citizens. Therefore, the practice of research requires a careful balancing of the respective interests in both data protection and data sharing. For these reasons, stakeholders who advocate the sharing of scientific data refer to it as 'responsible sharing'.[307] In this context, the tasks of maintaining confidentiality and safeguarding the privacy of research subjects are viewed as the requirements of research conduct, rather than barriers to data sharing. This is an important distinction and one that implies that sharing clinical trial data without compromising the privacy or confidentiality of research subjects is not only desirable but is also possible and can be achieved through transparent and open data sharing practices championed by institutions such as the EMA.

7.5.1 The sources of confidentiality

Researchers and research investigators have the primary responsibility for maintaining confidentiality and safeguarding the privacy of people participating in their research.[308] They are also responsible for collecting informed consent and informing participants about data use and how confidentiality will be maintained. Obligations of confidence stem from diverse sources of law and have been extended to various areas—including privacy, confidentiality, trade secrets, data protection, labour law, and professional and research ethics, among others. This section considers the key effects of these laws on the release of open data and the latest practice guiding the responsible sharing of clinical trial data.

In Australia, the obligations of confidentiality generally arise under the common law system, as:

- Implied by operation of our common law through the equitable doctrine of confidence

[306] *Ibid.*

[307] Institutes of Health (2017).

[308] Universities in particular require ethics committee approval for undertaking research involving human beings or human activity.

- Expressed through a contractual obligation
- Imposed through operation of legislation (e.g. disclosure of sensitive information)

The first doctrine is commonly implied through a relationship between the party disclosing information and the person to whom it is disclosed—for example, through a doctor-patient relationship or employer-employee relationship. In this regard, the employee has a duty of fidelity to the employer, who can prevent disclosure of information acquired in the course of employment ([439], pp. 860, 867).

Secondly, an obligation of confidentiality may arise from various contracts that govern the disclosure of confidential information—such as trade secrets, confidential agreements, or non-disclosure agreements. In the public research setting, such arrangements are typical in contracts with industry research sponsors who explicitly or implicitly require that confidentiality. Release of research data that contains confidential information is effectively prohibited unless the industry partner provides explicit permission.

Lastly, the obligation to maintain confidentiality can stem from statutes such as the *Privacy Act 1888* (Australia), the General Data Protection Regulation (European Union),[309] and the *Health Insurance Portability and Accountability Act of 1996* (United States) [440] or from various professional code of conduct principles enshrined in legislation. Under such legislation, and due to the recent changes to the global regulatory framework for the sharing of clinical trial data introduced by the European Medicines Agency (EMA) in 2014 [441], the practice of clinical data sharing has transformed quite dramatically in recent years. Legislative and policy changes require drug regulatory agencies to redact the records and/or data they share to de-identify personal details and to remove commercial confidential information. Given the global reach of research based in, or funded, by the European Union, the developments occurring on the continent are likely to influence the global practice of sharing clinical trial data as open data, with efforts mounted to drive the adoption of the interoperability of standards.

7.5.2 Latest approaches to the protection of privacy and sharing sensitive data for research

There have been significant recent developments in the European Union data protection law that will have an impact on research data sharing. The General Data Protection Regulation (GDPR) took effect on 25 May 2018.[310] For the first time, the Regulation is directly enforceable across the European Union and replaces transposition of the Directive at the national level, as was the case with the previous Directive.[311] However, the European Union member states are permitted minor differences in interpretation, with the European Court of Justice as the ultimate arbiter.

The principal tenets of the Regulation with regard to the processing and sharing of sensitive data in scientific research are as follows:

---

309 Regulation (EU) 2016/679 of the European Parliament and of the Council of 27 April 2016 on the protection of natural persons with regard to the processing of personal data and on the free movement of such data and repealing Directive 95/46/EC (General Data Protection Regulation) [42, 43].

310 See point 4 above.

311 Directive 95/46/EC.

- A risk-based and context-specific approach to data processing, aimed at ensuring that appropriate data protection measures are employed in data processing.[312]

- A highly decentralised approach to data handling and processing, vesting responsibilities for data processing in data controllers[313] and providing for decentralised accountability.[314] Data controllers need to adopt a proactive approach to data protection and are responsible for the assessment, implementation, and verification of the measures to ensure compliance with the Directive.

- The Directive specifically enables the processing of sensitive data for scientific research in the 'public interest',[315] requiring organisational and technical measures such as 'pseudonymisation'[316] and the designation of a data protection officer in the cases of large-scale and systematic processing of sensitive data.[317]

- Maintaining the broad notion of informed consent required to process data for future uses, which may not have been known at the time of obtaining informed consent.

The term 'scientific research' is not defined in the Regulation, yet a recent report of the GDPR Working Group[318] clarified that it means 'a research project set up in accordance with relevant sector-related methodological and ethical standards'.[319] Moreover, the processing of personal data for scientific research purposes 'should be interpreted in a broad manner'.[320] Recital 33 states:

> *It is often not possible to fully identify the purpose of personal data processing for scientific research purposes at the time of data collection. Therefore, data subjects should be allowed to give their consent to certain areas of scientific research when in keeping with recognised ethical standards for scientific research. Data subjects should have the opportunity to give their consent only to certain areas of research or parts of research projects to the extent allowed by the intended purpose.*[321]

The Working Group further clarified that scientific research projects can only include personal data on the basis of consent if they have a well-described

---

312 Enshrined in Article 25, in the 'data protection by design and default principle'.

313 Articles 5(2) and 24. Controllers are defined as the persons, companies, associations, or other entities that are in control of personal-data processing.

314 Article 40.

315 Article 9.2.j and 9.2.g.

316 Article 4(5) defines pseudonymisation as 'the processing of personal data in such a manner that the personal data can no longer be attributed to a specific data subject without the use of additional information, provided that such additional information is kept separately and is subject to technical and organisational measures to ensure that the personal data are not attributed to an identified or identifiable natural person'.

317 Articles 37 and 39.

318 The Working Party on the protection of individuals with regard to the processing of personal data. Guidelines on Consent under Regulation 2016/679 adopted on 28 November 2017.

319 *Ibid*, 27.

320 Directive at point 4, Recital 159.

321 *Ibid*, Recital 33.

purpose[322] and if processing of the data is compatible with the initial purposes for which personal data was originally collected.[323] If purposes are unclear at the start of a scientific research program, controllers will have difficulty pursuing the program in compliance with the Directive, which has introduced criteria for compatibility assessment. These aim to determine, on a case-by-case basis, whether further processing of personal data would meet the requirement of compatibility.

The Working Group also mentioned that transparency is an additional safeguard when the circumstances of the research do not allow for specific consent. A lack of purpose specification may be offset by controllers providing regular information on the development of the purpose as the research project progresses so that, over time, the consent will be as specific as possible. In that context, the data subject should have at least a basic understanding of the state of play, allowing that person to assess whether or not to use, for example, the right to withdraw consent pursuant to Article 7(3) of the Directive.

The processing of sensitive research data should be subject to appropriate safeguards for the rights and freedoms of the data subject, and so the Directive mentions techniques such as data minimisation, anonymisation, and data security.[324] Anonymisation is the preferred solution, provided that the purpose of the research can be achieved without the processing of personal data.

Similar decentralised approaches to data de-identification are currently being pursued in the United States. Policy 45 CFR part 46, known as the 'Common Rule' [442], requires de-identification of data prior to release for further research.

The HIPAA Privacy Rule[325] defines the direct personal identifiers (see **Table 6**)[326] and outlines two approaches commonly applied—firstly, expert determination, and secondly, safe harbour.

The first approach requires a statistical expert to apply statistical methods to render data not individually identifiable. This method often results in excessive information loss that can wipe out the analytical utility of the dataset [443].

The safe harbour approach is consistent with the de-identification approach pursued in Europe and requires masking of both direct and indirect identifiers. This process can be automated to a large degree.

7.5.3 Open sharing of sensitive commercial documents

An important aspect of the de-identification process is not only to safeguard the privacy of the research subject but also to enable publishing of the de-identified results online so as to enable the transparency of pharmaceutical research, particularly for regulatory approvals. Championed by the EMA, this approach to open access—in addition to safeguarding the privacy of research subjects—requires the redaction of confidential commercial information.

The requirement by the EMA for the public release of clinical summary reports submitted to it for gaining marketing authorisation or additional market exclusivity

---

322 Report of the Working Party at 30.

323 Directive at point 4, Article 6.4.

324 The processing of personal data for scientific purposes should also comply with other relevant legislations such as on clinical trials (see Recital 156 of the Directive at Point 4).

325 Arising from the *Health Insurance Portability and Accountability Act of 1996* to provide data privacy and security for medical information (https://www.hhs.gov/hipaa/for-professionals/privacy/index.html).

326 Source: *Health Insurance Portability and Accountability Act of 1996* (https://www.hhs.gov/hipaa/for-professionals/privacy/index.html).

1.	Name
2.	Geographic subdivisions smaller than a state. The initial three digits of a ZIP code can be retained if certain criteria are met.
3.	With the exception of year, all elements of dates directly related to an individual (such as birth date, admission date, discharge date, date of death).
4.	Telephone numbers
5.	Fax numbers
6.	Email addresses
7.	Social security numbers
8.	Medical record numbers
9.	Health plan beneficiary numbers
10.	Account numbers
11.	Certificate/licence numbers
12.	Vehicle identifiers and serial numbers, including license plate numbers
13.	Device identifiers and serial numbers
14.	Web Universal Resource Locators (URLs)
15.	Internet Protocol (IP) addresses
16.	Biometric identifiers, including finger and voice prints
17.	Full-face photographs and any comparable images
18.	Any other unique identifying number, characteristic, or code, except as permitted by paragraph (c) of HIPAA Safe Harbor section; and
19.	The covered entity does not have actual knowledge that the information could be used alone or in combination with other information to identify an individual who is a subject of the information.

Table 6.
Ensuring privacy—HIPAA 18 direct identifiers.

has met the resistance of pharmaceutical companies. A number of them have objected to the disclosure of the documents and initiated legal proceedings against the EMA. In February 2018, the General Court delivered judgements in the cases brought by Pari Pharma [444], PTC Therapeutics International [445], and MSD Animal Health Innovation [446]. The court dismissed all three cases as it considered that the companies had failed to provide any concrete evidence of how the disclosure of the contested documents would undermine their commercial interests.

These cases tested, for the first time, the application of the EMA policy on access to documents [346] in the context of the European Union Transparency Regulation [447]. That policy enabled the release of documents that the companies considered were submitted on a confidential basis, and these cases were the first to challenge the legality of the transparency of the EMA approach. Specifically, the EMA submitted that the balance between the commercial interests of the companies and the interests of the general public and public health should lead to disclosure as a default position, except in the cases where the company would clearly demonstrate that such disclosure would undermine its commercial interest.

To implement the policy, the EMA had developed a robust document redaction process and consulted the companies whose documents it sought to release. However, the EMA resisted the claim that the entire documents should be protected from disclosure. The arguments put forward by the EMA included that some of the contents were available in the public domain. The companies counterargued that their compilation of public and non-public data might enable competitors to gain a market advantage.

The Pari Pharma case was the first considered, and the resulting judgement framed the results in the other two. Specifically, the court dismissed the claim that the published documents were presumed confidential. It said that the documents could be subject to a presumption of confidentiality if there existed ongoing judicial or administrative proceedings, but in this case there were none. With regard to the substance of commercially sensitive information, the court said that these could include 'considerations relating to an inventive strategy'[327] or a 'new scientific conclusions'.[328] However, Pari Pharma failed to make the case that any individual pieces of information included in the report should be protected from disclosure.

In particular, the court held that Pari Pharma failed to 'describe in specific terms the professional and commercial importance of the information'[329] along with 'the utility of that information for other undertakings which are liable to examine and use it subsequently'[330] and that the company had failed 'to show specifically and actually how, once the documents have been disclosed, competitors would be able to enter the market'.[331]

Pari Pharma then tried to argue that there was no overriding public interest in disclosure as it was already served in another report. But the court said that, having concluded that the contested information was not commercially confidential, the EMA did not need to determine whether there was or was not an overriding public interest in disclosure. So the claims failed on all accounts.

In the meantime, the EMA continues to disclose reports submitted as part of the regulatory process. In light of this practice, companies continue to argue for maximum redaction and have refined their approach to submitting evidence presented to the EMA. However, last year the EMA rejected 76% of the requests by pharmaceutical companies to redact what they claimed was confidential information [448] and published over 1.3 million pages in 2017 alone.

7.5.4 Approaches to data sharing, managing privacy, and confidentiality in Australia

The current Australian Government has taken an active role in developing an integrated data system across the economy and has, at the time of finalisation of this book, introduced a roadmap towards a new data regulatory mechanism with a view to improving Australia's ability to capture the social and economic benefits from the existing data [449].

The proposed mechanisms aim to improve access to and derive value from public data by introducing a new data regulatory mechanism. The key elements of the proposed framework relevant to the sharing of research data include:

- Taking a risk-based approach to releasing available publicly funded datasets.

- Streamlining and standardising data sharing arrangements.

---

327 Pari Pharma at 25, at 78 and 79.
328 *Ibid*, 77.
329 *Ibid*, 108.
330 *Ibid.*
331 *Ibid*, 118.

- Accredited Data Authorities will engage with data custodians and users on matters relating to data availability and use. The authorities will make decisions on the data to be shared openly and that which requires restricted sharing. The authorities would also certify 'trusted users'.

- Data sharing agreements between data custodians, Accredited Data Authorities, and data users will be a key part of the governance framework.

- Development of National Interest Datasets across and between sectors, including public, private, not-for-profit, and academia.

- Introducing a *Data Sharing and Release Act*, which will set clear rules and expectations for data sharing and release, including making clear when data can be shared and embedding strong safeguards for sensitive data and effective risk management practices.[332]

While the objectives of the Australian Government are laudable, there are, however, significant problems with the proposed approach of 'balancing data sharing with secrecy' and adopting centralised and 'standardised' approaches to data sharing. A particular issue explored in detail in this book is that standardised approaches to data sharing have not been effective drivers of increased data availability and reuse. Similarly, developing closed and rigid communities of 'trusted users' is unlikely to achieve the desired spillover of data and knowledge to enable harnessing of the economic benefits of data. The proposed approach fails to recognise that privacy and security concerns only apply to highly sensitive datasets, which represent only a small subset of national datasets. Most data can be shared freely without any restrictions. However, as the proposal stands now, it appears that the Australian Government has adopted screening approaches across the whole board.

One of the defining features of our time is that the Internet and communication technologies have led to the reconfiguration of power structures and have promoted the rise of distributed social and research networks. In this environment, balancing data sharing with secrecy cannot be a zero-sum game. Any attempts to centrally regulate and restrict data release and use will be met with resistance from Australian citizens and researchers who currently control data and use it on a daily basis to extend the boundaries of science. These are important considerations for the Australian Government to incorporate into the proposed governance structures.

Conclusion

This chapter outlined the legal issues arising in stages of data release and data reuse, focusing on the recent developments and legislative proposals aimed at enabling researchers to share and reuse data while also respecting the emergent rules for responsible data sharing.

The examination found that copyright law poses serious challenges to data release and reuse in all three jurisdictions under examination—the United States, Australia and the European Union. The problems arise due to uncertainty surrounding the scope of copyright protection as it applies to the various forms of data, especially databases. The situation is even more complicated in the European Union which provides a double layer of sui generis and copyright protection. Therefore,

---

[332] *Ibid.*

using the data created by European research organisations carries an inherent risk of IP infringement. Another source of legal uncertainty is the ownership of data and the inability of users to identify data owners, which poses challenges to data licencing and subsequent reuse due to lack of clarity around the conditions governing data reuse.

Various mechanisms have emerged to deal with the challenges. A particular focus has been placed on enabling greater access to data produced by publicly funded research organisations. The question of data ownership appears to be less of a concern to researchers than the matter of the rights and responsibilities of data holders.

This is particularly the case with clinical trials, which collect vast amounts of data from patients and other research subjects. The sharing of the data requires informed consent, and recent years have seen patients demanding a greater say over the use of the data generated in clinical trials. The prevalent view in all jurisdictions is that privacy rights need to be balanced with the benefits accrued from public research and that in the cases where patient consent for future data reuse cannot be foreseen, the data may be used for research purposes in the public interest. This is the position taken by the General Data Protection Regulation.

The European Medicines Authority has championed a novel approach to publicly releasing data after redacting confidential information, and recent judgements have affirmed such sharing of clinical trial data and summary reports in the public interest.

The centralised data-screening approach proposed by the Australian Government seems to go in the opposite direction, despite the fact that [450] was largely modelled around the European approaches to data protection valid at the time. Centralised approaches to data sharing and vetting of prospective data users will be costly and are unlikely to bring about the desired benefits of increased data availability and reuse. An approach with restricted data sharing, too many review boards, too many arguments to be made for gaining access to data, and too many conditions placed on data reuse cannot lead to increased innovation and data uptake.

In this study, it has been shown that decentralised governance mechanisms have been central to the rise and uptake of open data and its reuse by stakeholders. For example, this has been the prevalent approach shaping European science policy, especially biomedicine and medical research, which have advanced as a result of the concerted efforts of heterogeneous stakeholders directly involved in the research conduct. Experiences with open data from CERN and from the EMA confirm that the benefits of open data can be best harnessed by allowing research and regulatory agencies themselves to set the rules for data sharing.

Furthermore, the European data system has primarily relied on trust among stakeholders and on soft-rule instruments, such as codes of professional conduct and research ethics, rather than on more rigid forms of legislative interventions. These three key elements—decentralisation, trust in data holders, and reliance on soft instruments—have been integrated into the new General Data Protection Regulation, which is arguably the most stringent piece of privacy legislation in the world. And yet, the approach adopted in Europe to data sharing is highly decentralised and open.

Chapter 8

The Staged Model for Open Scientific Data

This chapter outlines a way forward for open scientific data. Specifically, it evaluates the impact of open data mandates, identifies the problems associated with their implementation, and proposes ways to address them.

The chapter consists of three sections:

1. Before open data mandates
2. The mandates and their impact
3. The staged model for open scientific data
    - Open data and open publications require different approaches
    - One size does not fit all: the concept of research data
    - The need to make choices: the time and resources required
    - Misunderstood incentives: data exclusivity period
    - Proposed scope of the mandate: releasing data along different stages
    - Increased focus on data reusability: more than metadata
    - The need to develop individual and collective incentives
    - Data ownership should be vested in researchers
    - Legal problems with data reuse: text and data mining exemption

Introduction

The previous three chapters have identified the challenges associated with implementing open scientific data in practice at CERN and in the field of clinical trial data. Those chapters also identified emergent best practice in data curation and release. Drawing on the findings of the previous chapters, this chapter evaluates the impact of the open data mandates and proposes a model to address the problems arising in their implementation.

There are three main parts in this chapter. I first outline the ideological and policy setting within which the policies mandating open access to scientific data have emerged. This is followed by an overview of the main features of the mandates and identification of their drawbacks. The final section discusses those shortcomings in more detail and introduces a staged model for open scientific data.

It is argued that the open data mandates have created a momentum for data release globally. At the same time, the mandates alone are insufficient to effectively drive open data into the future because digital curation of research data for public release is both a very recent and a complex function, posing many challenges. The proposed model and its eight recommendations suggest options for dealing with the issues arising in implementation so as to ensure sustainability of open research data into the future.

8.1 Before open data mandates

Open scientific data is largely driven by the emergence of digital science, as outlined in Chapter 2. The transition from modern science[333] to digital science[334] started well before the open access movement. The World Data Center was established in 1955 to archive and distribute data collected during the 1957–1958 International Geophysical Year.[335] As a result, representatives of 13 governments agreed on scientific collaboration enabled by a free sharing of scientific observations and results from Antarctica [451]. In 1966 the Committee on Data in Science and Technology was founded by the International Council for Science to promote cooperation in data management and use [60].

Digital sharing of scientific data builds on these early foundations. It has accelerated in recent years largely due to technological advances in communication technologies and the proliferation of measurement and scientific equipment capable of collecting, processing, and storing vast amounts of data. Such equipment is now more readily available, and the costs associated with automated data harvesting and analysis have dropped significantly. To illustrate this point, I refer back to the Human Genome Project completed in 2003. Decoding the human genome, using the technology available at the time, took 10 years and cost over US$1 billion. Today, complex DNA analyses require only several days at a cost of around US$1000 each.[336]

The year 2003 also loosely marks the emergence of the open access movement, which brought renewed calls for greater availability of scientific data.[337] It was also the year the non-profit Public Library of Science (PLOS) in the United States launched *PLOS Biology* and high-profile journals such as *Nature*, *Science*, and *The Scientist* all published high-profile articles on open access to scientific publications [456–458].

Open scientific data needs to be seen in this historical context. It is not a completely novel concept, and it is not merely an extension of policies mandating open access to publications. Open scientific data is new in that it calls for research data to be freely available for access, reuse, and distribution by anyone—whether as

---

[333] Thomas Kuhn developed the concept of modern science and elaborated on the concept of scientific revolutions in 1962. Kuhn explains the process of scientific change as the result of various phases of paradigm change. He challenged the Mertonian view of progress in what he called 'normal science'. He argued for a model in which periods of conceptual continuity in 'normal science' were interrupted by periods of 'revolutionary science'. See Kuhn [100], Chapter 2, Section 2.2.

[334] The term 'digital science' is often referred to as 'open science' or 'Science 2.0'. See definitions in Glossary.

[335] Scientists from 67 countries participated in the data collection that year and agreed to share data generated from cosmic ray, climatology, oceanography, earth's atmosphere, and magnetic research, with a view to make the data available in machine-readable formats. See also Chapter 2, Section 2.2.

[336] Statistics sourced from the International Council for Science [452]. The early economic analysis of the Human Genome Project is included in Chapter 2, Section 2.4.

[337] The calls for enabling open access to research data came from different authoritative sources [45–51, 71, 453–455].

researchers, policymakers, industry partners, or any member of the public. While some scientific articles were previously available for anyone to use freely in digital formats, research data—the 'raw material' necessary to validate the outcomes published in those articles—is only now becoming freely available to the broader public as open data.

Indeed, open scientific data aims to encourage, for the first time in history, the participation in science creation, validation, and dissemination by both scientific and non-scientific actors. The production of scientific knowledge is now more centrally located within social relations—a shift that has been termed as *Mode 2* of knowledge production.[338] This also means that data is viewed in a different way to that found in the previous context of modern science defined by Thomas Kuhn. The key difference is the principle that where data is produced through publicly funded research, then the broader public should have a right to access it. Furthermore, according to the theory of *Mode 2* knowledge production, data is seen as having value through its reuse by a broader range of stakeholders than just the research community that initially collected it.[339]

Open scientific data further highlights the transformative changes in science conduct in the digital era. With increased availability of data in digital formats, computers alone can now validate and generate scientific outcomes—due to advances in artificial intelligence and quantum computing and the development of algorithms capable of solving problems by processing and calculating vast amounts of data. Following on from these developments is the argument that open scientific data challenges established research and science conduct and communication practices, as well as the monopoly of researchers over validating and creating scientific outcomes.

Such profound changes require careful change management and implementation processes. While some researchers welcome these developments and embrace the changes, others are naturally reticent or even sceptical about them. Despite recent progress, the transition to digital science is still in early stages. In some fields of science, especially social sciences, the transition has not even properly started [459]. For these reasons, this book argues the calls for engaging the broader public in science participation may come too early.

The argument draws on the findings of Chapters 5 and 6, which document the experiences with implementation of open data in particle physics and clinical trials. The finding of these chapters is that scientists in both fields are still learning how to implement open scientific data and how to deal with the many challenges associated with the processing, curation, release, and (re)use of open scientific data they produce. Their experiences with open data demonstrate that even a well-established and large data-centric organisation, such as CERN, is still experimenting with the parameters and descriptors that will make its particle physics data available in a form suitable for independent reuse by others.

By contrast, describing, sharing, and reusing clinical trial data in digital formats are a well-established practice in closed scientific circles. However, the free sharing of that data as open data is not developing quickly as a practice, despite the economic and social value the data holdings found to offer society [339, 460, 461]. Instead of looking for ways for facilitating the sharing of data more widely, some members of the research community took the view that disseminating clinical trial data as open data was risky as the data might be used maliciously or to uncover the identity of research subjects [462–464]. Those researchers who were willing to

---

338 *Mode 2* is a new paradigm of knowledge production that is characterised as socially distributed, application-oriented, transdisciplinary, and subject to multiple accountabilities ([33], p. 179).

339 *Ibid*, see also Wessels et al. [89], p. 56, Chapter 2, and Section 2.2.

share data often faced criticism for giving away data that could potentially be used to generate further publications or research revenue for their organisations.

The increased calls for opening up research data come at a time when major governments are decreasing their funding for research[340] and there is an increasing trend in the private sector to draw on public research.[341] Many governments now require publicly funded research organisations to increase the return on the investment in research by generating income through the protection and commercialisation of intellectual property, including though the creation of start-up enterprises [150]. The demand for commercialisation has affected the goals of government research funding. It is causing public sector research agencies to justify the success of research by providing a convincing argument for the future economic value of their science and technology bases [151]. Such agencies are also urged to demonstrate the broader social and environmental benefits of their research.

Australia is no exception. Many CSIRO researchers work on commercial projects with industry and are under the obligation to maintain confidentiality about the results. Also, all science-intensive research agencies in Australia now have a technology transfer function and try to create revenue from commercialising university intellectual property. However, the vast majority of university research in Australia remains publicly funded, and some 70% of CSIRO research is funded by the government. Thus, there is a strong case for allowing the public to share in the fruits of scientific research by having access to the data these research organisations create.

In recent years, the Federal Court of Australia has upheld the argument that science has a public function. In the *UWA vs Gray* case [414], a dispute over intellectual property rights claimed by a former university employee, Justice French, made specific acknowledgement that the function of universities is to offer education and research facilities and to award degrees and that this amounts to a public function.

Further, he stated that although universities do perform commercial activities, those enterprises had not displaced the public functions of universities in such a way that they became 'limited to that of engaging academic staff for its own commercial purposes'.[342]

In addition, Justice French held that academic freedoms are incompatible with any duty to maintain confidentiality of the kind required to protect, for commercial purposes, the intellectual property that might result from research activities within a university.[343] In sum, this judgement confirmed the principle that the public

---

340 Spending on R&D in government and higher education institutions in OECD countries fell in 2014 for the first time since the data was first collected in 1981. Countries with declining public R&D budgets include Australia, France, Germany, Israel, the Netherlands, Poland, Sweden, the United Kingdom, and the United States. See OECD [146].
In the United States, for the first time in the post-World War II era, the Federal Government no longer funds a majority of the basic research carried out in the country. Data from ongoing surveys by the National Science Foundation show that federal agencies provided only 44% of the US$86 billion spent on basic research in 2015. See Mervis [147].

341 Chesbrough has shown that technology companies require timely access to knowledge as they increasingly innovate by combining research outputs from external and internal sources and increasingly draw on research from universities and other public research organisations [11, 12].
For example, in the pharmaceutical sector in the United States alone, roughly 75% of the most innovative drugs, the so-called new molecular entities with priority rating, trace their existence to the National Institutes of Health [149].

342 *Ibid*, FCA 49 at 184.

343 *Ibid*, at 192.

function of universities is the priority, with commercial considerations subordinate to that.

This position underpins the case for open research data. It is within such an ideological and technological setting that the policies mandating open access to scientific data have emerged.

8.2 The open data mandates

Some of the world's leading research organisations are based in the United States. These were among the earliest institutions anywhere to recognise the potential of open scientific data.

The first policy statement for open access to research data is found in the *Bromley Principles* issued by the US Global Change Research Program in 1991 [169]. Five years later, the *Bermuda Principles*—developed as part of the Human Genome Project—set an international practice for sharing genomic data prior to publication of research findings in scientific journals.[344]

In 2003 open access to scientific data was first codified internationally, in the *Berlin Declaration on Open Access to Knowledge in the Sciences and Humanities* [63].[345] This emerged from a conference hosted by the Max Planck Institute in Munich and represents a landmark statement on open access to scientific contributions[346] including 'original scientific research results, raw data and metadata, source materials, digital representations of pictorial and graphical materials and scholarly multimedia material'.[347] Research organisations committed to implementing the objectives of open scientific data can sign the declaration, and over 600 have done so already.[348]

Awareness of the need to develop data management infrastructure took a huge step forward in 2010 when the National Science Foundation (NSF) in the United States announced that it would begin requiring data management plans with applications in the grant cycle starting from January 2011.[349] This policy has inspired research funders to introduce similar policies all over the world. The original NSF policy states:

> *Investigators are expected to share with other researchers, at no more than incremental cost and within a reasonable time, the primary data, samples, physical collections and other supporting materials created or gathered in the course of work under NSF grants. Grantees are expected to encourage and facilitate such sharing. Investigators and grantees are encouraged to share software and inventions created under the grant or otherwise make them or their products widely available and usable.*[350]

---

[344] The Human Genome Project is discussed in Chapter 2, Section 2.5.

[345] The Declaration is analysed in Chapter 3, Section 3.1.

[346] The Berlin Declaration does not use the term 'open research data' but rather refers to 'open knowledge contributions' which represent a broad definition of open research data. See also discussion concerning the definition of research data in Chapter 4.

[347] As of October 2007, there were 240 signatories, in early 2018 over 600 [63].

[348] *Ibid*, [172].

[349] Proposals submitted to NSF on or after 18 January 2011: ... must include a supplementary document of no more than two pages labelled 'Data Management Plan.' This supplementary document should describe how the proposal will conform to NSF policy on the dissemination and sharing of research results [185].

[350] See NSF Award and Administration Guide, Chapter 6—Other Post Award Requirements and Considerations, points 4(b) and (c) [16].

For several years prior to this statement, research funders had required grant recipients to share their data with other investigators. Yet none had policies on how this should be accomplished. The position has changed following the publication of the NSF policy, with many funders now requiring that recipients of grants enable open access to research data and, in many cases, also submit research data management plans at the grant proposal stage. Such policies aim to ensure that data resulting from publicly funded research is retained and can be reused over time—usually for 10 years.

The US government has taken significant steps to enable the dissemination of scientific outcomes arising from public research. In early 2013, the Office of Science and Technology Policy at the White House directed each federal agency with over US$100 million in annual research and development expenditure to develop plans to make 'the results of unclassified research arising from public funding publicly accessible to search, retrieve and analyse and to store such results for long-term preservation'.[351]

The coordinating body for science policy in the United Kingdom, UK Research and Innovation (the successor since April 2018 to Research Councils UK), has had policies on open access since 2005. Its common principles for open data of 2011 [465] take account of the evolving global policy landscape.

The European Commission was among the first of the large funders to test arrangements for encouraging open access to publicly funded research. In 2008, the Commission launched the Open Access Pilot as part of its Seventh Research Framework Programme. That was replaced in 2014, under the Horizon 2020 research and innovation project, with the Open Research Data Pilot for treating the data underlying publications—including curated data and raw data [21]. The Rules of Participation[352] establish the legal basis for open access to research data funded by the European Commission under the Horizon 2020 Work Programme, and the overarching principles are translated into specific requirements in the Model Grant Agreement[353]. The Commission has also developed a user guide that explains the provisions of the Model Grant Agreement to applicants and beneficiaries along with defined exceptions to data sharing.[354]

In addition to the measures taken by the European Commission, individual European countries have taken legislative steps to recognise open access to research outputs. These include Germany,[355] Italy,[356] the Netherlands[357] and Spain.[358]

---

[351] The White House (2013). *e Results of Federally Funded Scientific Research*. The research results include peer-reviewed publications, publications' metadata, and digitally formatted scientific data. The major shortcoming is that the memo does not mention metadata associated with research data. This omission is unfortunate because, in many cases, scientific data without metadata is unlikely to be reusable.

[352] Article 43.2 of Regulation (EU) No 1290/2013 of the European Parliament and of the Council laying down the rules for participation and dissemination in Horizon 2020, the Framework Programme for Research and Innovation (2014–2020) and repealing Regulation (EC) No 1906/2006.

[353] Multi-beneficiary General Model Grant Agreement, Version 4.1, 26 October 2017 (http://ec.europa.eu/research/participants/data/ref/h2020/grants_manual/amga/h2020-amga_en.pdf).

[354] The exceptions include the obligation to protect research results with intellectual property, confidentiality, and security obligations and the need to protect personal data and specific cases in which open access might jeopardise the project. If any of these exceptions is applied, then the data research management plan must state the reasons for not giving or restricting access. (Annotated Model Grant Agreement, Version 1.7, 19 December 2014, 215).

[355] Law October 1, 2013 (BGBl. I S. 3714) amending Article 38 Copyright Act.

[356] Par. 4, Law October 7, 2013, no. 112.

[357] Law June 30, no. 257 amending Article 25fa Copyright Act.

[358] Artículo 37 'Difusión en acceso abierto', Ley 14/2011, de 1 de junio, de la Ciencia, la Tecnología y la Innovación.

Elsewhere, significant policy developments are under way in several Latin American countries. The Chinese Academy of Sciences was an early signatory to the Berlin Declaration, and it actively participates in several open data projects.

Australia is hesitant to implement open research data practice, even though the country was one of the first in the world to adopt open access to public sector information. The country's two principal research funders—the National Health and Medical Research Council (NHMRC) and the Australian Research Council (ARC)—mandated open access to peer-reviewed publications in 2012. Starting from 2014, the ARC said that it 'strongly encourages' the depositing of data and any publications arising from a research project in an appropriate subject and/or institutional repository [466]. At the same time, 'research data and metadata' are expressly excluded from the scope of its open access policy.[359] This highlights the need to understand the meaning of 'open research data' within the ARC grants, as pointed out in Chapter 4 and further discussed in Recommendations 1–4 below.

The NHMRC mandate did not extend to open data until early 2018. Australia seemed to be falling behind the rest of the world in terms of open research data, even though the Australian Government was one of the first in the world to develop a national research infrastructure having established the Australian National Data Service as early as in 2008. It was not until 10 years later the NHMRC finally updated its policy, stating that it:

> *... strongly encourages researchers to consider the reuse value of their data and to take reasonable steps to share research data and associated metadata arising from NHMRC supported research [467].*

The introduction of open data mandates by research funders and governments is a welcome development, as Chapter 3 concludes. Research organisations and universities are largely dependent on grant funding. Suddenly, these institutions realised that to enable researchers to successfully compete for grants, they had to provide them with support in the formulation of data management plans. Libraries at many research organisations are now providing these services,[360] and researchers are changing their research data management practices as a result. Within only a few years, the policies introduced by research funders appear to have built a momentum for significant organisational and behavioural changes. Such changes are driving the increased retention and sharing of research data globally.

However, implementation of open data mandates presents many challenges for research organisations, as this book finds. The mandates neither specifically acknowledge nor deal with these challenges. The open data policies are more likely high-level statements of principles and expectations, rather than documents setting out rules and providing detailed instructions to research organisations. These factors make comparative analyses difficult.

To date, there is no agreement on what constitutes 'research data' and, consequently, what is the 'data' that researchers need to release.[361] Only a few of the policies include time limits for data release, and even fewer say what happens if there is no compliance. Very few policies address the funding requirements for

---

[359] The revised ARC Open Access Policy, version 2017.1, was issued on 30 June 2017 following consultations with the deputy vice chancellors (research) of Australian universities. Other publicly-funded research organisations do not appear to have been consulted.

[360] For example, all large Australian universities provide support to researchers with research data management (RDM). See Chapter 5, Section 5.2 [468–475].

[361] These issues are discussed in Chapters 4, Sections 4.1 and 4.2.

research data and supporting infrastructures, even though some funders include a provision in their grants for data curation for the duration of the relevant research project.[362] However, research data lifecycle generally extends beyond the duration of research projects.[363] Furthermore, the division of responsibilities for data annotation, curation, and preservation is not delineated. Some funders remain silent about the legal and ethical issues arising in research data sharing and reuse. Some appear to hold the perception that appropriate licencing mechanisms can effectively address the issues.[364]

These and other shortcomings and problems with implementation are detailed in Chapters 5–7, which provide a foundation for the development of the staged model for open scientific data that is introduced in the following sections.

8.3 The staged model for open scientific data

8.3.1 Open data and open publications require different approaches

The approach adopted for facilitating open access to scientific data has been strongly influenced by the experiences of research organisation in enabling open access to publications. Chapter 5 argued that research data management cannot be treated simply as a standardised library service for implementing open data mandates in practice. Yet this is exactly the approach taken by universities and many research organisations. While standardised approaches have generally proved to be suitable for developing open access to publications, such approaches are neither suitable nor appropriate for open scientific data. Librarians and research funders, who have played pivotal roles in facilitating open access to scientific publications, tend to apply uniform principles and approaches to open data as well. This creates challenges for researchers, who are required to comply with the open data mandates introduced by research funders but, at this stage, are unable to do so. There are several reasons for the confusion. In particular, there is the need for a more advanced understanding of the different natures of open data and open publications and of the different drivers and processes that have led to both.

Originally, open access was focused nearly exclusively on some 2.5 million articles that appear annually in 25,000 journals around the world, coming from all disciplines [476]. The rationale behind facilitating open access to publications was that, in the digital age, those articles should no longer be accessible only to users at such institutions as could afford the journal subscriptions. Instead, it was argued these articles could be made available to all potential users by depositing them on the web. Institutional repositories were created with open access-compliant software to make the articles interoperable, harvestable, navigable, searchable, and useable as if they were just one global repository—freely open to all.

The message about the feasibility and benefits of open access spreads quickly to academics and researchers, most of whom not only welcomed but gradually also embraced and began to actively promote the concept. Studies have shown that open access publications significantly increase research uptake and impact, as measured by downloads and citations [477–481]. Most publishers endorsed providing immediate open access, and researchers started depositing their articles on the web.

---

[362] See Chapter 3, especially Section 3.3. For example, the revised Research Councils (UK) Policy includes funding provisions.

[363] See Chapter 5, especially Section 5.1.

[364] See Chapter 3 and Chapter 7, Section 7.5.

However, it soon became apparent that the spontaneous deposit rate was not growing fast enough to make the ever-increasing volume of global annual research output available as open access. Researchers were surveyed, and their responses revealed significant concerns about copyright and about the time and effort that it could take to deposit. The same surveys established that researchers would readily provide open access if their institutions and research funders would mandate it.[365] So the only enablers needed were uniform mandates from research funders and appropriate copyright licencing mechanisms. Once these were introduced, librarians started to implement the new arrangements in collaboration with researchers.

Encouraged by these experiences, the same stakeholders started to call for extending the open access mandate to scientific data. Given the successful implementation of open access to publications, it was thought that mandates from scientific institutions and research funders would be the golden keys to increase the digital sharing of research data.

However, the mandates mushroomed well before any experiences with open data were generated by researchers. Several years down the track, it is becoming obvious that, for the most part, these approaches and assumptions were overly enthusiastic, if not unrealistic—largely because of the different nature of scientific data across different scientific disciplines but also because of the different incentives for collecting and sharing research data. Many of these differences are highlighted below.

For now, I summarise scientific publications and scientific data as two different concepts that require different approaches to their release, management, and curation. In the early stages of the open data debate, these distinctions went unnoticed and only became evident once the open data mandates from research funders became difficult to implement in practice.

8.3.2 One size does not fit all: the concept of research data

Despite the many examples of data provided in the open data policies and the many parameters and conditions that qualify data as 'open', 'findable', and 'intelligible', the term 'research data' (as it is used in practice) conveys different meanings to different people.[366] Research funders, researchers, librarians, and lawyers working in research organisations all approach the term differently. Funders and publishers typically mention research data that underpins publications; researchers talk about files, databases, and spreadsheets they collect and work within the course of research projects; librarians are preoccupied with metadata, data citations, and software; lawyers would like to see 'data' described as facts, raw facts, or compilations of facts in databases.

This can create confusion, as Chapter 4 argues. If researchers are to comply with the policies of funders and publishers, they need to understand what 'data' they need to make available. Similarly, if librarians are to provide effective assistance to researchers with data management, they need to be certain about the research outputs to be considered and how they need to be classified and described.

The nub of the problem with defining 'research data' is that data is a dynamic concept, unlike information.[367] The contents of 'data' vary in the context of its use, as examined in Chapters 4 and 7.[368] What represents 'data' to one researcher may

---

365 However, over 90% of the researchers sampled said that if open access was mandated, then they would comply, with over 80% indicating that they would do so willingly [482, 483].

366 See Chapter 4, Sections 4.2 and 4.3.

367 See Chapter 2, Section 2.2.

368 Chapter 4, Section 4.1 and 4.2, and Chapter 7, Section 7.1.

be 'noise'[369] for another researcher working on the same project, as Borgman pointed out [167]. However, the emerging consensus is that the meaning of 'data' needs to be interpreted through the lenses of researchers.[370] Generally, all outputs that are accepted in the scientific community as necessary to validate research findings are included among research data. The terms 'research data' and 'scientific data' are often used interchangeably, irrespectively of the subject collecting the data —whether the subject is a researcher or whether the data collection is semiautomated (such as through online questionnaires) or fully automated (such as data harvested by scientific equipment).

'Research data' may therefore take many forms, come in different formats, and arrive from various sources. In the physical and life sciences, researchers typically generate data from their own experiments or observations. In the social sciences, data can either be generated by the researchers themselves or sourced from elsewhere, such as from statistics collected by government departments. The notion of 'data' is least well-established in the humanities, although the rapid development of digital research in those disciplines has seen the use of the term become more common. In the humanities, the source of data is generally cultural records—archives, published materials, or artefacts [167, 484]. This variety of research practices across different disciplines results in a variety of practices for the collection and preparation of open access. The research community has yet to come to a uniform understanding of these matters [485].

Another facet of 'research data' is the sharing of it at various stages of granularity and processing levels. These range from top-level data underpinning scientific publications to various working versions incorporating different levels of analysis, cleaning, reorganising, and processing; to raw data collected in field research or harvested by scientific equipment.[371]

The open data mandates fail to acknowledge this fact, which is unfortunate, because agreement on the stages at which data needs to be shared across scientific disciplines would instantly assist researchers to make the data management task easier. In general terms, the lower the level of granularity of the data shared, the greater the possibilities for research reproducibility and data reuse. But this is conditional—the data must be supported by rich metadata and detailed description of the assumptions made by the original data collectors along the different levels of their research and data analysis and with the statistical methods used to analyse and aggregate the data and the methods used to clean the data and reduce 'noise'.[372]

Finally, there is consideration of the varying level of control of research data. Scientific organisations around the world implement numerous approaches and models of research data with varying levels of access control. At one end of the spectrum is the sharing of research data by anyone and with everyone. On the other end is a complete ban on data sharing gathered as part of certain research projects or across entire disciplines or institutions. Even though it is now generally accepted that sharing of publications is desirable and should be encouraged and pursued to

[369] Data noise is additional meaningless information included in data, for example, duplicate or incomplete entries. 'Noise' also includes any data that cannot be understood and interpreted correctly by machines, such as unstructured text.

[370] For example, the Australian National Data Service accepts records of data that are considered to be important to the Australian research community [231].

[371] For example, the sharing of clinical trial data can happen at the stage of the raw data collected in case report forms during trials, to the coded data stored in computerised databases, to the summary data made available through journals and registries. See also Chapter 6, Section 6.3.

[372] See definition of 'noise' at point 52 above.

the maximum extent possible, such an agreement is yet to emerge on the scope for the open sharing of research data.

Recommendation 1

The open data policies must incorporate the various facets of scientific data—that is, data which is heterogeneous, is complex, and differs across various scientific disciplines, various levels of granularity, and various levels of processing and control.

Research funders, publishers, and learned societies should, in close collaborations with researchers, facilitate the discussion to clarify the notion of data, its stages of processing, and the requirements for data sharing at each of these stages.

8.3.3 The need to make choices: the time and resources

Unlike academic publications, in which the objective is to publish as open access as many peer-reviewed outputs as possible, simply publishing more open data is unlikely to yield the same benefits. Choices need to be made about what data to keep and to preserve into the future and why. There are several reasons for this.

Firstly, preserving and curating all data collected in scientific experiments are not possible at this stage of technological development and at recoverable cost. This is because the burden of preparing and maintaining usable open access data repositories requires far more effort and resources than preparing publications for digital release. In this context, research data needs to be treated as an independent 'product', rather than part of research. What is more, the development of infrastructures is required to make the data discoverable, retrievable, interpretable, and usable.

The additional time and effort required from researchers cannot be overestimated. This is an important point of difference between open publications and open data. Publications are generally readily available in digital formats, and releasing them in electronic formats does not require any additional effort from researchers.

Preparing data for digital release is far more labour-intensive, especially in organisations implementing controlled access to data. Data curation requires detailed description of the datasets and the methods used to process it. The stages of receiving and processing applications for data release, then developing agreements on its use and related contracts, then producing and transferring data, and finally responding to any subsequent requests for clarification involve a diverse range of people throughout the data sharing organisation [366].

Research organisations typically have limited resources to handle these requests, which can result in clashes with other demands on staff time, such as research tasks. In the absence of support from research funders to prepare the datasets, some research bodies may request that applicants pay the cost of the staff time required to fulfil requests for sharing data or that they cover it from their own research budgets.

The sharing of scientific publications is generally straightforward and uniform across the world. Publications may exist in many copies and in many collections but need to be catalogued only once. Libraries are well-experienced in doing this and share such digital services across institutions. University libraries make agreements about what publications each will collect, promoting the concentration of resources and providing access to community members ([167], p. 75). While the same can be done with data collections, the experiences with data use and reuse are only just starting to emerge. Research data is more analogous to archival materials—each set is unique and requires its own metadata and provenance records.[373] Data is only meaningful and reusable if supported by properly recorded metadata and other data descriptors.

[373] *Ibid*, 307.

More work is required to describe unique items or to merge them into common structures. And even more work is required to keep the data collections up to date. While the effort associated with curation of publications is generally complete at the stage of release, data also requires post-release curation and tracking of issues such as software versions and other data processing systems.

Another reason why choices need to be made about what data to keep and curate as open data is the limitation on available computing power, data storage facilities, and other resources. Even CERN, an organisation at the forefront in the development of quantum computing in the world, has to make many hard choices about what 'data' to preserve into the future. The CERN processes and data decision points are detailed in Chapter 5.

Clearly, the resources required to curate and preserve open scientific data are immense and go well beyond the resources required to develop digital data repositories in the same manner as providing open access to publications. The open data mandates fail to recognise the resource implications, especially the efforts required from researchers to prepare data for release and the time required for any subsequent consultations with other researchers wishing to reuse the data. These efforts need to be recognised and rewarded.

Recommendation 2

Research funders and policymakers should allocate funding for the documentation, curation and preservation of research data that requires additional effort and time from researchers.

Choices need to be made about what data to preserve and why. Researchers are best positioned to make such choices provided data sharing is properly resourced.

8.3.4 Misunderstood incentives: data exclusivity period

A striking difference between open publications and open data is that increased impact is not the primary incentive for publishing research data. While it is true that the release of research data can increase use of the resulting scientific publications,[374] the purpose of the data itself is a prerequisite for conducting the research and writing the publication. Stevan Harnard summarised these differences well as early as in 2010 when he said:

> *Scientists and researchers are not data gatherers, they are analysers and interpreters of the data. They do gather and generate data and often at the cost of much time and effort. But researchers do so in order to be able to able to exploit and mine the data they have gathered or generated. What they publish in articles are the results of these analyses, that is why they are researchers and it is on that result that their careers and rewards depend [489].*

While researchers are generally keen to make their refereed articles available for open access immediately after publication, researchers are generally reticent to share their data freely immediately after gathering the data or immediately upon publication of the first data analyses. The reasons for this are many and are not well understood. Those known include the incentives for career progression and the prospects for scrutinising and, in some cases, even maliciously challenging research findings published in articles.

However, the most important reason is the significant time and effort required to process and describe the data. For these reasons, it has become obvious that

[374] A number of studies across several scientific fields have shown increased impact of publications supported by data [115, 486–488].

researchers in most disciplines insist on exclusive exploitation rights over their data, even if the data collection process is publicly funded. The period of exclusive exploitation required to produce the necessary publications varies by research disciplines and even by research projects.

At this time, most research organisations remain silent about the length of the exclusivity period required for their data. The lack of discussion on this issue is a significant impediment to open scientific data and needs careful consideration and negotiation between researchers, research funders and research organisations.

Setting unrealistic deadlines may achieve no more than setting no deadlines. This is especially the case as researchers themselves often do not have rights to the data they collect—a situation that is different from the legal rights they have, at least initially, in publications. The length of the period needs to be agreed at the beginning of research project. One way of achieving agreement would be to negotiate the length of exclusivity at the stage of preparing data management plans.

The stakeholders in the process also need to recognise that circumstances can arise for which the immediate release of research data is required in the public interest—such as to assist in dealing with a public health emergency or a national security interest.

Recommendation 3

Research funders and publishers need to seek consensus among research stakeholders that:

a. Researchers who generate original data will have the right of exclusive first use for a reasonable period.

b. The length of the period of exclusive use will vary by research discipline and even by research project and should be determined at the outset of each project in consultation between researchers and research funders.

c. The length of the agreed period of exclusive use should not exceed the maximum limits defined in the commonly agreed community norms and protocols for each scientific discipline.

d. Exceptions to this period of the exclusive use of data will apply in circumstances that are of urgent public interest—for example, in the case of a public health emergency.

8.3.5 Scope of the mandate: releasing open data along different stages

The key impediments to the practice of open data are the lack of recognition for the various types of research data and the lack of recognition that research data can be shared at various stages of processing and granularity. These issues were outlined in the previous sections and are discussed in detail in Chapters 5 and 6.[375] In this section, I introduce a staged approach for enabling open access to data that addresses the gaps—a modified version of the approach to research data as it has evolved at CERN. This approach can also be adopted to open research data in other organisations.

CERN has classified its data along four different levels of processing, which are summarised in **Table 7**.[376]

Level 1 data, the data underpinning scientific publications, is available simultaneously with publications and is mandatory.

---

[375] See Chapter 5, Section 5.3.2.

[376] This table is based on the four Open Access Policies in place across CERN [287, 293, 304, 310].

	Data type	Primary users	Data access level
level 1	Data directly related to publications that provide documentation for the published results ('underlying data').	Interested scientific members or the general public (= any internet user).	Open data
level 2	Simplified data formats (selected datasets).	Outreach and education providers and users.	Open data
level 3	Reconstructed data, simulation data, and the analysis software needed to allow a full scientific analysis.	High energy physicists.	Restricted data
level 4	Raw data and access to the full potential of the experimental data.	Restricted CERN users (data constructors and data-takers) working in one of the four collaborations.	Highly restricted data

Table 7.
Data processing levels at CERN.

Level 2 data consists of carefully selected and highly pre-processed datasets, such as those where students can search for the Higgs Boson. These datasets are released sporadically, mostly for educational purposes. CERN found its outreach education programs utilising *Level 2* data were highly successful and popular among high school students in many countries. This engagement has helped to develop data literacy and to promote awareness of particle physics among students.

Level 3 data is data ready for scientific analyses and processing and requires expert use. The data is 'reconstructed'—the level of processing that would roughly correspond to data cleaning and removing 'noise' in datasets in other research organisations.

Level 4 data is called experimental data in the field of particle physics. It is the data collected from the Large Hadron Collider with minimal processing steps. This data is highly restricted and requires enormous computing power and resources for processing and descaling. CERN is, however, open to the possibility of sharing selected experimental datasets with expert users.

The data classification at CERN highlights another difference between open data and open publications. Access to open publications is generally available to anyone, whether as a member of the general public or of a scientific audience. Any person of reasonable intelligence can read the publication and is able to interpret and to assimilate the knowledge included in the publication to a certain degree.

This is not the case with open data in general and open scientific data in particular. A person of reasonable intelligence is unlikely to be able to interpret and to adequately utilise lower-level scientific data, even if the data is properly described and supported by relevant software. Freely accessible research data across all scientific disciplines may not be of widespread interest to the general public.

On occasion, good reasons may exist for restricting access to scientific data, especially raw data, to those scientists capable of using it in line with precisely defined research methods and established principles for research ethics. At the same time, the arguments presented by researchers against data sharing need careful examination before accepting any exceptions for not sharing data.

The key issue to keep in mind is that both open access publications and open access data collections gain in value as they grow ([167], p. 67). Therefore, many of the benefits of large open data collections will also only be discovered as the collections grow. This presents opportunities for broadening open access to lower-level data. However, at this point, neither the experimental data is described to the level of detail that would enable independent reuse, nor are the non-expert users able to process the data outside CERN.

	Data type	*Primary users*	*Data access level*	*When to deposit*
level 1	Data underpinning the findings in publications. ('underlying data').	Expert users and non-expert users (= all internet users).	Open data	**Default open access.** Underlying data and publications should be released simultaneously on the date of the publication. Data exclusivity period should not apply to Level 1 data.
level 2	Selected pre-processed datasets.	Expert users to test open data in practice. Non-expert users for education and outreach.	Open data	*Optional.* At any time. Data exclusivity may apply.
level 3	Working level data and software needed to allow a full scientific analysis.	Expert-users.	Restricted data	*Data exclusivity period will apply.* **After expiration of the exclusivity period, Level 3 data should be reclassified and released as Level 2 open data provided such a release would not incur substantial costs.**
level 4	Raw data and access to the full potential of the scientific, clinical and laboratory equipment.	Restricted expert-users.	Highly restricted data	*Data exclusivity period will apply.* The use of data to be monitored.

Table 8.
Staged model for facilitating open access to research data.

With this in mind, it is important for research funders across the different scientific disciplines to ascertain the levels at which scientific data is generally collected and processed across each scientific discipline. The funders should then set the boundaries for the levels at which the data holds the highest potential to be reused by other researchers (expert users) and by other interested users (non-expert users). The staged model summarised in **Table 8** can serve as a guideline for such deliberations.

The model puts a renewed emphasis on mandatory sharing of 'underlying data' that should be released concurrently with publications.

There should be no delays in releasing the *Level 1* data. A period of data exclusivity would not apply, because *Level 1* data represents highly selected and highly processed subsets of the lower-level research data. *Level 1* data is directly related to the results published. Once the findings are in the public domain, the reasoning that data underpinning those results can have a commercial value may not be plausible, as recently tested in cases to which the European Medicines Agency was a party.[377] Therefore, *Level 1* data should be released on the date of publication in all instances.

Level 2 data would be optional and would allow researchers as well as non-expert users to experiment with research data, enabling them to explore ways for reusing data produced by others and for embedding the data in their own research practice (see also Recommendation 6).

Level 3 data would be shared among expert users during a data exclusivity period, a situation which is not too dissimilar from the current practice among expert users in clinical trials and in particle physics experiments. Under this scenario, expert users would be authorised to access and to freely utilise the data and support tools directly in institutional repositories, or the data would be shared under data use agreements.

---

[377] See Chapter 7, Section 7.5.3.

However, after expiry of the exclusivity period, *Level 3* data would be published as open data and reclassified as *Level 2* data. Research funders along with librarians working in research organisations should be responsible for monitoring the expiry of the exclusivity period and release the data as open data when appropriate, provided there would be no substantial additional costs.

The need for sharing *Level 3* data after the expiry of the exclusivity period is especially relevant to those scientific disciplines where data infrastructures are well-developed and where open data is already embedded in research practice—such as in geospatial and earth sciences, materials sciences, biomedical research, computational engineering, and digital humanities.

Level 4 data can be governed by the same access mechanisms as *Level 3* data. However, the data would not be reclassified or released as open data after the expiry of the exclusivity period unless there would be a compelling business case for curating and preserving the data. This is because the curation and preservation of *Level 4* is costly and extremely labour-intensive.[378]

Recommendation 4

1. The open data mandates should:
   a. Put a renewed emphasis on mandatory sharing and unlimited use of the data underpinning the results published in scientific publications ('underlying data').
   b. Simultaneously develop transparent norms and protocols that would govern the levels of processing, dissemination, and reuse of 'working to raw level data' (*Level 3* and *Level 4* data) in each scientific discipline.
2. Researchers and learned societies should play a key role in coordinating the development of the open data norms and levels of data access for both scientific and non-scientific users in each discipline.
3. Open sharing of 'working level data' (*Level 3* data) should be the default practice in those scientific fields in which data infrastructures are well-developed and where open data is already embedded in research practice—such as in clinical and biomedical research, geospatial and earth sciences, materials sciences, computational engineering, and digital humanities.
4. The data exclusivity period would apply to releasing all but 'underlying data' (*Level 1* data).

8.3.6 Increased focus on data reusability

Chapter 2 found that the theories advocating open data release—namely, the theories of knowledge-based society[379] and science production in the digital era[380]—fail to recognise that data reuse is necessary for the envisaged benefits of open data to accrue. These theories of knowledge production and dissemination envisage that mere data release will bring out the desired economic and social benefits of open science.

---

[378] See Chapter 5, Section 5.2.4.

[379] According to Castelfranchi, a knowledge society generates, shares, and makes available to all members of the society knowledge that may be used to improve the human condition [32, 89, 95, 490].

[380] See Gibbons [33] at point 9.

The staged model proposed in this chapter rebuts this argument, positing that simply providing *access* to data in the public domain is useless to society unless that data is *reused*. In fact, facilitating open access to data is a potential burden to society if substantial costs in curating data are required and the data is not subsequently reused or produces other benefits. The crucial importance of data reuse in realising the benefits of open data does not appear to figure in the understanding of open data by research funders, even though reusability of open data is one of the conditions typically placed on open data.

Reusability can be achieved by providing rich metadata with attendant software and algorithms. However, there is little understanding of what makes metadata rich and how exactly metadata facilitates reusability. Experiences at CERN and with clinical trials both confirm that there is far more to metadata than computer-automated reports and that substantial human inputs are required to describe the data and all the steps taken to process and analyse it.

Based on the CERN experience, the notion of metadata needs to be expanded to include detailed documentation of all assumptions underpinning the data-gathering process, the cleaning and processing of the data, and the statistical and mathematical methods used to analyse the data—including all the decisions made along the different stages. Only researchers who collect and process the original data are capable of furnishing such descriptions. What is more, these steps need to be recorded at the time of data collection and analysis and, as such, need to be embedded in the research workflow.

Open data in large research organisations cannot be treated just as a 'product' resulting from research. Open data is an essential part of that research. It took CERN several years to define and fine-tune the parameters that make its particle physics data reusable. In particular, there was the need for data format and software version control.

The library team at CERN conducted several pilot studies and collected information about how researchers record their research workflows [301]. This was followed by an extensive consultation process and testing that eventually resulted in the new library service, which captures each data processing step and the resulting digital objects [302]. To facilitate future reuse of multiple research objects, researchers at CERN need to plan data preservation from an early stage of their experiments. For this reason, the decisions about recording 'metadata' in research organisations should also be made early in the research process.

Another area not yet explored by research funders that requires further attention is the nature of the factors that would motivate researchers to reuse the open data produced by others.

There appears be to an assumption, among both researcher funders and scientists, that once data is released, it will be reused by interested parties, as happens with open publications. While a correlation exists between the increased citations of publications supported by research data,[381] the incentives for data reuse are not well understood.

In some cases, researchers may opt to combine data from different sources, but some may prefer to collect their own data even if data produced by others is readily available as open data. This is because embedding open data in research practice is not yet common and requires new approaches and new reward mechanisms, as canvassed in the following section.

---

[381] *Ibid*, p. 61.

Recommendation 5
To ensure the maximum value from open data:

a. The potential for reusability should be the top criterion for evaluating any deposit of open data and when making decisions about investing resources in further curation or preservation.

b. Metadata and/or other detailed annotation and description of open data should form a mandatory part of every research data file submitted to repositories.

c. Software (code) and algorithms used to process the data should also be properly documented and shared wherever this is feasible.

8.3.7 The need to develop individual and collective incentives

The future success of open data practice lies primarily in the development of incentives that would motivate researchers both to release their own data and to reuse data produced by others. While many new metrics are currently under consideration—for example, altmetrics discussed in Chapter 6—all the new metrics are based on the measurement of 'data impact'. There are, however, several problems with this approach. The first is that researchers are rewarded for their 'publication impact', not 'data impact'.

The second problem is that 'data impact' does not lead to career progression. It follows that increased impact is not the key incentive for publishing research data (see discussion on Recommendation 3) and, therefore, data citations are unlikely to sufficiently motivate researchers to curate and release open data. So how could we better motivate researchers to put substantial time and effort into curating data?

A better incentive might be to acknowledge the original data creators as 'co-authors' of any publications arising from the reuse of their original data. Such an acknowledgement would have an immediate impact on researchers' career progression and would also stimulate collaborations among researchers, especially as early experiences with open data suggest that their benefits can be maximised in consultation with the original data creators.

However, the above recommendation highlights another problem that the current research performance metrics are biased in favour of individual performance, encouraging researchers to compete rather than to collaborate with each other. This approach is not appropriate to promote collaborations in the digital era that often require input from researchers across several disciplines and across different organisations. The research performance metrics need adjustment to promote and reward collective efforts.

The approach championed by CERN can serve as inspiration for other organisations. Large research teams always publish collectively—it is not unusual for a research publication to list over 3000 authors. The key to managing performance in such teams is the control over who is entitled to be considered a member and, consequently, to be included as an author in the publication. CERN has developed detailed guidelines for the approval process, and these incentives are definitely working. The spirit of collaboration is present in all communications with CERN.

An extension of this approach could be joint PhDs, a concept already allowed by some higher educational institutions but still uncommon in the scientific community.

Recommendation 6

a. Ensure that acknowledgement of the original creators of open data as 'co-authors' is included in any publications arising from reuse of the data.

b. Develop other performance metrics that will encourage researchers to curate and release research data and metrics that encourage the reuse of data developed by others.

c. Design such metrics so as to promote the formation of collaborations and collegial working relationships among researchers.

8.3.8 Uncertainty surrounding data ownership and confidentiality

An issue that arises from facilitating open access to, and the reuse of, publicly funded research data has highlighted the need to determine the legal ownership of data and to provide clarification on who should have the right to restrain unauthorised disclosure of confidential information, as Chapter 7 concludes.

This need arises because of two reasons.

Firstly, the various types of research data can be protected by copyrights and only data owners can licence the data under open licences. The uncertainty about data ownership has been identified as the root cause of subsequent problems affecting data licencing, the lack of interoperability, and the lack of clarity around the conditions governing data reuse.

Secondly, most researchers employed in research organisations have a duty of fidelity to their employer that prevents them from disclosing information acquired in the course of their employment ([491], 13.2 and 13.7). In Australia, this duty offers extensive protection for the employer and can include research data, especially in those research organisations that engage in collaborations with industry.

In such cases, the duty of confidentiality may also arise under a contract signed between the organisation and the industry partner where there usually is a term to prevent unauthorised disclosure of information.[382] Under these arrangements, the decision to release research data may be vested in a 'data steward'—the researcher or data manager with the responsibility to assess whether such release would constitute an authorised disclosure of confidential information—rather than be a decision for the owner of research data.

The effect of these provisions on researchers is that they often do not know who can clear the data for release or they are simply afraid to share research data, even in those cases where the data is not subject to any confidentiality provisions. A recent authoritative survey of researchers identified intellectual property and confidentiality as the top reasons for not sharing data.[383] Researchers are indeed afraid to share data when they are unsure whether it is appropriate for them to do so.

With regard to ownership of research data, there are two key legal regimes governing its ownership. The first is the copyright regime under which, as a general rule, the owner of the copyrighted work is the person who creates it by translating

---

[382] See Monotti [492] and *Ormonoid Roofing and Asphalts Ltd v Bitumenoids Ltd* [1930] NSWStRp 88; (1930) 31 SR (NSW) 347.

[383] In 2014 the publisher Wiley conducted an extensive survey of researcher attitudes to data sharing. The company contacted 90,000 researchers across many research organisations and received 2250 responses. Of those, 42% stated that they are hesitant to share their data because of intellectual property or confidentiality issues. See further discussion in Chapter 6, Section 6.3.6.

the idea into a fixed, tangible expression.[384] The second regime involves various contractual arrangements that may transfer or assign ownership of research data. The most common contractual arrangements guiding the ownership of research data are employment agreements and research funding agreements.

As employees of a university or a research organisation, researchers in most cases assign the rights to the data they produce (in the course of their employment) to their employers. In sponsored research, the research organisation typically retains ownership of the data but grants the role of data steward to the principal investigator.

In industry-funded research, the data typically belongs to the sponsor, although the right to publish the data can also be extended to the investigator. Where publicly funded research data is created under research collaboration between researchers working in different organisations, data ownership becomes even more unclear. Collaboration may involve a number of organisations, external researchers, funding bodies, government agencies, and commercial entities. The data ownership policies of the collaborating parties might be different or even conflicting.

The situation is also complicated because many researchers assume (often wrongly) that they own the data they collect in the course of their research. This position stems from their understanding that data and databases can be subject to copyright and, therefore, researchers are the legitimate owners because they have 'created' it—similar to the position with academic publications. However, only students and external visiting researchers typically own copyright that they create in the course of research or studies [492]. Likewise, researchers who create copyright outside their employment own it. But if the research is performed in the course of employment and the research organisation contributes resources, then the resulting data is likely to be owned by the organisation.[385]

Regardless of the legal position on data ownership, all researchers seem to maintain a sense of ownership over the data they produce. The role of researchers is also crucial in managing and documenting research data along the various stages of its processing and curation. Given these additional responsibilities placed on researchers for documenting and curating research data, vesting ownership of the data in researchers (or even better research teams) would be a logical step. The right of ownership would enable them to exercise greater autonomy over that data.

However, the prevalent view is that research data should belong to organisations, not individuals or research teams, since only organisations can be responsible data custodians and guarantors of data security and preservation. This notion of ownership is at odds with the open data mandates that place the responsibility for data deposit with researchers. Since researchers are not the legitimate owners of research data, they may be unable to fulfil this requirement and share the data under a licence, especially if the data was created in a joint project. In such a case, data release may be dependent on the consent of all co-owners.[386]

Another relevant point is that much scientific data is computer-generated and therefore it is unlikely to be subject to copyright protection and so should be placed in the public domain. Accordingly, researchers and research organisations need to become aware of the fact that determining copyright ownership may be irrelevant

---

384 In copyright legislation this general rule is usually qualified by a specific rule that gives the employer copyright in certain circumstances and the crown under the crown copyright provisions.

385 *Ibid.*

386 For example, in Australia a co-owner of copyright is unable to exploit (copy or reproduce), grant an exclusive licence, or assign the copyright work without the consent of the other co-owner.

to computer-generated data. Furthermore, research organisations need to ensure that the data release in the public domain actually occurs.

To sum up, there is a need to delineate the notion of data ownership and confidentiality and to clearly define the attendant responsibilities for data management and sharing. It is not desirable for both research funders and organisations to be silent on these issues. While this book does not offer a recommendation in this regard, it highlights the importance of addressing uncertainties surrounding confidentiality and ownership of research data. Ultimately, data generated using public funds should be public property, and everyone has a responsibility to ensure that maximum value is derived from it. Data ownership needs to be managed so as to balance the interests of all—scientists, research funders, research organisations, and society as a whole.

Recommendation 7

Policymakers should Commission further research into data ownership and confidentiality with a view to achieving greater sharing of research data as open data.

Large research funders such as the European Commission and the National Institutes of Health are best positioned to provide direction for the research.

8.3.9 Introducing text and data mining exemption into copyright law

With the increasing availability of research data in the public domain, various types of reuse of that data will inevitably come to the forefront of the open data debate. Text and data mining,[387] often referred to as data analysis, is necessary to extract value and insights from large datasets. Such processes typically involve accessing the materials, extracting and copying the data, and then recombining it to identify patterns [494]. In Australia, subsequent to the definition of 'originality' established by the courts in the proceedings described in Chapter 7, such extraction of data and facts from protected work should not be subject to copyright protection.[388] However, since data mining typically requires the making of a (temporary) copy of the data, it is likely that this act would classify as copyright infringement.

Some countries, such as the United States, consider an activity such as making a copy as falling under the scope of the 'fair use' doctrine[389] of copyrighted works. Meanwhile, the United Kingdom has recently introduced a text and data mining exemption that covers such data uses but only for non-commercial research.[390]

The scope of the exemption in the United Kingdom is quite narrow, and it has the effect of hindering the realisation of the full value of open research data. A similar exemption is currently under consideration in the European Parliament, and the scope of the proposed exemption is broader than that in the United Kingdom—if

[387] The Australian Law Reform Commission defines data mining as 'automated analytical techniques that work by copying existing electronic information, for instance articles in scientific journals and other works, and analysing the data they contain for patterns, trends and other useful information' [493].

[388] Such uses would be classified as non-expressive use. The key principle here is that copyright law protects the expression of ideas and information and not the information or data itself.

[389] Par. 107 of the US Copyright Act 17 USC. The fair use requires a consideration whether the use of a work adds value to the original, for example, if used as raw material, transformed in the creation of new information, new aesthetics, new insights, and understandings.

[390] See Regulation 3 of the Copyright and Rights in Performances (Research, Education, Libraries, and Archives) Regulations 2014, No. 1372, adding Article 29A to the UK Copyright, Designs and Patents Act 1988. The Regulations came into force on 1 June 2014.

adopted, it would allow any Internet user to perform text and data mining for any purpose, whether commercial or non-commercial [429]. The proposed exemption cannot be overridden by contract, and some scholars have suggested that this principle should be extended to technology protection measures [495].

France, Germany, and Estonia have recently also introduced similar text and data mining exemptions, albeit more limited in their scope.

In Australia, text and data mining is not covered by the existing exemptions and could be considered copyright infringement if a substantial part of the text/data is reproduced. Limited text mining may be covered by the fair dealing exception if conducted for the purposes of research or study. However, the copying of an entire dataset would exceed a 'reasonable portion'[391] of the work and constitute infringement.

Australia currently does not have a text and data mining exemption but has, on several occasions, considered introducing a fair use system similar to that of the United States in place of the current fair dealing system. Despite that interest, action on the proposals is lagging, and, consequently, Australian research organisations seem disadvantaged. In the 2013 enquiry conducted by the Australian Law Reform Commission, the CSIRO argued that:

> *... if laws in Australia are more restrictive than elsewhere, the increased cost of research would make Australia a less attractive research destination [497].*

Furthermore, the CSIRO was of the view that

> *... the commercial/non-commercial distinction is not useful, since such a limitation would seem to mean that 'commercial research' must duplicate effort and would be at odds with a goal of making information (as opposed to illegal copies of journal articles, for example) efficiently available to researchers.*[392]

In line with this reasoning, it is proposed that—in the absence of fair use—a text and data mining exemption should be introduced into the *Copyright Act 1968* [496] (Cth).

Recommendation 8

Introduce the text and data mining exemption into copyright law—to enable data users to access, extract, combine, and mine data and datasets that currently are governed by various licence, contractual, copyright, technological protection, and legal regimes.

The exemption should eliminate legal uncertainty regarding the various data reuses associated with text and data mining. Such data reuses should be allowed to take place without the right holder's prior authorisation under conditions to be specified in the law.

8.4 Conclusion

In this chapter, I have argued that facilitating open access to research data requires vastly different approaches from those for enabling open publications. This is because research data are heterogenous, complex and differ across various scientific disciplines, various levels of granularity and various levels of processing and control.

---

[391] *Copyright Act 1968* [496] (Cth) s 40(5), setting out what is a 'reasonable portion' with respect to different works.

[392] *Ibid*, 11.69.

Open data mandates as they stand today fail to acknowledge that diversity and the fact that research data can be shared as open data at any point. The staged model proposed in this chapter calls for discussion across scientific disciplines to define the content of the data they hold and the stages of its processing. In the case of CERN and clinical trial data, the stages of data processing and sharing are well defined, and it is hoped that the proposed model can stimulate discussion about the levels of data processing in other research disciplines.

Rigorous data management practices and input from researchers are required to prepare the data for reuse for unknown audiences and for unknown purposes. However, these requirements should not be excuses for not sharing data. The proposed model calls for default open access to data that underpins results published in scientific publications (Level 1 data). Such data should be deposited in online repositories concurrently with publications, and research funders should take measures to ensure that their open data mandates include specific provisions to that effect. In cases of clinical data, the mandates that specifically required data archival in repositories along with a data accessibility statement included in the manuscript achieved the highest deposit rates.

The proposed model recognises the value open data can deliver if it is used for education and outreach purposes, as demonstrated with Level 2 data, especially the data showcasing the Higgs boson recently discovered at CERN. The related open dataset has reached thousands of high school and university students, and it has been used as a case study to promote data literacy and the development of computing skills among budding scientists. Such uses also help other research organisations in particle physics to replicate the experiments conducted at CERN and learn from them.

The proposed model encourages organisations to showcase their own research and to encourage the general public and expert users to reuse open data in innovative ways. Those experiments are necessary to promote the use of open data, embed it in research practice, and discover new reuses of open data in collaborative spaces.

The proposed model also recognises that not all research data can be of interest to the general public and that there are certain risks associated with sharing of some types of data—especially risks of breaching the privacy of patients involved in clinical trials and the risks of data misuse and misinterpretation of the original research. The staged model also recognises that lower-level data (Level 3 and 4 data) may not be shared immediately after the publication of research results and that such data may only be competently reused by expert users. For these reasons, the proposed model calls for clarification of the data levels that should be made available as open data to these two types of users—expert and non-expert users.

At the same time, the model makes the case for greater transparency in enabling access to low-level research data to experts, immediately after the expiry of a data exclusivity period. The length of that period would vary among scientific disciplines and even research projects and needs to be negotiated between researchers, their organisations, and research funders. Generally, it should not exceed the maximum limits defined in commonly agreed community norms and protocols.

If implemented, the proposed model would instantly improve access to high-level research data as open data, thus enabling any Internet user—whether researcher or non-researcher—to access and reuse the data for any purpose. By clearly defining the required competencies, skills, and attributes necessary to effectively reuse research data, the model would also lead to more transparent and improved data sharing among experts.

Specifically, it is anticipated that the proposed model would lead to a more nuanced discussion about the conditions and parameters that would qualify experts to promptly access low-level research data without restrictions, such is the case with

Level 3 LHC data that CERN makes available to physicists around the globe. In the field of clinical trials, a promising development on the same level of data access (Level 3 to Level 4) would be to enable the sourcing of background data for clinical trials directly from patients' electronic health records, smartphones, health insurance data, and other government databases.

The future of open data is in its use. The only way to make open data successful is to reuse it and prove that it can deliver the envisaged benefits. For this potential to be realised, open scientific data must be embedded in research practice and reused by other researchers or non-researchers. The proposed model posits that the potential for reusability should be the key criterion for evaluating any deposit of open data and when making decisions about investing resources in further data curation and preservation.

The future of open scientific data therefore lies in the hands of researchers. Only they can prove the value of the data by its reuse. Research funders and research organisations need to encourage them by developing appropriate incentives for forming collaborations and then sharing and reusing research data developed by others.

Finally, the law should not stand in the way of scientific progress, and it should not pose challenges in data release and reuse. Every dataset needs to have a clear owner so that the data can be properly licenced and be capable of reuse by others without any restrictions. Researchers should not be afraid to share, mine, and analyse research data in their quest to unearth new scientific knowledge. It is important for policymakers to ensure that data can be reused freely.

The proposed text and data mining exemption holds a great potential to enable Australian research organisations, businesses, and the broader public to reap the benefits of open scientific data.

Chapter 9

Conclusion: Towards Achievable and Sustainable Open Scientific Data

This chapter summarises the findings of the study by answering the research questions posed. The chapter consists of four parts:

1. Vision: What are the expected benefits associated with the curation and release of open scientific data?
2. Policy: What is the scope of the open data policies recently introduced by research funders and publishers?
3. Practice: How are selected data-centric public research organisations implementing open data? What are the legal and other challenges emerging in the process of implementation? Is open scientific data an achievable objective?
4. A way forward: What can be done to promote open access to scientific data across different research disciplines? Is there a need to revise the open data mandates?

Introduction

This book began with the call from research funders and publishers for increased access to research data so as to facilitate its increased uptake and reuse by others. The principal triggers for the renewed emphasis on sharing research data are the open data policies introduced by research funders and publishers in many jurisdictions in the world.

In this final chapter, we take a step back to review the findings of this study to evaluate the effect of these policies on the practice of data sharing as open data. I start with an overview of the expected benefits of open scientific data and the assumptions that led governments to introduce the policies. This is followed by a summary of the scope of the mandates and then an outline of the challenges associated with the practice of open data at CERN and in clinical trials. The final section briefly summarises the staged model for open scientific data introduced in the previous chapter.

9.1 Vision: what are the expected benefits associated with the curation and open release of scientific data?

The research data landscape has changed considerably in recent years. The open data policies introduced by research funders and publishers since 2010 have created a momentum, driving research data curation and release globally, this book finds.[393]

[393] See conclusion in Chapter 3 of this book.

Open data is developing concurrently with the open publications sector, which has accelerated the speed and ease of making research publications freely available in digital formats.[394] The last few years have also seen the emergence of data journals and discipline-specific data repositories that enable researchers to deposit their research data along with publications.[395]

These developments are underpinned by the strong endorsements of open data practice by major public research funders—including the National Institutes of Health in the United States, the European Commission,[396] stringent regulatory authorities such as the European Medicines Agency (EMA),[397] and esteemed research organisations such as CERN and NASA, among many others. These actors have championed open scientific data and are developing major infrastructures for data deposit and discoverability.

Implicit in these developments is the understanding of the common objectives and benefits of open scientific data—to advance and democratise science by increasing the uptake and reuse of scientific knowledge and data, to increase the quality and transparency of published scientific results, to enable the verification and reproducibility of scientific results, and to facilitate the continuing shift towards digital modes of science production and dissemination.[398] Also implicit in these benefits is the desire to find solutions to some of the biggest challenges facing humanity and the planet today—global warming, food security and poverty, the insatiable demand for energy and resources, increased pollution, growing urbanisation, and the quest for increased knowledge, longevity, and an improved quality of life that increasingly depend on the application of science and technology.[399]

In this world of rapid technological changes, in which scientific knowledge increasingly means power and market advantage,[400] the demand for scientific knowledge and data is also increasing.[401] While most research remains publicly funded,[402] recent years have seen an uptake of open innovation strategies by companies—especially those that source knowledge from external sources,[403] as evidenced in growing demand for collaborations and partnerships with universities and public research organisations.[404] Such partnerships and innovation strategies have resulted in the increased commoditisation of science by businesses—a trend that is especially evident in the biological and medical sciences as well as in engineering.[405]

In this context, scientific data in the public domain has the potential to impact the economic context in which power and control over science are distributed in society. Open scientific data ensures that the outcomes of public science remain available without any restrictions and for reuse by anyone, including future generations of researchers working in the public and private sectors, and anywhere in the world. Such a practice brings about huge economic benefits for countries that invest

394 See Chapter 3, Sections 3.2 and 3.3, and Chapter 8, Sections 8.2 and 8.3.1.

395 See Chapter 3, Section 3.2.

396 *Ibid.*

397 See Chapter 6, Section 6.2 and Chapter 7, Section 7.5.3.

398 See Chapter 2, Sections 2.3 and 2.4.

399 See Chapter 1, Section 1.1.1.

400 See Chapter 2, Section 2.2 and Footnote 57.

401 *Ibid*, Footnote 57.

402 See Chapter 2, Section 2.5, Footnote 99.

403 See Chapter 2, Section 2.5.

404 *Ibid*, Footnote 100.

405 See Chapter 2, Section 2.2 and Chapter 1, Section 1.1.1, Footnote 33.

in the development of open data, as evidenced in the Human Genome Project and the Global Positioning System (GPS)—two early, large-scale open data initiatives.

The Human Genome Project cost the US government US$3.8 billion to develop and up until today has generated around US$750 billion in biotechnology industry output in that country.[406] Compare US$750 billion with just over US$1 billion received from biotechnology licencing revenue by the top 15 universities in the United States and just over US$400 million of commercial income received from IP licencing by that country's biomedical research institutes.[407]

The economic benefit that the United States has accrued from GPS technology up until 2013 was estimated at about US$56 billion.[408] Compare this with the less than US$3 billion received as income from the commercialisation of research by all universities in the United States in 2016,[409] with over 85% of universities finding themselves unable to realise enough income to cover the costs of running their technology transfer offices.[410]

The economic justification of innovation is clearly on the side of open data, and governments should not be afraid to invest in the development of open technologies. The potential benefits for local economies are enormous.

9.2 Policy: what is the scope of the open data policies recently introduced by research funders and publishers?

Research funders and publishers have played a critical role in driving open scientific data. Beyond federal governments, private not-for-profit research funders such as the Bill and Melinda Gates Foundation and Wellcome Trust have adopted open data policies. These policies have changed the game and have, within a span of around 5 years, led researchers and their organisations to curate, document, and share their data.[411] Most funders have some form of policy regarding *research data management* (RDM)—ranging from requiring data management plans at the proposal stage through to expectations about depositing and sharing data. In response to these policies, research organisations have developed or strengthened internal RDM functions.

These policy adjustments vest the responsibility for data curation and release in researchers. The policies vary in their scope and in the specific requirements for sharing research data. Some policies 'recommend' or 'strongly encourage' data sharing, while others 'require' it. Several policies explicitly 'mandate' data sharing for research that receives grant money and stipulate requirements on when, how, and what data should be deposited and where.[412] The Public Library of Science mandates data availability as a condition of publication. Other journals, such as *Nature* and *Science*, expect researchers who publish within their pages to provide data 'on request', without requiring the deposit of data on the date of publication.

The first evaluations of these policies have found a strong correlation exists between the existence of data policies and data deposit practice.[413] Another

---

406 Chapter 2, Section 2.5, under Human Genome Project.

407 See Chapter 2, Section 2.5, Footnote 124.

408 *Ibid*, under Global Positioning System.

409 See Chapter 2, Section 2.5, Footnote 124.

410 *Ibid.*

411 See Chapter 3, Conclusion, and Sections 3.2 and 3.3.

412 See Chapter 3, Section 3.4.

413 See Chapter 6, Section 6.1, Footnote 15.

important finding is that more prescriptive policies—those with a mandate for data deposit along with a statement on data sharing included in the manuscript, have achieved the greatest deposit rates.[414]

However, a major theme that has emerged in this book is that the meaning of 'research data' varies across scientific disciplines, across various levels of data processing, and can originate from many different sources.[415] In addition, research practices vary widely across scientific disciplines and so does the collection and preparation of open access data.

The inability to clearly acknowledge and articulate the heterogenous nature of research data is a major shortcoming of the open data mandates; this book has argued.[416] In particular, the opening up of research data requires adopting an open mindset and the acknowledgement that 'one size does not fit all'; a mindset that finds RDM is an ongoing process that is as important a driver of improved science as is the resulting open data. Another key finding is that the quality of open data is far more important than quantity. More open scientific data, by itself, does not necessarily lead to more open science, more easily reproducible science, or improved and data-driven science.

This study cautions against any standardised approach to defining 'data'. While such approaches have generally proved useful when developing open access to publications, such approaches are neither suitable nor appropriate for open scientific data, this book argues.[417] If open scientific data is to be sustainable, then cultural, research practice, and organisational issues must first be addressed.

Yet librarians and research funders, who play pivotal roles in facilitating open access to scientific publications, tend to apply the same 'standardised' principles and approaches to research data. In particular, many librarians are calling for the standardisation of research data formats and metadata descriptors for inclusion in the policies of research funders and publishers.[418] This creates confusion and challenges for researchers, who are required to comply with the mandates introduced by research funders but are unable to do so because the complexity and heterogenous nature of open data simply makes it impossible for them to apply the same set of rules to every research project and dataset.

Common language and search structures can indeed facilitate discoverability of data. However, every dataset is unique, requiring different languages to describe the data and provide all supporting documentation, software, algorithms, and metadata so as to facilitate the reuse of the data. In this sense, research data is more analogous to archival materials rather than to open publications.

The experience from CERN is that only researchers can develop the necessary data descriptors and that these descriptors need to be rigorously tested and embedded in research practice before any common language and data structures can be contemplated.[419] In other words, attempts at research data standardisation need to be driven bottom-up, by researchers. External approaches that would impose common descriptors on research data would be unhelpful unless the descriptors are already firmly established in research practice. Given the recent and novel nature of open scientific data, such pilots are only just now starting to emerge. The notion of research data and its structuring and sharing require more refinement.

---

[414] *Ibid*, Footnote 17.

[415] See Chapter 4, Sections 4.1 and 4.2.

[416] See Chapter 4, Conclusion.

[417] See Chapter 8, Sections 8.1 and 8.2

[418] See Chapter 3, Section 3.4.

[419] See Chapter 5, Sections 5.3 and especially 5.3.4.

In the meantime, open data as a default practice seems appropriate for data underpinning scientific publications—to facilitate the validation of results. Yet 'open by default' is not, at this stage, feasible for data produced in clinical trials and data collected in particle physics experiments, even though well-documented and well-curated digital data, including raw data and metadata, is generally available. Most of the data can only be shared with expert collaborators. Carefully selected subsets of the data are, however, increasingly becoming available as open data for educational purposes. Open data is also paving the way for making scientific experiments more accessible to wider audiences.

9.3 Practice

9.3.1 How are selected data-centric public research organisations implementing open data? Is open scientific data an achievable objective?

In assessing early experiences with open scientific data at CERN and with clinical trial data, this book finds that curating scientific data for public release is far more complex and costly than governments and research funders had envisaged.

The major complication is that implementing open scientific data requires appropriate RDM. Public research organisations in general, and universities in particular, have very limited experience in this area.[420] Furthermore, the key stakeholders in the process have different, often conflicting, interests, and concerns about research data.

For researchers, the need to ensure the ethics and validity of secondary data analyses and the recognition of their efforts vested in data curation are the most prominent concerns. From the perspective of research sponsors and publishers, safeguarding their economic interests through intellectual property and confidentiality remain important considerations that directly challenge the practice of open scientific data.

Understanding the requirements for responsible data sharing and ensuring compliance with these requirements pose fresh challenges to research organisations. Maintaining the privacy of subjects involved in data collection, particularly in clinical trials, is an additional concern for medical research institutes. Furthermore, digital curation of research data is labour and resource-intensive and requires substantial investments in data infrastructures and new business models. In this context, many research organisations point out that open scientific data should not be an unfunded mandate. This is particularly the concern among researchers collecting clinical trial data, who fear that the funding needed for data curation will diminish the resources available to conduct new trials.[421]

The lessons learnt with implementing open data at CERN can prove helpful to other research organisations active in different areas of science. One particular area of emerging best practice is that the implementation of open data within organisations needs to be embraced and discussed by all—researchers, management and librarians. At CERN, such discussions were initiated through the development of internal open data preservation and sharing policies within the four main research teams. The vigorous debate that occurred at many different levels during the process transformed the whole organisation, including its conduct of data-driven research.[422] The resulting open data policies have created a shared understanding of

[420] See Chapter 5, Section 5.1.

[421] See Chapter 6, Section 6.2.4, Footnotes 72 and 73.

[422] See Chapter 5, Sections 5.3, and Conclusion.

the processes leading to data reusability and established the potential for data sharing with external users.[423]

One particular finding at CERN was that the value of open scientific data lies primarily in its quality, determined by two factors—robust data management practices within organisations and the potential in open data for future use and reuse.[424] From this came the development of the Open Data portal at CERN.

Despite these learnings and insights, CERN has not yet made available as open data all the data it produces. It has divided prospective users into four groups—ranging from a base level, offering direct access by anyone to the data underlying publications, through to the restricted access to the entire raw dataset only available to selected expert collaborators. This user hierarchy is necessary because CERN does not, at this time, have the data-processing capacity to accommodate universal and unrestricted access and also because some of the data requires knowledge of particle physics to understand and reuse it.[425]

In medicine, the sharing of clinical trial and genomic data has been an established practice for several years. It has gained new momentum with the release of open data mandates by research funders, by publishers, and especially by the EMA. New requirements for data sharing have also lead to greater transparency and increased data sharing in industry. Open sharing of data submitted to regulatory authorities has been tested by courts, which have upheld, in all cases, the open approach championed by the EMA.[426]

The key consideration in sharing patient-level data as open data is the protection of privacy and confidentiality. Research organisations have dealt with these concerns for many years and have in place well-tested procedures for research ethics along with data sharing protocols.[427] These are supported by the rigorous training of researchers, including the certification of researchers who collect and work with data involving human subjects.

However, recent unauthorised data sharing and privacy breaches by several large companies have brought renewed attention from policymakers to ensuring data privacy and confidentiality. As the result of the widespread publicity for privacy breaches at companies such as Facebook and Yahoo, policymakers are seeking to interfere with established decentralised research practice and to institute centrally controlled mechanisms to manage the privacy and confidentiality of data, with the vetting of prospective users.[428] In particular, this is the policy approach adopted by governments in the United Kingdom, New Zealand and, very recently, in Australia. There is a proposal to apply this approach to research data and, on first sight, it appears that it would apply to all research data.[429]

Such centralised approaches are unlikely to yield the desired economic and social benefits that open data presents. If there is one lesson learnt from the remarkable growth of the biomedical industry in Europe and the United States, it is that decentralised and open research can accelerate the pace of discovery and innovation, fuel economic growth and strengthen global competitiveness. This potential can only be realised if research data is available broadly and is reused by others.

---

[423] *Ibid.*

[424] See Chapter 5, Conclusion.

[425] See Chapter 5, Section 5.2.2.

[426] See Chapter 7, Section 7.5.3.

[427] See Chapter 6, Sections 6.2.1 and 6.2.2, and Chapter 7, Section 7.5.

[428] See Chapter 7, Section 7.5.4.

[429] *Ibid.*

Another important issue that has emerged in the implementation of open data, both at CERN and in clinical trials, is the necessity to define the levels of processing and other parameters that can make data reusable by others. Best practice in both fields confirms that research data, software and metadata—the three components of research data generally specified in the policies of research funders and publishers—are not sufficient to enable independent data reuse.[430]

Also required is a detailed description of the assumptions made by the original data collectors during the different stages of their research and data analysis, along with the statistical methods used to clean, process, aggregate and analyse the data. Such steps are rarely recorded as part of research practice and more study is needed to determine the scope and level of documentation required to achieve data reusability across different scientific disciplines and projects.

With this in mind, it is important for research funders across the different scientific disciplines to ascertain the levels at which scientific data is generally collected and processed across each scientific discipline. Funders should then set the boundaries for the levels at which the data holds the highest potential for reuse by others, whether as researchers (expert users) or as other interested users.

In addition, there is the need for reconsideration of the calls by research funders and policymakers for research reproducibility. This study finds that sharing of research data as open data does not necessarily or easily lead to research reproducibility. Low-level data (raw data) are generally required for this purpose and such data may not be readily available for sharing as open data or they can be costly to curate. Even where low-level data and all supporting analyses, algorithms and software are meticulously documented and are made available, experts in the same field of science may not achieve duplicate results by reusing the same data and applying the same techniques.[431]

Moreover, reproducibility studies can be costly, as evidenced in clinical trials and experienced first-hand by biomedical companies trying to replicate the research of competitors.[432] Therefore, reproducibility should only be the desired and stated objective in carefully selected research areas or research projects—such as those designed by drug regulators or those commissioned by courts to verify ambiguous claims made by pharmaceutical companies in their marketing applications for the approval of new products. Reproducibility should not be held as the 'golden standard' for science,[433] and it should not be one of the key objectives for open scientific data that research funders advocate.

9.3.2 What are the legal and other challenges emerging in the process of implementation?

Depositing research data in the public domain has highlighted the need to determine the legal owner of the dataset.[434] Uncertainties around the application of copyright to the various forms of data, and around data ownership in the research sector and in academia, have been identified as the root causes of subsequent problems affecting data licencing and the lack of clarity around conditions governing data reuse.[435]

---

[430] See Chapter 8, Section 8.3.6.

[431] See Chapter 6, Section 6.4.3.

[432] *Ibid.*

[433] *Ibid.*

[434] See Chapter 7, Section 7.2 and Conclusion and Chapter 8, Section 8.3.8.

[435] *Ibid.*

A further concern is the duty of fidelity that researchers have to their employers, which may prevent them from disclosing information acquired in the course of their employment.[436] The duty of confidentiality may also arise in collaborations with private sector sponsors. This book recommends more analysis of the relationship between the ownership of research data, in its different forms, and the interplay of that with possible copyright protection and confidentiality issues.[437]

Reuse of open data can give rise to legal problems, especially in the context of text and data mining, which is necessary to extract value and insight from datasets.[438] Since data mining typically requires the making of a (temporary) copy of the dataset, it is likely that the act of copying would amount to copyright infringement.

In this matter, compared with their counterparts in the United States, Europe and in other parts of the world, Australian research organisations seem disadvantaged. Such an inhibition for text and data mining also makes Australia a less attractive destination for data-driven businesses. This study proposes introducing a text and data mining exemption into the Australian *Copyright Act 1968* [496].[439]

9.3.3 Is open scientific data an achievable objective?

Taken together, the lessons learnt from the implementation of open scientific data—along with the financial and research benefits accrued from open data to this point, the potential future benefits and the increased need in the digital era for researchers to gain faster access to research data to conduct research—lead to the conclusion in this book that open scientific data is indeed an achievable objective and should become a priority for all research organisations.

However, curating all publicly funded research data as open data is not possible with current technology, nor it is currently achievable at recoverable cost. There remain necessary choices about what data to select for curation and release as open data.

The staged model proposed in this book offers some suggestions on how choices can be made so as to balance the individual responsibilities of researchers for curating research data with the collective benefits likely to accrue to other researchers and to society through reuse of the data.

9.4 A way forward: what can be done to promote open access to scientific data across different research disciplines? Is there a need to revise the open data mandates?

This book found that the open data mandates as they stand today do not acknowledge the diversity of research data as it occurs across different research disciplines and at different stages of processing and control. No uniform answers exist for the question of what defines data, and therefore, it is also difficult to determine what data is worth preserving into the future.

The staged model proposed in the preceding chapter encourages research organisations to define the content of the data they hold as well as to define the stages of its processing. This model, along with eight recommendations, presents a roadmap towards more achievable and sustainable open scientific data.

---

[436] See Chapter 7, Section 7.5 and Chapter 8, Section 8.3.8.

[437] *Ibid.*

[438] See Chapter 7, Section 7.4 and Chapter 8, Section 8.3.9.

[439] *Ibid.*

The proposed model includes four levels of data processing and release. It calls for default and immediate open access to data that underpins results published in scientific publications (Level 1 data). The staged model recognises the value open that data can deliver if it is used for educational and outreach purposes, as demonstrated with Level 2 data at CERN. The proposed model also recognises that not all research data can be of interest to the general public and that there are certain risks associated with sharing some types of data. Therefore, the model proposes that Levels 3 and 4 data may not be shared immediately after the publication of research results and that such data should be restricted for reuse by expert users with relevant competence.[440]

The factors that drive the independent reuse of open data are not known at this stage and will emerge over time as open data collections increase and gain in value. For now, open data practice may not be easy to implement, yet the individual and organisational lessons learnt are significant discoveries on the transformational journey to digital science.

As technologies evolve and as our ability to work with open data increases, the value of open data will increase also. Those governments, researchers, and organisations that learn to share their research data, and that learn to harness the value of data released by others, will become the visionaries to lead us into a data-enriched future.

> *"We must believe that we are gifted for something, and that this thing, at whatever cost, must be attained."*
>
> *Marie Skłodowska-Curie*

[440] See Chapter 8, Section 8.3.

Glossary

Attribution	Highlighting the creator/publisher of some data to acknowledge their efforts, conferring reputation.
Big data	Very large data sets that may be analysed computationally to reveal patterns, trends and associations.
Citation	Providing a link or reference to the data itself, in order to communicate provenance or drive discovery.
Clinical summary report	Integrated full report of an individual study of any therapeutic, prophylactic or diagnostic agent conducted on patients.
Data	Reinterpretable representation of information in a formalised manner suitable for communication, interpretation or processing (open archival information system definition).
Database	A collection of factual information held in electronic form.
Data breach	The loss, theft or other unauthorised access to data containing sensitive personal information that results in the potential compromise of the confidentiality or integrity of the data.
Data sharing plan	A brief description of how research data collected in research projects will be distributed and shared with others having a valid purpose for access to the data.
Data linking	A method of exposing and connecting data on the Web from different sources.
Data matching	Bringing together data from different sources, comparing it and possibly combining it, provided a common link can be found to interconnect at least one field in the datasets.
Data mining	Automated analytical techniques that work by copying existing electronic information —for instance, articles in scientific journals and other works, and analysing the data they contain for patterns, trends and other useful information.
Data noise	Also called noisy data, these are unwanted fields or information (such as duplicate entries) that degrades the quality of data signals.
Data object	An identifiable data item with data elements, metadata and an identifier (definition from the FAIR principles).
Data reuse	Any subsequent use of the original data by someone other than the originator(s).
Data signal	As opposed to data noise, this refers to meaningful data patterns that can be gleaned from data. The strength of the data signal increases by removing noise.
Data sharing	The practice of making data from scientific research available for secondary uses.
Data sharing plan	A brief description of how research data collected in research projects will be distributed and shared with others having a valid purpose for access to the data.
Data use	The first data use is by an individual or research team that originally gathered or collated the data. If the data originator(s) use(s) the same dataset for any later purpose, relating to the original project or not, that also counts as a 'data use'. See also 'data reuse'.
Gold open access	Providing free and permanent access to the final version of an article immediately after publication, and for everyone.
Green open access	Also referred to as self-archiving, is the practice of placing a version of an author's manuscript into a repository, making it freely accessible for everyone.
Information	Any type of knowledge that can be exchanged. In an exchange, information is represented by data.
Informed consent	The process in which a patient learns about and understands the purpose, benefits and potential risks of a medical or surgical intervention, including clinical trials, and then agrees to receive the treatment or participate in the trial.
Metadata	Structured information that describes, explains, locates, or otherwise makes it easier to retrieve, use, or manage an information resource. (National Information Standards Organisation).
Open access	Refers to free, unrestricted online access to research outputs such as journal articles and books. OA content is open to all, with no access fees.
Open data	Data that can be freely used, shared and built-on by anyone, anywhere, for any purpose (Open Knowledge Foundation).
Open science	Transparent and accessible scientific knowledge, whether as publications or data, that is freely shared and developed through collaborative networks.
Patient level data	The individual data separately recorded for each participant in a clinical study.
Raw data (or source data)	Unprocessed data sourced directly from research subjects or harvested by scientific equipment. In the context of clinical trials, raw data are observations about individual participants used by the investigators.
Reproducibility	In general terms, reproducibility involves replicating research experiments or verifying the research results by reusing the original data and following the same data methods. There is no shared understanding of this term among scientists.

Semantic data Data tagged with metadata and can be used to derive the relationships between data.
Sponsored research A research project commissioned by a private sector entity from a publicly funded research organisation.
Underlying data Research data underlying the findings published in scientific publications.

Appendix A: major international research data networks

Based on OECD (2017). Coordination and Support for International Data Networks.

	Acronym	Name	Geographic coverage	Discipline
1		AddNeuroMed	Regional (Europe)	Dementia research
2	ACTRIS	Aerosols. Clouds and Trace gases Research Infra - Structure	Regional (Europe)	Environmental data etc.
3	ADNI	Alzheimer's Disease Neuroimaging Initiative	US (International links)	Dementia research
4	Argo	Argo	Global	Oceanography and meteorology
5	CBRAIN	Canadian Brain Research Imaging Platform	Canada (International links)	Neuroimaging, cognitive neuroscience etc.
6	CLARIN	Common Language Resources and Technology Infrastructure	Regional (Europe)	Humanities and social sciences
7	CESSDA	Consortium of European Social Science Data Archives	Regional (Europe)	Social Sciences
8	DARIAH	Digital Research Infrastructure for the Arts and Humanities	Regional (Europe)	Arts and Humanities
9	ELIXIR	ELIXIR	Regional (Europe)	Life Sciences
10	EMBL-EBI	European Molecular Biology Laboratory - European Bioinformatics Institute	Regional (Europe)	Life sciences,
11	GBIF	Global Biodiversity Information Facility	Global	Life sciences,
12	GIRO	Global Ionospheric Radio Observatory	Global	Biodiversity Ionospheric physics etc.
13	GODAN	Global Open Data for Agriculture and Nutrition	Global	Agriculture and nutrition
14	GEO	Group on Earth Observations	Global	Earth Observations (Multidisciplinary)
15		Helix Nebula	Regional (Europe)	Various disciplines. mainly focusing on large sciences
16	ICSU-WDS	ICSU World Data System	Global	multidisciplinary
17	IPCC-DDC	Intergovernmental Panel on Climate Change - Data Distribution Center	International	Climate change
18	INCF	International Neuroinformatics Co-ordinating Facility	International	Neuroscience
19	IODP	International Ocean Discovery Program	Global	Seafloor drilling, ocean samples/observations
20	IVOA	International Virtual Observatory Alliance	Global	Astronomy
21	ICPSR	Interuniversity Consortium for Political and Social Research	Global	Social sciences
22	IUGONET	Interuniversity Upper atmosphere Global Observation NETwork	Japan (international links)	Space physics
23	LIGO	Laser Interferometer Gravitational-Wave Observatory	International	Gravitational physics
24	NITRC	Neuroimaging Informatics Tools and Resources Clearinghouse	USA (international inks)	Neuroimaging etc.
25		OpenAIRE	Regional (European)	All disciplines
26	H3ABioNet	Pan African Bioinformatics Network	Regional (Africa)	Bioinformatics and genomics
27	PaNdata	Photon and Neutron data infrastructure initiative	Regional (Europe)	Neutron and photon laboratories (Multidiscipline)
28		SeaDataNet	Regional (Europe,	Oceanography
29	SBP studies	Swedish Brain Power studies	Mediterranean and Baltic regions)	Brain research
30		UK Biobank	Sweden (international links)	Universal health data
31	WOCM-GCM	World Data Centre for Microorganisms - Global Catalogue of Microorganisms	UK (international inks)	Biodiversity
32	WLCG	Worldwide LHC Computing Grid	Global	Astrophysics, Nuclear & Particle Physics

Author details

Vera J. Lipton
Zvi Meitar Institute for Legal Implications of Emerging Technologies
Harry Radzyner Law School, IDC Herzliya, Israel

*Address all correspondence to: vera.lipton@bigpond.com

Bibliography

[1] Einav L, Levin JD. The data revolution and economic analysis. National Bureau of Economic Research Working Paper, No. 19035. Cambridge, MA; 2013. Available from: http://www.nber.org/papers/w19035

[2] Stanford University. Harnessing the power of data in health. In: Stanford Medicine 2017 Health Trends Report. Stanford: University; 2017

[3] Internet Source Stats. Internet Usage Statistics: The Internet Big Picture. 30 June 2018 update. 2018. Available from: https://www.internetworldstats.com/stats.htm [Accessed: 25 January 2019]

[4] Shah A. Poverty facts and stats. Global Issues. 7 January 2013. 2013. Available from: http://www.globalissues.org/article/26/poverty-facts-and-stats [Accessed: 10 June 2018]

[5] Cribb J. The case for open science. Broadcast for ABC Radio National Ockham's Razor. 2010. November (unpublished)

[6] Larsen PO, von Ins M. The rate of growth in scientific publication and the decline in coverage provided by Science citation index. Scientometrics. 2010;**84**(3):575-603. Available from: http://www.ncbi.nlm.nih.gov/pmc/articles/PMC2909426/

[7] European Commission. Online Survey on Scientific Information in the Digital Age. Studies and Reports. Luxembourg: Publications Office of the European Union; 2012. Available from: http://ec.europa.eu/research/science-society/document_library/pdf_06/survey-on-scientific-information-digital-age_en.pdf

[8] McCain KW. Communication, competition, and secrecy: The production and dissemination of research-related information in genetics. Science, Technology and Human Values. 1991;**16**(4):491-516

[9] Tenopir C, Allard S, Douglass K, Aydinoglu A, Wu L, Read E, et al. Data sharing by scientists: Practices and perceptions. PLoS ONE. 2011;**6**(6): e21101. DOI: 10.1371/journal.pone.0021101

[10] OECD. Main Science and Technology Indicators. Available from: http://www.oecd.org/sti/msti.htm

[11] Chesbrough HW. Open Innovation: The New Imperative for Creating and Profiting from Technology. Boston: Harvard Business School Press; 2003

[12] Chesbrough HW, Vanhaverbeke W, West J, editors. Open Innovation: Researching a New Paradigm. Oxford University Press; 2008

[13] European Commission. Open Innovation, Open Science, Open to the World. A vision for Europe. Directorate-General for Research and Innovation. Policy statement. Brussels: European Commission, Directorate General for Research and Innovation; 2016

[14] Fecher B, Friesike S. Open Science: One term, five schools of thought. In: Batling S, Friesike S, editors. Opening Science: The Evolving Guide on How the Internet is Changing Research. Springer Open: Collaboration and Scholarly Publishing; 2014

[15] Suber P. Timeline of the Open Access Movement. 9 February. 2009. Available from: http://www.earlham.edu/~peters/fos/timeline.htm [Accessed: 10 June 2018]

[16] National Science Foundation. NSf data sharing policy. 2010. Available from: http://www.nsf.gov/pubs/

policydocs/pappguide/nsf11001/aag_6.jsp#VID4 [Accessed: 10 June 2018]

[17] UK Research and Innovation. https://www.ukri.org/

[18] Research Councils of the United Kingdom. Policy on Open Access. 2011. Available from: http://www.rcuk.ac.uk/research/openaccess/policy/ [Accessed: 10 June 2018]

[19] European Commission. Recommendation SWD (2012) 221 of 17.7.2012 on Access to and Preservation of Scientific Information. Available from: https://ec.europa.eu/research/science-society/document_library/pdf_06/recommendation-access-and-preservation-scientific-information_en.pdf

[20] European Commission. Recommendation C 4890 of 17.7.2012 on access to and preservation of scientific information. Brussels. 17 July 2012

[21] European Commission. Guidelines on Open Access to Scientific Publications and Research Data in Horizon 2020, version 3.2. Directorate-General for Research and Innovation. 21 March. The EU Framework Programme for Research and Innovation, version 16 December 2013, 2. 2017. Available from: http://ec.europa.eu/research/participants/data/ref/h2020/grants_manual/hi/oa_pilot/h2020-hi-oa-pilot-guide_en.pdf

[22] Australian National Data Service. Project Registry Site. Available from: https://projects.ands.org.au/ [Accessed: 10 June 2018]

[23] Data to Decisions CRC. Available from: https://www.d2dcrc.com.au/about/ [Accessed: 10 June 2018]

[24] National Health and Medical Research Council. Open Access Policy. Australia. January 2018. Available from: https://www.nhmrc.gov.au/grants-funding/policy/nhmrc-open-access-policy

[25] Wellcome Trust. Statement on Genome Data Release. 1997. Available from: https://wellcome.ac.uk/funding/guidance/statement-genome-data-release [Accessed: 10 June 2018]

[26] Wellcome Trust. Position Statement in Support of Open and Unrestricted Access to Published Research. 2005. Available from: http://www.wellcome.ac.uk/docWTD002766.html [Accessed: 10 June 2018]

[27] Swam A. Policy Guidelines for the Development and Promotion of Open Access. Paris: UNESCO; 2012

[28] Fitzgerald AM. Open Access Policies, Practices and Licensing: A Review of the Literature in Australia and Selected Jurisdictions. Brisbane, Queensland: School of Law, Queensland University of Technology; 2009

[29] UNESCO. Revised draft strategy on UNESCO's contribution to the promotion of open access to scientific information and research. 20 October adopted at the 36th session of the UNESCO General Conference held in Paris on 20 October 2011. 2011. Available from: http://www.unesco.org/new/fileadmin/MULTIMEDIA/HQ/CI/CI/images/GOAP/OAF2011/213342e.pdf

[30] UNESCO. Open Access to Scientific Information. Available from: http://www.unesco.org/new/en/communication-and-information/access-to-knowledge/open-access-to-scientific-information/

[31] Wilkinson MD, Dumontier M, Aalbersberg IJ, Appleton G, Axton M, Baak A, et al. The FAIR guiding principles for scientific data management and stewardship. Scientific Data. 2016;3:160018. DOI: 10.1038/

sdata.2016.18. https://www.nature.com/articles/sdata201618

[32] Castelfranchi C. Comment. Six critical remarks on science and the construction of the knowledge society. Journal of Science Communication. SISSA—International School for Advanced Studies. 2007;1-3

[33] Gibbons M, Limoges C, Nowotny H, Schwartzman S, Scott P, Trow M. The New Production of Knowledge: The Dynamics of Science and Research in Contemporary Societies. London: SAGE Publications; 1994

[34] Merton R. Science and technology in a democratic order. Journal of Legal and Political Sociology. 1942;**1**:115

[35] Polanyi M. The republic of science. Minerva. 1962;**1**(1):54-73

[36] Castells M. The Rise of the Network Society. Cambridge, Mass/Oxford: Blackwell Publishers; 1996

[37] Radder H. The Commodification of Academic Research. Pittburgh, PA: University of Pittsburgh Press; 2010. p. 9. Available from: http://upress.pitt.edu/htmlSourceFiles/pdfs/9780822962267exr.pdf

[38] Lessig L. Free Culture: How Big Media Uses Technology and the Law to Lock Down Culture and Control Creativity. New York: Penguin; 2004

[39] Mayer-Schonberger V, Cukier K. Big Data: A Revolution That Will Transform How We Live, Work, and Think. Boston: Houghton Mifflin Harcourt; 2013

[40] Weinberger D. Too Big to Know: Rethinking Knowledge Now that the Facts Aren't the Facts, Experts Are Everywhere, and the Smartest Person in the Room Is the Room. New York: Basic Books; 2012

[41] Academies N. Facilitating Interdisciplinary Research. Washington: National Academy Press, Committee on Science, Engineering, and Public Policy; 2005. p. 2. DOI: 10.17226/11153

[42] European Parliament. Regulation (EU) 2016/679 on the Protection of Natural Persons with Regard to the Processing of Personal data and on the Free Movement of Such Data; 27 April 2016

[43] General Data Protection Regulation. Directive 95/46/EC Official Journal L. 4 May 2016;119/2:1-88

[44] The European Data Potection. Directive 2002/58/EC on privacy and electronic communication. 12 July 2002

[45] Fitzgerald BF. Legal Framework for E-Research: Realising the Potential. Sydney: Sydney University Press; 2008

[46] Lessig L. The Future of Ideas: The Fate of the Commons in a Connected World. Random House; 2001

[47] Willinsky J. The Access Principle: The Case for Open Access to Research and Scholarship. Massachusetts Institute of Technology; 2006

[48] Suber P. Open access to the scientific journal literature. Journal of Biology. 2002;**1**(1):3

[49] Wilbanks J. Another reason for opening access to Research. British Medical Journal. 2006;**333**(7582):1306-1308

[50] US National Research Council. Bits of Power. Washington: US National Research Council; 1997

[51] OECD. OECD Principles and Guidelines for Access to Research Data from Public Funding. Paris: OECD Publications; 2007

[52] Lessig L. Code 2.0. Basic Books. 2006. p. 198

[53] Harnad S et al. The access/impact problem and the green and gold roads to open access. Serials Review. 2004;**30** (4):310

[54] Ginsparg P. First steps towards electronic Research communication. Computers in Physics. 1994;**8**(4):390-396. Available from: http://dl.acm.org/citation.cfm?id=187178.187185

[55] Bernard N, Geller M. A prehistory of electronic journals: The EIES and BLEND projects. In: Tuttle M, Darling KD, editors. Advances in Serials Management. Greenwich, CT: JAI Press; 1995. pp. 27-47

[56] Budapest Open Access Initiative. Budapest Declaration on Open Access. 2002. Available from: http://www.budapestopenaccessinitiative.org/read

[57] Korsmo FL. The origins and principles of the world data center system. Data Science Journal. 2010;**8**:55-65. Available from: https://www.researchgate.net/publication/270166513_The_Origins_and_Principles_of_the_World_Data_Center_System

[58] National Academies. The International Geophysical Year. Available from: http://www.nas.edu/history/igy/

[59] Antarctic Treaty. 1959. Available from: https://www.ats.aq/e/ats.htm [Accessed: 10 June 2016]

[60] Lide DR, Wood GH. CODATA @ 45 Years: 1966 to 2010, the Story of the ICSU Committee on Data for Science and Technology (CODATA) from 1966 to 2010. Paris: CODATA; 2012. Available from: http://www.codata.org/about/CODATA@45years.pdf

[61] Global Change Research Program. Policy statements on data management for global change research. Policy Statements. Washington; 2 July 1991

[62] ICSU/CODATA. Scientific Access to Data and Information. Available from: http://www.codata.org/codata/data_access/policies.html [Accessed: 10 June 2018]

[63] The Berlin Declaration. The Berlin Declaration on Open Access to Knowledge in the Sciences and Humanities. Adopted on 22 October 2003. Max Planck Institute. Available from: http://openaccess.mpg.de/Berlin-Declaration [Accessed: 10 June 2018]

[64] Crane D. Invisible Colleges: Diffusion of Knowledge in Scientific Communities. Chicago: University of Chicago Press; 1972

[65] Inspire. High-energy physics literature database. Available from: http://inspirehep.net/ [Accessed: 10 June 2018]

[66] OECD. Declaration on Access to Research Data from Public Funding. OECD Legal Instruments. 2004. Available from: http://acts.oecd.org/Instruments/ShowInstrumentView.aspx?InstrumentID=157

[67] OECD. Science, Technology and innovation for the 21st century. Meeting of the OECD Committee for Scientific and Technological Policy at Ministerial Level, 29–30 January 2004—Final communique. 2004. Available from: http://www.oecd.org/science/sci-tech/sciencetechnologyandi nnovation forthe21stcenturymeetingoftheoecd committeeforscientificand technological policyatministeriallevel29-30j anuary2004-finalcom munique.htm

[68] OECD. OECD Principles and Guidelines for Access to Research Data from Public Funding. 2017. Available

from: https://www.oecd.org/sti/sci-tech/38500813.pdf

[69] National Science Foundation. Scientists Seeking NSF Funding Will Soon Be Required to Submit Data Management Plans. Media release. 10 May 2010. Available from: https://www.nsf.gov/news/news_summ.jsp?cntn_id=116928

[70] Jankowski N, editor. E-Research: Transformation in Scholarly Practice Routledge Advances in Research Methods. London: Routledge; 2009

[71] Royal Society. Science as an open enterprise. The Royal Society Policy Centre Report. 02/12/2012. Available from: https://royalsociety.org/topics-policy/projects/science-public-enterprise/report/

[72] Wouters P, Beaulieu A. Imagining e-science beyond computation. In: Hine C, editor. New Infrastructures for Knowledge Production: Understanding e-Science. London: Information Science Publishing; 2006. pp. 48-70

[73] Kahin B, Foray D, editors. Advancing Knowledge and the Knowledge Economy. MIT Press; 2006

[74] Neef D. Knowledge Economy: Resources for the Knowledge-Based Economy. Butterworth-Heinemann; 1997

[75] Westeren KI, editor. Foundations of the Knowledge Economy: Innovation. Learning and Clusters: Edward Elgar Publishing; 2012

[76] Blair AM. Too Much to Know: Managing Scholarly Information before the Modern Age. New Haven, CT: Yale University Press; 2010

[77] Brown JS, Paul D. The Social Life of Information. Boston: Harvard Business School Press; 2000

[78] Burke P. A Social History of Knowledge: From Gutenberg to Diderot. Cambridge, UK: Polity Press; 2000

[79] Burke P. A Social History of Knowledge. II: From the Encyclopaedia to Wikipedia. Cambridge, UK: Polity Press; 2012

[80] Case DO. Looking for Information: A Survey of Research on Information Seeking, Needs, and Behaviour. 2nd ed. San Diego: Academic Press; 2006

[81] Day RE. The Modern Invention of Information: Discourse, History, and Power. Carbondale: Southern Illinois University Press; 2001

[82] Ingwersen P, Kalervo J. The Turn: Integration of Information Seeking and Retrieval in Context. Dordrecht: Springer; 2005

[83] Liu A. The Laws of Cool: Knowledge Work and the Culture of Information. Chicago: University of Chicago Press; 2004

[84] Meadows J. Understanding Information. Muenchen: K. G. Saur Verlag; 2001

[85] Svenonius E. The Intellectual Foundation of Information Organization. Cambridge, MA: MIT Press; 2000

[86] Buckland MK. Information as thing. Journal of the American Society for Information Science American Society for Information Science. 1991;**42**:351-360

[87] Furner J. Conceptual analysis: A method for understanding information as evidence, and evidence as information. Archival Science. 2004;**4**:233-265

[88] E-learn. Making Sense of Data and Information: A Volume in Management Extra. Taylor and Francis/Elsevier; 2007

[89] Wessels B et al. Open Data and the Knowledge Society. Leiden: Amsterdam University Press; 2017

[90] Argote L, Ingram P. Knowledge transfer: A basis for competitive advantage in firms. Organizational Behavior and Human Decision Processes. 2000;**82**(1):150-169

[91] Cohen WM, Levinthal DA. Absorptive capacity: A new perspective on learning and innovation. Administrative Science Quarterly. 1991; **35**:128-152

[92] Mowery DC, Oxley J, Silverman B. Strategic alliances and interfirm knowledge transfer. Strategic Management Journal. 1996;**17**(2)

[93] Consultative Committee for Space Data Systems. Reference model for an open archival information system. 2012; **2**. Available from: https://public.ccsds.org/Pubs/650x0m2.pdf

[94] The Consultative Committee for Space Data Systems (CCSDS). Reference model for an open archival information system (OAIS). Consultative Committee for Space Data Systems. **2**:1-12. Available from: http://public.ccsds.org/publications/archive/650x0b1.pdf; http://public.ccsds.org/publications/RefModel.aspx [Accessed: 10 June 2018]

[95] Drucker PF. The Age of Discontinuity: Guidelines to our Changing Society. New York, NY: Harper & Row; 1969

[96] Mansell R, Wehn U, editors. Knowledge Societies: Information Technology for Sustainable Development. Oxford: Published for the United Nations Commission on Science and Technology for Development by Oxford University Press; 1998

[97] Stehr N. Knowledge Societies: The Transformation of Labour, Property and Knowledge in Contemporary Society. London: Sage; 1994

[98] Merton R. The Sociology of Science: Theoretical and Empirical Investigations. University of Chicago Press; 1973. p. 175

[99] Ritzer G. The Blackwell Companion to Major Contemporary Social Theorists. Malden, Massachusetts/Oxford: Blackwell; 1973. p. 13

[100] Kuhn, Thomas S. The Structure of Scientific Revolutions. 3rd ed. Chicago, IL: University of Chicago Press; 1996

[101] Bronowski J. The Origins of Knowledge and Imagination. Yale University Press; 1978

[102] Toffler A. Third Wave. Bantam Books; 1980

[103] Toffler A. Previews and Premises: An Interview with the Author of Future Shock and the Third Wave. Black Rose Books; 1987

[104] Australian Broadcasting Corporation. Life Matters. Radio program, interview with Norman Swann, Radio National; 5 March 1998

[105] Schimank U. Wissenschaft als gesellschaftliches Teilsystem. In: Maasen S, Kaiser M, Reinhart M, Sutter B, editors. Handbuch Wissenschaftssoziologie. Wiesbaden: Springer Fachmedien; 2012. pp. 113-123. Available from: https://link.springer.com/chapter/10.1007/978-3-531-18918-5_9

[106] Nentwich M. Cyberscience: Research in the Age of the Internet. Vienna: Austrian Academy of Sciences Press; 2003. pp. 63-64

[107] Fuller S. In search of vehicles for knowledge governance: On the need for institutions that creatively destroy social

capital. In: Stehr N, editor. The Governance of Knowledge. Transaction: New Brunswick, NJ; 2004. pp. 41-78

[108] Ciuriak D. The Economics of Data: Implications for the Data-Driven Economy. Centre for International Governance Innovation; 2018 5 March. Available from: https://www.cigionline.org/articles/economics-data-implications-data-driven-economy

[109] Gasser U, Faris R, Heacock R. Internet Monitor 2013: Reflections on the Digital World. Berman Center for Internet and Society Research Publication No. 27. Harvard University; 2013

[110] Global Issues. Poverty Facts and Stats. 2013. Available from: http://www.globalissues.org/article/26/poverty-facts-and-stats [Accessed: 10 June 2018]

[111] Meho L, Yang K. Impact of data source on citation counts and rankings of LIS faculty: Web of Science versus Scopus and Google scholar. Journal of the American Society for Information Science and Technology. 2007;**58**(13): 2015-2125

[112] Meho L. The rise and rise of citation analysis. Physics World. 2007; **29**(1):32

[113] Lemley MA, Shapiro C. Probabilistic patents. Journal of Economic Perspectives. 2005;**19**(2): 75-98

[114] Houghton J, Sheehan P. Estimating the potential impacts of Open access to research findings. Economic Analysis and Policy. 2009;**29**(1):127-142

[115] Piwowar HA, Day RS, Frisma DB. Sharing detailed research data is associated with increased citation rate. PLoS One. 2007;**2**(3):308

[116] Roy ASA. Stifling new cures: The true cost of lengthy clinical drug trials. In: FDA Report. Manhattan Institute for Policy Research; 2012

[117] Oldenburg H. Philosophical Transactions of the Royal Society. 1665; **1**(1). Available from: http://rstl.royalsocietypublishing.org/content/1/1/0.2.extract

[118] Rao C. Man of Science, Man of God. Institute for Creation Research. 2008. Available from: http://www.icr.org/article/science-man-god-robert-boyle/ [Accessed: 10 June 2018]

[119] National Research Council. Preparing the Workforce for Digital Curation. Washington, DC: National Academy Press; 2015. Available from: http://www.nap.edu/catalog/18590/preparing-theworkforce-for-digital-curation

[120] Nelson JS. U.S. Geological Survey. Earth Resources Observation and Science (EROS) Center—Fiscal Year 2010 Annual Report. U.S. Geological Survey. 2011. Available from: http://pubs.usgs.gov/of/2011/1057/pdf/of2011-1057.pdf

[121] Uhlir PF, Schröder P. Open data for global science. Data Science Journal. 2007;**6**:36–53. Available from: http://datascience.codata.org/articles/abstract/10.2481/dsj.6.OD36/

[122] National Research Council. The Case for International Sharing of Scientific Data: A Focus on Developing Countries: Proceedings of a Symposium. Washington, DC: The National Academies Press; 2012. DOI: 10.17226/17019

[123] European Commission. Enter the Data Economy: EU Policies for a Thriving Data Ecosystem. EPSC Strategic Notes, Issue 21. 2017. Available from: https://ec.europa.eu/epsc/sites/epsc/files/strategic_note_issue_21.pdf

[124] Mandel M. Data, Trade, and Growth, TPRC 412: The 41st Research

Conference on Communication. The Progressive Policy Institute: Information and Internet Policy; 2013

[125] European Commission. Fact Sheet Data cPPP. 2014. Available from: https://ec.europa.eu/research/industrial_technologies/pdf/factsheet-cppp_en.pdf

[126] Rossi B. The Value of Big Data and the Internet of Things to the UK Economy. Information Age. 2016. Available from: https://www.information-age.com/big-data-and-internet-things-add-322bn-uk-economy-2020-report-123461008/ [Accessed: 10 June 2018]

[127] International Data Corporation Research. Worldwide Big Data Technology and Services Forecast, 2015–2019. October 2015. Available from: https://www.idc.com/getdoc.jsp?containerId=US40803116 [Accessed: 10 June 2018]

[128] Pollock R. The Economics of Public Sector Information, CWPE 0920. Cambridge: University of Cambridge; 2009. Available from: http://www.econ.cam.ac.uk/dae/repec/cam/pdf/cwpe0920.pdf

[129] Weiss P. Borders in Cyberspace: Conflicting Public Sector Information Policies and their Economic Impacts. Silver Spring: National Oceanic and Atmospheric Administration; 2002

[130] Vickery G. Review of Recent Studies on PSI Reuse and Related Market Developments. Brussels: European Commission; 2010a. Available from: http://ec.europa.eu/newsroom/dae/document.cfm?doc_id=1093

[131] Dekkers M et al. MEPSIR: Measuring European Public Sector Information Resources. Brussels: European Commission; 2006. Available from: http://www.epsiplus.net/psi_library/reports/mepsir_measuring_european_public_sector_res ources_report

[132] PIRA. Commercial Exploitation of Europe's Public Sector Information. Brussels: European Commission; 2000

[133] DotEcon. The Commercial Use of Public Information (CUPI). 2006. http://www.oft.gov.uk/OFTwork/publications/publication-categories/reports/consumerprotection/oft861

[134] Houghton J. Costs and Benefits of Public Sector data Provision. Commissioned Report. Melbourne: Australian National Data Service; 2011

[135] Beagrie N et al. Economic Evaluation of Research Data Infrastructur. London: Economic and Social Research Council; 2012. Available from: http://www.esrc.ac.uk/_images/ESDS_Economic_Impact_Evaluation_tcm8-22229.pdf

[136] Beagrie N, Houghton JW. The Value and Impact of the Archaeology Data Services: A Study and Methods for Enhancing Sustainability. Bristol and London: Joint Information Systems Committee; 2013a. Available from: http://www.jisc.ac.uk/whatwedo/programmes/preservation/ADSImpact.aspx [Accessed: 10 June 2018]

[137] Beagrie N, Houghton JW. The Value and Impact of the British Atmospheric Data Centre. Bristol and London: Joint Information Systems Committee and the Natural Environment Research Council UK; 2013b. Available from: http://www.jisc.ac.uk/whatwedo/programmes/di_directions/strategicdirections/badc.aspx [Accessed: 10 June 2018]

[138] Beagrie N, Houghton JW. The Value and Impact of Data Sharing and Curation: A Synthesis of Three Recent Studies of UK Research Data Centres. Bristol and London: JISC; 2014.

Available from: http://repository.jisc.ac.uk/5568/ [Accessed: 10 June 2018]

[139] Beagrie N, Houghton JW. The Value and Impact of the European Bioinformatics Institute. Full Report to EMBL-EBI by Charles Beagrie Limited. 2016. Available from: http://www.beagrie.com/EBI-impact-report.pdf

[140] Houghton J, Gruen N. Open Research Data. Report prepared for the Australian National Data Service. 2014

[141] Stallman RM. In: Gay J, editor. Free Software, Free Society: Selected Essays of Richard M. Stallman. Boston: The Free Software Foundation; 2002

[142] Berman F, Cerf V. Who will pay for public access to research data? Science. 2013;**341**:616-617. Available from: http://sites.nationalacademies.org/cs/groups/pgasite/documents/webpage/pga_084791.pdf

[143] Google Blogoscoped. Google Stops Research Datasets Program. 2008. Available from: http://blogoscoped.com/archive/2008-12-23-n33.html

[144] European Commission. European Open Science Cloud. Avaiable from: https://ec.europa.eu/research/openscience/index.cfm?pg=open-science-cloud [Accessed: 10 June 2018]

[145] European Open Science Cloud (EOSC). Declaration and its Principles, Guiding the Implementation of the EOSC. adopted at the EOSC Summit of 12 June 2017 in Brussels. 2017. Available from: https://ec.europa.eu/research/openscience/pdf/eosc_declaration.pdf#view=fit&pagemode=none

[146] Organisation for Economic Cooperation and Development. Research funding cuts threaten global innovation, University World News, Issue 00493. 2016, 9 December 2016. Available from: http://www.universityworldnews.com/article.php?story=20161209233443636

[147] Mervis J. Data check: U.S. government share of basic research funding falls below 50%. Science. 2017. Available from: http://www.sciencemag.org/news/2017/03/data-check-us-government-share-basic-research-funding-falls-below-50

[148] Rohn J, Curry S, Steele A. Research funding slumps below 0.5% GDP: putting us last in the G8. The Guardian. 2015. Available from: https://www.theguardian.com/science/occams-corner/2015/mar/13/science-vital-uk-spending-research-gdp

[149] Angell M. The Truth behind the Drug Companies: How They Deceive Us and What to Do about It. New York: Random House; 2004

[150] OECD. Public Research Policy, STIL Outlook. Available from: https://www.oecd.org/sti/outlook/e-outlook/stipolicyprofiles/competencestoinnovate/publicresearchpolicy.html [Accessed: 10 June 2018]

[151] Weiss L. America Inc.: Innovation and Enterprise in the National Security State. Cornell University Press; 2014

[152] Department of Education and Training. Finance 2016: Financial Reports of Higher Education Providers. Report, Australia. 2018. Available from: https://docs.education.gov.au/node/47911

[153] National Human Genome Research Institute. A Brief History of the Human Genome Project. 2012. Available from: http://www.genome.gov/12011239 [Accessed: 10 June 2018]

[154] Cook-Deegan R, Heaney C. Patents in genomics and human genetics. Annual Review of Genomics and Human Genetics. 2010;**11**:383-425. DOI:

10.1146/annurev-genom-082509-141811

[155] Rogers J. Genome sequencing: Wellcome news? In: Radford T, editor. Frontiers 03: New Writing on Cutting-Edge Science by Leading Scientists. Trowbridge: Atlantic Press; 2003

[156] Tripp S, Grueber M. Economic Impact of the Human Genome Project. Columbus: Battelle Memorial Institute; 2011

[157] Pool S, Erickson J. The High Return on Investment for Publicly Funded Research, Center for American Progress. 10 December 2012. Available from: https://www.americanprogress.org/issues/economy/reports/2012/12/10/47481/the-high-return-on-investment-for-publicly-funded-research/

[158] Mazzucato M. The entrepreneurial state: Debunking the public vs. private myth in risk and innovation. Anthem Press; 2013

[159] Mazzucato M. A Mission-Oriented Approach to Building the Entrepreneurial State. A report commissioned by Innovate UK. 2015. Available from: https://www.gov.uk/government/publications/a-mission-oriented-approach-to-building-the-entrepreneurial-state

[160] Beijing Genomics Institute. Rapid open-source genomic analyses accelerated global studies on deadly *E. coli* O104:H4. Science Daily. 2011a. Available from: https://www.sciencedaily.com/releases/2011/07/110727171501.htm [Accessed: December 28, 2013]

[161] Lynn TE. China helps unravel new *E. coli* for embattled Europe. Reuters. 3 June 2011. Available from: http://www.reuters.com/article/2011/06/03/us-ecoli-china-idUSTRE75224620110603 [Accessed: December 28, 2013]

[162] NASA. Global Positioning System History. 2012. Available from: https://www.nasa.gov/directorates/heo/scan/communications/policy/GPS_History.html [Accessed: June 10, 2018]

[163] GPS World Staff. The Economic Benefits of GPS. GPS World. 1 September 2015. Available from: http://gpsworld.com/the-economic-benefits-of-gps/

[164] Valdivia WD. University Start-ups: Critical for Improving Technology Transfer. The Brookings Institution. 20 November 2013. Available from: https://www.brookings.edu/research/university-start-ups-critical-for-improving-technology-transfer/ [Accessed: June 10, 2018]

[165] Hugget B. Top US universities, institutes for life sciences in 2015. Nature Biotechnology. 2017;**35**:203

[166] Cervantes M, Meissner D. Commercialising public research under the Open innovation model: New trends. OECD Foresight and STI Governance. 2014;**8**(3):70-81. Available from: https://www.researchgate.net/publication/290945411_Commercialising_Public_Research_under_the_Open Innovation Model New Trends

[167] Borgman C. Big Data, Little Data, No Data: Scholarship in the Networked World. Cambridge, MA: The MIT Press; 2015

[168] Chesbrough HW. Open innovation: A new paradigm for understanding industrial innovation. 2006

[169] Bromley A. Data Management for Global Change Research Policy Statements. US Global Change Research Program. 1991. Available from: https://digital.library.unt.edu/ark:/67531/metadc11862/ [Accessed: June 10, 2018]

[170] Bermuda Meeting Affirms Principle of Data Release. 1997.

Available from: https://www.genome.gov/25520385/online-education-kit-1997-bermuda-meeting-affirms-principle-of-data-release/

[171] ICSU/CODATA Ad Hoc Group on Data and Information. Access to Databases: Principles for Science in the Internet Era. 2002. Available from: http://www.codata.info/resources/databases/data_access/principles.html

[172] Berlin Declaration. The 'Signatories'. Max Planck Institute. Available from: http://openaccess.mpg.de/319790/Signatories.

[173] World Library of Science. A Global Community for Science Education. Available from: http://www.nature.com/wls

[174] OECD Declaration on Access to Research Data from Public Funding. Available from: http://acts.oecd.org/Instruments/ShowInstrumentView.aspx?InstrumentID=157

[175] Organisation for the Economic Cooperation and Development. OECD Principles and Guidelines for Access to Research Data from Public Funding. OECD Press; 2010. pp. 9-11

[176] Denton Declaration: An Open Data Manifesto. Adopted at the University of North Texas on 22 May 2012. Available from: https://openaccess.unt.edu/denton-declaration

[177] Family Educational Rights and Privacy Act (FERPA). (20 U.S.C. § 1232g; 34 CFR Part 99)

[178] Health Insurance Portability and Accountability Act (HIPAA) of 1996; 2008

[179] Toronto International Data Release Workshop Authors. Prepublication data sharing. Nature. 2009;**461**:168. DOI: 10.1038/461168a

[180] Shoefield PN et al. Post-publication sharing of data and tools. Nature. 2009; **461**:171-173

[181] Panton Principles. Panton Principles for Open Data in Science. Available from: http://pantonprinciples.org/ [Accessed: June 10, 2018]

[182] Research Data Alliance. Legal interoperability of research data: Principles and implementation guideline. 8 September 2016. Available from: http://www.codata.org/uploads/Legal%20Interoperability%20Principles%20and%20Implementation%20Guidelines_Final2.pdf

[183] National Institutes of Health (2013). Data Sharing Policies. Available from: http://www.nlm.nih.gov/NIHbmic/nih_data_sharing_policies.html [Accessed: June 10, 2018]

[184] Insel T. 'Open Data', Director's Blog, National Institute of Mental Health. 13 June 2014. Available from: http://www.nimh.nih.gov/about/director/2013/open-data.shtml

[185] National Science Foundation. (n.d). Dissemination and Sharing of Research Results. Division of Institution and Award Support. Available from: http://www.nsf.gov/bfa/dias/policy/dmp.jsp. [Accessed: June 10, 2018]

[186] Tufts University. Research Guides@Tufts, Federal Funding Agencies: Data Management and Sharing Policies. 2013

[187] European Commission. Riding the Wave: How Europe Can Gain from the Rising Tide of Scientific data. Final report of the High level Expert Group on Scientific Data. October 2010c

[188] European Commission. A Digital Agenda for Europe, Communication from the Commission to the European Parliament, the Council, the European Economic and Social Committee of the

Regions, COM/2010/0235 Final. 2010a. 245. Availabe from: https://eur-lex.europa.eu/procedure/EN/199329

[189] European Commission. Europe 2020 Flagship Initiative Innovation Union. Communication from the Commission to the European Parliament, the Council, the European Economic and Social Committee and the Committee of the Regions, COM2010b. p. 546. Available from: https://eur-lex.europa.eu/procedure/EN/199719

[190] European Commission. A Reinforced European Research Area Partnership For Excellence AND Growth. Communication from the Commission to the European Parliament, the Council, the European Economic and Social Committee and the Committee of the Regions, COM2012b. p. 392. Available from: https://eur-lex.europa.eu/procedure/EN/201831

[191] European Commission. Towards better access to scientific information: Boosting the benefits of public investments in research. Communication from the Commission to the European Parliament, the Council, the European Economic and Social Committee of the Regions, COM/2012/401 final. 2012c. 4890. Availabe from: https://ec.europa.eu/research/science-society/document_library/pdf_06/era-communication-towards-better-access-to-scientific-information_en.pdf

[192] Margoni T, Caso R, Ducato R, Guarda P, Moscon V. Open Access, Open Science, Open Society. University of Glasgow; 2016. Available from: http://eprints.gla.ac.uk/129357/

[193] Article 43.2 of Regulation (EU) No 1290/2013 of the European Parliament and of the Council Laying Down the Rules for Participation and Dissemination in Horizon 2020, the Framework Programme for Research and Innovation (2014–2020) and Repealing Regulation (EC) No 1906/2006. Available from: https://eur-lex.europa.eu/legal-content/EN/TXT/?uri=celex%3A32013R1290

[194] European Research Council. Open Access Guidelines for Researchers Funded by the ERC. June 2012. Available from: http://erc.europa.eu/sites/default/files/document/file/open_access_policy_researchers_funded_ERC.pdf

[195] Europe PMC. Available from: http://europepmc.org/ [Accessed: June 10, 2018]

[196] Cornell University Library. Arxiv. Available from: http://arxiv.org/ [Accessed: June 10, 2018]

[197] UK Research and Innovation. About us. 2018. Available from: https://www.ukri.org/about-us/

[198] RCUK Common Principles on Data. Available from: http://www.rcuk.ac.uk/research/datapolicy/

[199] Ryan B. Supporting research data management costs through grant funding. Blog, Research Councils UK, 9 July 2013. Available from: http://blogs.rcuk.ac.uk/2013/07/09/supporting-research-data-management-costs-through-grant-funding/

[200] Tanner S. When Data Hits the Fan. Available from: http://simon-tanner.blogspot.com.au/2013/07/uk-government-promotes-open-data-public.html [Accessed: June 10, 2018]

[201] Digital Curation Centre. Overview of Research Funder Policies. Available from: http://www.dcc.ac.uk/resources/policy-and-legal/overview-funders-data-policies#sthash.NkYRudy0.dpuf

[202] Research Councils UK. Policy on Open Access. 2011. Available from: http://www.rcuk.ac.uk/research/openaccess/policy/

[203] Davidson J. Chapter 5: Supporting early-career researchers. In: Mackenzie A, Martin L, editors. Mastering Digital Librarianship. Facet Publishing; 2014. pp. 82-102

[204] Australian National Data Service. Projects funded under the 'Seeding the Commons Program'. Available from: https://projects.ands.org.au/getAllProjects.php?start=sc

[205] Australian Research Council. The Australian Code for the Responsible Conduct of Research. Available from: http://www.nhmrc.gov.au/_files_nhmrc/publications/attachments/r39.pdf

[206] Australian Research Council. The ARC Centre of Excellence Funding Agreement. Available from: http://www.arc.gov.au/ncgp/ce/ce_fundingagreement.htm

[207] Government of Canada. Tri-Agency Open Access Policy on Publications. December 2016. Available from: http://www.science.gc.ca/default.asp?lang=En&n=F6765465-1

[208] Dryad Digital Repository. Available from: http://datadryad.org/ [Accessed: June 10, 2018]

[209] Nature. Availability of Data, Materials and Methods. Editorial policy. N. D. Available from: http://www.nature.com/authors/policies/availability.html [Accessed: June 10, 2018]

[210] Journal of the Royal Society Interface. Available from: http://rsif.royalsocietypublishing.org/site/misc/preparing-articles.xhtml#question15 [Accessed: June 20, 2015]

[211] Vasilevsky et al. Reproducible and reusable research: Are journal data sharing policies meeting the mark? Peer J. 2017;**5**:e3208

[212] Vasilevsky N, Brush M, Paddock H, Ponting L, Tripathy S, Larocca G, et al. On the reproducibility of science: Unique identification of research resources in the biomedical literature. Peer J. 2013;**1**:e148

[213] Xiaolin Z. Development of open access in China: Strategies, practices, challenges. Insight. 2014;**27**:55-60. DOI: 10.1629/2048-7754.111

[214] van Noorden R. Chinese agencies announce open access policies. Nature. 2014. DOI: 10.1038/nature.2014.15255

[215] Chinese Academies of Sciences. The Institutional Repositories Grid. Available from: http://www.irgrid.ac.cn/ [Accessed: June 10, 2018]

[216] Organisation for Economic Cooperation and Development OECD. Main Science and Technology Indicators (2014 data). 2014. Available from: http://www.oecd.org/sti/msti.htm

[217] Eurostat (Statistical Office of the European Union). R & D Expenditure. Statics Explained. March 2018. Available from: http://ec.europa.eu/eurostat/statistics-explained/index.php/R_%26_D_expenditure

[218] Kenya Open Data. Home page. Available from: https://opendata.go.ke

[219] Morocco Open Data. Home page. Available from: http://data.gov.ma

[220] Open Data Tunisia. Home page. http://www.data.gov.tn

[221] Open Government Tanzania. Home page. Available from: http://www.opengov.go.tz

[222] Transparency Sierra Leone. Available from: http://www.transparencysierraleone.gov.sl

[223] Edo State Government. Official Data Repository Portal. Available from: http://data.edostate.gov.ng/

[224] The Nigeria Extractive Industries Transparency Initiative. Available from: http://neiti.org.ng/

[225] Ghana Open Data. Available from: http://data.gov.gh

[226] Open Data for Africa. Home page. Available from: http://opendataforafrica.org/

[227] English Oxford Living Dictionaries Available from: https://en.oxforddictionaries.com/definition/data [Accessed: 10 June 2018]

[228] Oxford English Reference Dictionary. 2nd ed. OUP; 2002

[229] Rosenberg D. Data before the fact. In: Gitelman L, editor. 'Raw data' is an Oxymoron. Cambridge, MA: The MIT Press; 2013. pp. 15-40

[230] Uhlir P, Cohen D, editors. Report from Developing Data Attribution and Citation Practices and Standards: An International Symposium and Workshop, National Academy of Sciences' Board on Research Data and Information. Washington DC: National Academies Press; 2012. Available from: http://www.nap.edu

[231] Australian National Data Service, What is Research Data?. Available from: https://www.ands.org.au/guides/what-is-research-data [Accessed: June 10, 2018]

[232] National Institutes of Health. NIH Grants Policy Statement. Available from: http://grants.nih.gov/grants/policy/nihgps_2013/nihgps_ch8.htm#_Toc271264947 [Accessed: June 10, 2018]

[233] National Academy of Sciences, National Academy of Engineering and Institute of Medicine (2009). Ensuring the Integrity, Accessibility, and Stewardship of Research Data in the Digital Age

[234] Digital Curation Centre. Example DMPs and guidance. Available from: http://www.dcc.ac.uk/resources/data-management-plans/guidance-examples [Accessed: June 10, 2018]

[235] University of Glasgow. Research Data Policy. Available from: https://www2.le.ac.uk/services/research-data/documents/GlasgowRDPolicy.docx [Accessed: June 10, 2018]

[236] Australian Code for the Responsible Conduct of Research, Section 2.1., University of Technology, Queensland. Available from: https://www.nhmrc.gov.au/guidelines-publications/r39 [Accessed: March 2016]

[237] Queensland University of Technology. Management of Research Data. Policy. 2015. Available from: http://www.mopp.qut.edu.au/D/D_02_08.jsp [Accessed: March 2016]

[238] University of Melbourne. Management of Research Data and Records Policy. Available from: http://policy.unimelb.edu.au/MPF1242 [Accessed: June 2018]

[239] Monash University. Research Data Management Policy. Available from: https://www.monash.edu/__data/assets/pdf_file/0011/797339/Research-Data-Management-Policy.pdf [Accessed: June 10, 2018]

[240] Engineering and Physical Sciences Research Council. Expectations. Available from: https://epsrc.ukri.org/about/standards/researchdata/expectations/ [Accessed: June 10, 2018]

[241] European Commission. Horizon 2020 Annotated Model Grant Agreements, Version 4.1. The EU Framework Programme for Research and innovation. 26 October 2017b. Available from: http://ec.europa.eu/research/participants/data/ref/h2020/grants_manual/amga/h2020-amga_en.pdf

[242] White House. Increasing Access to the Results of Federally Funded Scientific Research. Memorandum to the Heads of Executive Departments and Agencies. 5

[243] Borgman C. Scholarship in the Digital Age: Information, Infrastructure, and the Internet. Cambridge, MA: MIT Press; 2007

[244] Stodden V. The legal framework for reproducible scientific research licencing and copyright. Computing in Science and Engineering. 2009;**11**(1): 35-40

[245] Pasquetto IV et al. On the reuse of scientific data. Data Science Journal. 2017;**16**(8):1-9. DOI: 10.5334/dsj2017-008

[246] Wallis JC, Rolando E, Borgman CL. If we share data, will anyone use them? Data sharing and reuse in the long tail of science and technology. PLoS One. 2013; **8**(7):e67332. DOI: 10.1371/journal.pone.0067332

[247] SPARC Europe. What is open data? Available from: https://sparceurope.org/what-we-do/open-data/what-is-open-data/ [Accessed: June 10, 2018]

[248] Open Knowledge Foundation. What is Open? Available from:https://okfn.org/opendata/ [Accessed: June 10, 2018]

[249] OECD. Co-ordination and support of international research data networks. OECD Science, Technology and Industry Policy Papers, No. 51. Paris: OECD Publishing; 2017a. 10.1787/e92fa89e-en

[250] The Royal Society. Science as an Open Enterprise. 2012. Available from: https://royalsociety.org/~/media/policy/projects/sape/2012-06-20-saoe.pdf

[251] Uhlir PF, editor. For Attribution–Developing Data Attribution and Citation Practices and Standards: Summary of an International Workshop. Washington, D.C.: National Academies Press; 2012 Available from: http://www.nap.edu/catalog.php?record_id=13564

[252] Zimmerman AS. Not by metadata alone: The use of diverse forms of knowledge to locate data for reuse. International Journal on Digital Libraries. 2007;**7**(1–2):5-16. DOI: 10.1007/s00799-007-0015-8

[253] Lorentz Center. Jointly designing a data FAIRPORT. Conference Report. 2014. Available from: https://www.lorentzcenter.nl/lc/web/2014/602/extra.pdf [Accessed: June 10, 2018]

[254] National Institutes of Health. Data Science at NIH. Available from: https://datascience.nih.gov/commons [Accessed: June 10, 2018]

[255] Horizon 2020 Annotated Model Grant Agreements, Version 1.6. 2 May 2014. Available from: https://ec.europa.eu/research/participants/data/ref/h2020/grants_manual/amga/h2020-amga_en.pdf

[256] University of Cambridge. Research Data Management. Available from: https://www.data.cam.ac.uk/

[257] Princeton University. RDM Home. Available from: http://library.princeton.edu/research-data-management

[258] Harvard Library. Data Management. Available from: https://guides.library.harvard.edu/dmp

[259] Stanford Libraries. Data Management Services. Available from: https://library.stanford.edu/research/data-management-services

[260] Cornell University. Data Management Planning. Available from: https://data.research.cornell.edu/content/data-management-planning

[261] Kristin B. Data Management for Researchers: Organize, Maintain and Share your data for Research Success (Research Skills) (Kindle Location 321). Pelagic Publishing. Kindle Edition. 2016

[262] Lee DJ, Stvilia B. Practices of research data curation in institutional repositories: A qualitative view from repository staff. PLoS One. 2017;**12**(3): e0173987. DOI: 10.1371/journal.pone.0173987

[263] Digital Curation Centre. DCC Curation Lifecycle Model. Available from: http://www.dcc.ac.uk/drupal/resources/curation-lifecycle-model

[264] Gladney HM. Long-term preservation of digital records: Trustworthy digital objects. American Archivist. 2009;**72**:401-435 Available from: http://americanarchivist.org/doi/pdf/10.17723/aarc.72.2.g513766100731832

[265] Bicarregui J, Gray N, Henderson R, Jones R, Lambert S, Matthews B. Data management and planning for big science projects. 2012. Available from: http://inspirehep.net/record/1128200/plots?ln=en

[266] Springer Nature. What is Open Access? Available from: https://www.springer.com/gp/authors-editors/authorandreviewertutorials/open-access/what-is-open-access/10286522

[267] CERN. Exploring the Mysteries of the Universe through Video Collaboration. Available from: https://21fvm71z6eomz3v3luqi11am-wpengine.netdna-ssl.com/wp-content/uploads/Case-Studies/CSW-CERN-US.pdf [Accessed: June 10, 2018]

[268] CERN. Member states. Available from: https://home.cern/about/member-states [Accessed: June 10, 2018]

[269] CERN (European Organization for Nuclear Research). ALICE - Accelerating Science. Available from: https://home.cern/about/experiments/alice [Accessed: June 10, 2018]

[270] High Scalability. How Big Is A Petabyte, Exabyte, Zettabyte, Or A Yottabyte?. 2012. Available from: http://highscalability.com/blog/2012/9/11/how-big-is-a-petabyte-exabyte-zettabyte-or-a-yottabyte.html [Accessed: June 10, 2018]

[271] CERN (European Organization for Nuclear Research). Computing. https://home.cern/about/computing [Accessed: 10 June 2018]

[272] CERN (European Organization for Nuclear Research). CERN Data Centre Passes the 200-Petabyte Milestone. Available from: https://home.cern/about/updates/2017/07/cern-data-centre-passes-200-petabyte-milestone [Accessed: June 10, 2018]

[273] Worldwide LHC Computing Grid (WLCG). Memorandum of Understanding for Collaboration in the Deployment and Exploitation of the Worldwide LHC Computing Grid. Available from: http://wlcg.web.cern.ch/collaboration/mou

[274] Worldwide LHC Computing Grid (WLCG). About. Available from: http://wlcg-public.web.cern.ch/about [Accessed: June 10, 2018]

[275] CERN. Worldwide LHC Computing Grid, Tier0 and Tier1 Centres, and the CERN Analysis Facility. Available from: https://espace2013.cern.ch/WLCG-document-repository/MoU%20docs/Annexes/Annex-1/2017/Annex1_Tier1centres_20JUN2017.pdf [Accessed: June 10, 2018]

[276] CERN. Worldwide LHC Computing Grid, Tier2 Centres. Available from: https://espace.cern.ch/

WLCG-document-repository/MoU%20docs/Annexes/Annex-2/2017/Tier2-Centres_03FEB2017.pdf [Accessed: June 10, 2018]

[277] CERN. The Worldwide LHC Computing Grid. Available from: http://home.cern/about/computing/worldwide-lhc-computing-grid [Accessed: June 10, 2018]

[278] CERN (European Organization for Nuclear Research). Proposed LHCOPN Operational Model. Available from: https://twiki.cern.ch/twiki/bin/view/LHCOPN/OperationalModel#Foundations

[279] Oxford A. The Technology Behind CERN: The Hunt for the Higgs Boson. Software, December 28, 2012

[280] Litmaath M. A short introduction to the Worldwide LHC computing grid. Presentations. Available from: https://espace.cern.ch/visits-nl-scholen/Presentations/wlcg-intro-4.pdf

[281] Herterich P, Dallmeier-Tiessen S. Data citation services in the high-energy physics community. Digital Library Magazine. 2016;**22**(1/2)

[282] Aad G et al. Combined measurement of the Higgs boson mass in pp collisions at $\sqrt{s}=7$ and 8 TeV with the ATLAS and CMS experiments. Physical Review Letters. 2015;**114**: 191803. DOI: 10.1103/PhysRevLett.114.191803

[283] CERN (European Organization for Nuclear Research). Experiments. Available from: https://home.cern/about/experiments [Accessed: June 10, 2018]

[284] CERN (European Organization for Nuclear Research). LHCb. Available from: https://home.cern/about/experiments/lhcb [Accessed: June 10, 2018]

[285] Open Data CERN. Data Policies. Available from: http://opendata.cern.ch/collection/Data-Policies [Accessed: June 10, 2018]

[286] DPHEP Study Group. Data preservation in high energy physics. In: arXiv Preprint. arXiv:0912.0255. 2009

[287] CERN (European Organization for Nuclear Research). ATLAS Data Access Policy. Available from: http://opendata.cern.ch/record/413 [Accessed: June 10, 2018]

[288] Open Data CERN. Home page. Available from: http://opendata.cern.ch/ [Accessed: June 10, 2018]

[289] CERN. CMS Guide to Research Use of CMS Open Data. Available from: http://opendata.cern.ch/docs/cms-guide-for-research [Accessed: June 10, 2018]

[290] Rao A. CERN CMS releases 300 terabytes of research data from LHC. CERN Media Release. 2016. Available from: https://phys.org/news/2016-04-cms-terabytes-lhc.html

[291] Library of Congress. MARC 21 Format for Bibliographic Data. Available from: https://www.loc.gov/marc/bibliographic/

[292] ISO 26324:2012. Information and Documentation—Digital Object Identifier System. Available from: https://www.iso.org/standard/43506.html

[293] CERN (European Organization for Nuclear Research). CMS Collaboration. 2012 'CMS Data Preservation, Re-use and Open Access Policy'. 10.7483/OPENDATA.CMS.UDBF.JKR9. Available from: http://opendata.cern.ch/record/411 [Accessed: June 10, 2018]

[294] Data Citation Synthesis Group. Joint Declaration of Data Citation Principles. In: Martone M editor.

San Diego CA: FORCE11. 10.25490/a97f-egyk; 2014

[295] Cowton J et al. 'Open data and data analysis preservation services for LHC experiments'. 21st International Conference On Computing In High Energy and Nuclear Physics. IOP Publishing, Journal of Physics: Conference series. 2015;**664**(2015): 032030. DOI: 10.1088/1742-6596/664/3/032030

[296] Nobelprize.org. The Nobel Prize in Physics. 2013. Available from: http://www.nobelprize.org/nobel_prizes/physics/laureates/2013/

[297] Higgs Boson Machine Learning Challenge. Available from: https://www.kaggle.com/c/higgs-boson/> [Accessed: June 10, 2018]

[298] Gentil-Beccot A, Mele S, Brooks TC. Citing and reading behaviours in high energy physics. Scientometrics. 2009;**84**(2):345-355

[299] INVENIO. Open Source Framework for Large-Scale Digital Repositories. Available from: http://invenio-software.org/

[300] Nobelprize.org. The Nobel Prize in Physics. 2004. Available from:http://www.nobelprize.org/nobel_prizes/physics/laureates/2004/advanced.html [Accessed: June 10, 2018]

[301] Dallmeier Tiessen S, Herterich P, Igo-Kemenes P, Simko T, Smith T. CERN Analysis Preservation—Use Cases. 2015. Available from: https://zenodo.org/record/33693; https://docplayer.net/14993957-Cern-analysis-preservation-cap-use-cases-sunje-dallmeier-tiessen-patricia-herterich-peter-igo-kemenes-tibor-simko-tim-smith.html [Accessed: June 10, 2018]

[302] Chen X et al. CERN analysis preservation: A novel digital Library service to enable reusable and reproducible research. In: Fuhr N, Kovács L, Risse T, Nejdl W, editors. Research and Advanced Technology for Digital Libraries. TPDL, Lecture Notes in Computer Science. Vol. 9819. 2016. pp. 347-356, 348. DOI: 10.1007/978-3-319-43997-6_27 [Accessed: June 10, 2018]

[303] Cranmer K, Heinrich L, Jones R, South DM. Analysis preservation in ATLAS. In: 21st International Conference on Computing in High Energy and Nuclear Physics. Vol. 664. IOP Publishing. Journal of Physics: Conference Series; 2015, 2015. p. 032013, 3. DOI: 10.1088/1742-6596/664/3/032013. Available from: http://iopscience.iop.org/article/10.1088/1742-6596/664/3/032013/meta

[304] CERN (European Organization for Nuclear Research). ALICE Data Preservation Strategy. Available from: http://opendata.cern.ch/record/412 [Accessed: June 10, 2018]

[305] Catmore J et al. New petabyte-scale data derivation framework for ATLAS. IOP Publishing, Journal of Physics: Conference Series. 2015;**664**(072007). DOI: 10.1088/1742-6596/664/7/072007

[306] Jones RWL et al. ATLAS data preservation. Publishing Journal of Physics: Conference Series. 2015;**664**(032017):4

[307] Larkoski A, Marzani S, Thaler J, Tripathee A, Xue W. Exposing the QCD splitting function with CMS open data. Physical Review Letters. 2017;**119**(13). DOI: 10.1103/PhysRevLett.119.132003

[308] International Masterclasses in the LHC Era. CERN Courier. June 2014;**54**(5):37–39. Available from: https://home.cern/students-educators/updates/2014/07/international-masterclasses-lhc-era

[309] Jones R. Big data at the large hadron collider: ATLAS data preservation and access policy. Power

point presentation dated 15 July 2014. 2014. (unpublished)

[310] CERN (European Organization for Nuclear Research). LHCb External Data Access Policy. Available from:http://opendata.cern.ch/record/410 [Accessed: June 10, 2018]

[311] Dimasi JA, Grabowski HG. The cost of biopharmaceutical R&D: Is biotech different? Managerial and Decision Economics. 2007;**28**:469-479

[312] Frydman JG. Patient-driven research: Rich opportunities and real risks. Journal of Participatory Medicine. 2009;**1**. Available from: https://www.medscape.com/viewarticle/713872

[313] Fogel J, Ribisl KM, Morgan PD, et al. Underrepresentation of African Americans in online cancer support groups. Journal of National Medicine Association. 2008;**100**:705-712

[314] Grant RW, Cagliero E, Chueh HC, Meigs JB. Internet use among primary care patients with type 2 diabetes: The generation and education gap. Journal of General Internal Medicine. 2005;**20**: 470-473

[315] Han JY, Kim JH, Shim M, McTavish FM, Gustafson DH. Social and psychological determinants of levels of engagement with an online breast cancer support group: Posters, lurkers, and non-users. Journal of Health Communication. 2012;**17**:365-371

[316] Im EO, Chee W, Liu Y, et al. Characteristics of cancer patients in internet cancer support groups. Computers, Informatics, Nursing. 2007; **25**(6):334-343 https://www.ncbi.nlm.nih.gov/pmc/articles/PMC2504028/

[317] Owen JE et al. Use of health-related online support groups: Population data from the California health interview survey complementary and alternative medicine study. Journal of Computer-Mediated Communication. 2010;**15**:427-446

[318] Klemm P et al. Online cancer support groups: A review of the research literature. Computers, Informatics, Nursing. 2003;**21**(3):136-141

[319] Vilhauer RP. Perceived benefits of online support groups for women with metastatic breast cancer. Women and Health. 2009;**49**(5):381-404. DOI: 10.1080/03630240903238719

[320] Kratz JE, Strasser C. Researcher perspectives on publication and peer review of data. PLoS One. 2015;**10**: e011761

[321] Hrynaszkiewicz I, Norton ML, Vickers AJ, Altman DG. Preparing raw clinical data for publication: Guidance for journal editors, authors, and peer reviewers. British Medical Journal. 2010;**340**:181-182

[322] Van de Wetering FT, Scholten R, Haring T, Clarke M, Hooft L. Trial registration numbers are underreported in biomedical publications. PLoS One. 2012;**7**:e49599

[323] Jones CW et al. Non-publication of large randomized clinical trials: Cross sectional analysis. British Medical Journal. 2013;**347**:6104-6104

[324] McGauran N et al. Reporting bias in medical research—A narrative review. Trials. 2010;**11**:37

[325] Doshi P, Goodman SN, Ioannidis JPA. Raw data from clinical trials: Within reach? Trends in Pharmacological Sciences. 2013;**34**(12): 645-647

[326] Zarin DA. Participant-level data and the new frontier in trial transparency. New England Journal of Medicine. 2013;**369**(5):468-469

[327] Savage CJ, Vickers AJ. Empirical study of Data sharing by authors

publishing in PLoS journals. PLoS ONE. 2009;**4**(9):e7078, 1. DOI: 10.1371/journal.pone.0007078

[328] Wicherts JM, Borsboom D, Kats J, Molenaar D. The poor availability of psychological research data for reanalysis. American Psychology. 2006; **61**:726-728

[329] Vines TH et al. Mandated data archiving greatly improves access to research data. The FASEB Journal. 2013; **27**(4):1304-1308

[330] Piwowar HA. Who shares? Who doesn't? Factors associated with openly archiving raw research. PLoS One. 2011; **6**:e18657

[331] Lipkin M. Shared decision making. JAMA Internal Medicine. 2013;**173**: 1204-1205

[332] Lloyd K, White J. Democratizing clinical research. Nature. 2011;**474**:277-278

[333] Tinetti ME, Basch E. Patients' responsibility to participate in decision making and research. JAMA. 2013;**309**: 2331-2332

[334] Domecq JP, Prutsky G, Elraiyah T, et al. Patient engagement in research: A systematic review. BMC Health Services Research. 2014;**14**:89

[335] Thornton S. Beyond rhetoric: We need a strategy for patient involvement in the health service. British Medical Journal. 2014;**348**:g4072

[336] Sacristán JA, Aguarón A, Avendaño-Solá C, Garrido P, Carrión J, Gutiérrez A, et al. Patient involvement in clinical research: Why, when, and how. Patient Preference and Adherence. 2016;**10**:631-640. DOI: 10.2147/PPA.S104259

[337] Gupta UC. Informed consent in clinical research: Revisiting few concepts and areas. Perspectives in Clinical Research. 2013;**4**(1):26-32. DOI: 10.4103/2229-3485.106373

[338] Food and Drug Administration, Informed Consent for Clinical Trials, United States. Available from: https://www.fda.gov/ForPatients/ClinicalTrials/InformedConsent/default.htm

[339] Institute of Medicine. Sharing Clinical Trial Data: Maximizing Benefits, Minimizing Risk. Washington, DC: The National Academies Press; 2015. 10.17226/18998

[340] Humphries C. New disease registry gives patients some privacy. MIT Technology Review. 14 March 2013. Available from: https://www.technologyreview.com/s/512456/new-disease-registry-gives-patients-some-privacy/

[341] Suver C. Innovation in informed consent Sage bionetworks toolkit. Presentation given at UBC REB Retreat, 21 October 2015. Available from: https://ethics.research.ubc.ca/sites/ore.ubc.ca/files/documents/Innovation_in_IC_Sage_Bionetworks_Toolkit_CSuver.pdf

[342] Bierer BE. Guiding principles for clinical trial data sharing. Paper Presented at IOM Committee on Strategies for Responsible Sharing of Clinical Trial Data: Meeting Two, 3–4 February, Washington, DC; 2014

[343] Koenig F, Slattery J, Groves T, Lang T, Benjamini Y, Day S, et al. Sharing clinical trial data on patient level: Opportunities and challenges. Biometrical Journal. 2015;**57**(1):8-26. DOI: 10.1002/bimj.201300283

[344] Decision of the European Ombudsman Closing His Inquiry Into Complaint, 2560/2007/BEH against the European Medicines Agency. Available from: https://www.ombudsman.europa.

eu/cases/decision.faces/en/5459/html.bookmark#_ftn1

[345] European Commission. Regulation of the European Commission No 1049/2001. [Accessed: May 30, 2001]

[346] European Medicines Agency. European Medicines Agency Policy on Access to Documents (Related to Medicinal Products for Human and Veterinary Use), POLICY/0043. 30 November 2010b. Available from: http://www.ema.europa.eu/docs/en_GB/document_library/Other/2010/11/WC500099473.pdf

[347] Wathion N and European Medicines Agency. Finalisation of EMA policy on publication of and access to clinical trial data. Summary report. 2014. Available from: http://www.ema.europa.eu/docs/en_GB/document_library/Report/2014/09/WC500174226.pdf

[348] European Medicines Agency. Publication and access to clinical-trial data. Draft Policy. 2013 Available from: http://www.ema.europa.eu/docs/en_GB/document_library/Other/2013/06/WC500144730.pdf

[349] European Medicines Agency policy on Publication of Clinical Data for Medicinal Products for Human Use. The Policy Is In Accordance Article 80 of Regulation (EC) No 726/20041. 2014. Available from: http://www.ema.europa.eu/docs/en_GB/document_library/Other/2014/10/WC500174796.pdf

[350] FDA, CFR—Code of Federal Regulations Title 21, Par. C. Available from: https://www.accessdata.fda.gov/scripts/cdrh/cfdocs/cfcfr/CFRSearch.cfm?fr=20.61

[351] Drug Price Competition and Patent Term Restoration Act, Public Law. 24 September 1984. pp. 98-417, 98th Cong

[352] Brennan Z. FDA Withdraws Proposed Rule on Public Disclosure of Info on Unapproved Gene Therapies'. Regulatory Focus™. 10 November 2016. Available from: https://www.raps.org/regulatory-focus™/news-articles/2016/11/fda-withdraws-proposed-rule-on-public-disclosure-of-info-on-unapproved-gene-therapies

[353] Woodcock J. FDA's New Pilot Program Aims for More Transparency about New Drug Approvals. FDA Voice. Blog, Posted on 19 March 2018. Available from: https://blogs.fda.gov/fdavoice/index.php/2018/03/fdas-new-pilot-program-aims-for-more-transparency-about-new-drug-approvals/

[354] Lanthier M, Miller KL, Nardinelli C, Woodcock J. An improved approach to measuring drug innovation finds steady rates of first-in-class pharmaceuticals, 1987–2011. Health Affairs. 2013;**32**(8):1433-1439

[355] Doshi P, Dickersin K, Healy D, Vedula SS, Jefferson T. Restoring invisible and abandoned trials: A call for people to publish the findings. British Medical Journal. 2013;**346**:f2865

[356] Krumholz HM, Gross CP, Blount KL, Ritchie JD, Hodshon B, Lehman R, et al. Sea change in open science and data sharing: Leadership by industry. Circulation: Cardiovascular Quality and Outcomes. 2014;**7**(4):499-504

[357] European Federation of Pharmaceutical Industries and Associations (EFPIA). EFPIA and PhRMA release joint principles for responsible clinical trial data sharing to benefit patients. 2013. Available from: https://www.efpia.eu/news-events/the-efpia-view/statements-press-releases/130724-efpia-and-phrma-release-joint-principles-for-responsible-clinical-trial-data-sharing-to-benefit-patients/

[358] Food and drug Administration. Small business report to Congress

mandated by the Food and Drug Administration Safety and Innovation Act. 31 May 2013. Available from: https://www.fda.gov/downloads/RegulatoryInformation/LawsEnforcedbyFDA/SignificantAmendmentstotheFDCAct/FDASIA/UCM360058.pdf

[359] Greenwald T. Patients Take Control of their Health Care Online. MIT Technology Review. 2013. Available from: https://www.technologyreview.com/s/518886/patients-take-control-of-their-health-care-online/

[360] World Health Organization, Joint Statement on Public Disclosure of Results From Clinical Trials Signed on 18 May 2017. Available from: http://www.who.int/ictrp/results/jointstatement/en/

[361] National Research Council. Private Lives and Public Policies: Confidentiality and Accessibility of Government Statistics. Washington, DC: National Academy Press; 1993

[362] National Institutes of Health. Summary Table of HHS/NIH Initiatives to Enhance Availability of Clinical Trial Information. 15 September 2016. Available from: https://www.nih.gov/news-events/summary-table-hhs-nih-initiatives-enhance-availability-clinical-trial-information

[363] Hudson KL, Collins FS. Sharing and reporting the results of clinical trials. Journal of the American Medical Association. 2014. DOI: 10.1001/jama.2014.10716

[364] European Medicines Agency. (N.D.). Clinical data available. Policy document. Available from: https://clinicaldata.ema.europa.eu/web/cdp/background [Accessed: June 10, 2018]

[365] European Medicines Agency, Online access to clinical data for medical products for human use. Available from: https://clinicaldata.ema.europa.eu [Accessed: June 10, 2018]

[366] Sydes MR et al. Sharing data from clinical trials: The rationale for a controlled access. Clinical Trials. 2015; **16**:104. Available from: https://trialsjournal.biomedcentral.com/articles/10.1186/s13063-015-0604-6

[367] Wiley Open Science Researcher Survey. 2016. Available from: https://figshare.com/articles/Wiley_Open_Science_Researcher_Survey_2016/4748332

[368] Wiley Network, Open Science Trends you Need to Know About. Available from: https://hub.wiley.com/community/exchanges/discover/blog/2017/04/19/open-science-trends-you-need-to-know-about?referrer=exchanges [Accessed: June 10, 2018]

[369] Elsevier and the Centre for Science and Technology Studies (2017). Open Data: The Researcher Perspective. Available from: https://www.elsevier.com/__data/assets/pdf_file/0004/281920/Open-data-report.pdf

[370] Van den Eynden V, Knight G, Vlad A, et al. Survey of Wellcome researchers and their attitudes to open research. figshare. 31 October 2016. Available from: https://doi.org/10.6084/m9.figshare.4055448.v1

[371] Bornmann L. Do altmetrics point to the broader impact of research? An overview of benefits and disadvantages of altmetrics. Journal of Informetrics. 2014;**8**(4):895-903. DOI: 10.1016/j.joi.2014.09.005

[372] Konkiel S. Altmetrics. A 21st-century solution to determining research quality. Information Today. 2013;**37**(4) Available from: http://www.infotoday.com/OnlineSearcher/Articles/Features/Altmetrics-A-stCentury-

Solution-to-Determining-Research-Quality-90551.shtml

[373] Peters I, Kraker P, Lex E, et al. Research data explored: An extended analysis of citations and altmetrics. Scientometrics. 2016;**107**:723. DOI: 10.1007/s11192-016-1887-4

[374] Piwowar HA, Chapman WW. Public sharing of research datasets: A pilot study of associations. Journal of Informetrics. 2010;**4**:148-156

[375] Reuters T. Repository Evaluation, Selection, and Coverage Policies for the Data Citation Index within Thomson Reuters Web of Knowledge. 2012. Available from: http://wokinfo.com/products_tools/multidisciplinary/dci/selection_essay

[376] Costas R, Meijer I, Zahedi Z, Wouters P. The value of research data—Metrics for data sets from a cultural and technical point of view, a knowledge exchange report. 2012. Available from: http://www.knowledge-exchange.info/datametrics

[377] National Academy of Sciences. Sharing of Research Results. Washington: National Academies Press; 2009. Available from: www.ncbi.nlm.nih.gov/books/NBK214573/

[378] Jasny BR, Chin G, Chong L, Vignieri S. Again, and again, and again... Science. 2011;**334**(6060):1225. DOI: 10.1126/science.334.6060.1225

[379] Stodden VC. Reproducible research: Addressing the need for data and code sharing in computational science. Computing in Science and Engineering. 2010;**12**(5):8-12. DOI: 10.1109/MCSE.2010.113

[380] Ioannidis J, Khoury M. Improving validation practices in 'Omics' Research. Science. 2011;**334**(6060):1230-1232. DOI: 10.1126/science.1211811

[381] Open Data Institute, Publisher's Guide to Open Data Licensing. Available from: https://theodi.org/article/publishers-guide-to-open-data-licensing/ [Accessed: June 10, 2018]

[382] World Trade Organization (WTO). Trade-Related Aspects of Intellectual Property Rights'. Available from: https://www.wto.org/english/tratop_e/trips_e/trips_e.htm

[383] World Intellectual Property Organization (WIPO). WIPO Copyright Treaty (WCT). Available from: http://www.wipo.int/treaties/en/ip/wct/

[384] Ricketson S, Richardson M, Davison MJ. Intellectual Property: Cases, Materials and Commentary. Chatswood, NSW: Lexis Nexis Butterworth; 2013, Part 4

[385] IceTV Pty Ltd v Nine Network Australia Pty Ltd (2009a) 239 CLR 458

[386] Telstra Corporation Limited v Phone Directories Company Pty Ltd (2010) FCA 44

[387] Desktop Marketing Systems Pty Ltd v Telstra Corporation Ltd (2002) 119 FCR 491 at 407

[388] Fitzgerald, Anne M, Dwyer N. Copyright in databases in Australia. 2017. Available from: https://eprints.qut.edu.au/50425/

[389] IceTV Pty Ltd v Nine Network Australia Pty Ltd (2009b) HCA 14

[390] Telstra Corporation Ltd v Phone Directories Company Pty Ltd (2010a) 264 ALR 617

[391] Telstra Corporation Ltd v Phone Directories Company Pty Ltd (2010b) FCAFC 149

[392] Productivity Commission Inquiry Report. (2017). Data Availability and Use Report No. 82, Canberra. Australia,

March. Available from: https://www.pc.gov.au/inquiries/completed/data-access/report/data-access.pdf

[393] Copyright Act of 1976, 17 U.S.C. (1976)

[394] Feist Publications, Inc. v. Rural Telephone Service Co. 499 U.S. 340; 1991

[395] Directive 2009/24/EC. Available from: https://eur-lex.europa.eu/legal-content/EN/ALL/?uri=CELEX%3A32009L0024

[396] Directive 2006/115/EC. Available from: https://eur-lex.europa.eu/LexUriServ/LexUriServ.do?uri=OJ:L:2006:376:0028:0035:EN:PDF

[397] Directive 93/83/EEC. Available from: https://eur-lex.europa.eu/legal-content/EN/ALL/?uri=celex:31993L0083

[398] Directive 93/98/EEC. Available from: https://eur-lex.europa.eu/legal-content/en/ALL/?uri=CELEX:31993L0098

[399] Directive 96/9/EC. Available from: https://eur-lex.europa.eu/legal-content/EN/TXT/?uri=celex%3A31996L0009

[400] Directive 2001/29/EC. Available from: https://eur-lex.europa.eu/LexUriServ/LexUriServ.do?uri=OJ:L:2001:167:0010:0019:EN:PDF

[401] Directive 2001/84/EC. Available from: https://eur-lex.europa.eu/LexUriServ/LexUriServ.do?uri=CELEX:32001L0084:EN:HTML

[402] Directive 2012/28/EU. Available from: https://eur-lex.europa.eu/legal-content/EN/TXT/?uri=celex%3A32012L0028

[403] Directive 2014/26/EU. Available from: https://eur-lex.europa.eu/legal-content/EN/TXT/?uri=celex%3A32014L0026

[404] Dietrich N, Guibault L, Margoni T, Siewicz K, Wiebe A. Possible forms of legal protection: An EU perspective. In: Guibault L, Wiebe A, editors. Safe to be Open: A Study on the Protection of Research Data and Recommendations for Access and Usage. Universitätsverlag Göttingen; 2013. p. 23

[405] ECJ Case C-604/10. Football Dataco Ltd et al v Yahoo! UK Ltd GRUR at 386; 2012

[406] ECJ Case C-203/02. British Horseracing Board Ltd v William Hill Organization Ltd (BHB). ECR I-10415; 2004

[407] Davison M. Database protection: Lessons Europe, Congress, and WIPO. Case Western Reserve Law Review. 2016;**57**(4)

[408] CJEU, case C-2-2/12, Innoweb BV v Wegener ICT Media BV and Wegener Mediaventions BV. ECLI 850; 2013

[409] Judgement of the Court (Fifth Chamber). 19 December 2013. Available from: http://curia.europa.eu/juris/celex.jsf?celex=62012CJ0202&lang1=en&type=TXT&ancre=

[410] Right Environment for Digital Networks and Services. 6 May 2015. Available from: https://ec.europa.eu/digital-single-market/en/right-environment-digital-networks-and-services [Accessed: June 10, 2018]

[411] European Commission. Public consultation on the database directive: Application and impact. 24 May–30 August 2017. Available from: https://ec.europa.eu/info/consultations/public-consultation-database-directive-application-and-impact-0_en

[412] Gideon Emcee Christian. Building a Sustainable Framework for Open

Access to Research Data through Information and Communication Technologies, International Development Research Centre Canada. 2009

[413] Productivity Commission. Intellectual Property Arrangements: Draft Report. Canberra: Australian Government; 2016

[414] University of Western Australia (UWA) v Gray (No 20) (2008) FCA 49. FCAFC 116; 2009

[415] Van Caenegem W. VUT v Wilson, UWA v Gray and university intellectual property policies. Australian Intellectual Property Journal. 2010;**21**(3):148-163

[416] University of Western Australia v Gray. 179 FCR 346; 2009

[417] Fishbein EA. Ownership of research data. Academic Medicine. 1991; **66**(3):129

[418] Columbia University. 'Responsible Conduct of Research'. Available from: http://ccnmtl.columbia.edu/projects/rcr/rcr_data/foundation/index.html

[419] Evans BJ. Much ado about data ownership. Harvard Journal of Law and Technology. 2011:25. Available from: http://jolt.law.harvard.edu/articles/pdf/v25/25HarvJLTech69.pdf

[420] Moore v Regents of the University of California and Ors 793 P 2d 479 . Supreme Court of California;1990

[421] Newborn Screening Saves Lives Reauthorization, Act of 2014. 113th Congress (2013–14). Available from: https://www.congress.gov/bill/113th-congress/house-bill/1281

[422] US Department of Health and Human Services (18 January 2017). Final Rule Enhances Protections for Research Participants, Modernizes Oversight System. Available from: http://wayback.archive-it.org/3926/20170127095200/https:/www.hhs.gov/about/news/2017/01/18/final-rule-enhances-protections-research-participants-modernizes-oversight-system.html

[423] European Commission. Digitising European Industry Reaping the Full Benefits of a Digital Single Market. Communication from the Commission to the European Parliament, the Council, the European Economic and Social Committee of the Regions, COM/2016/0180 Final; 19 April 2016a

[424] Van Asbroeck B, Debussche J, César J. Building the European Data Economy, Data Ownership. White paper. Bird & Bird. 2017

[425] CJEU, case C-128/11, UsedSoft GmbH v Oracle International Corp. ECLI: 407

[426] Hoeren T. Big Data and the Ownership in Data: Recent Developments in Europe. EIPR. 2014;**36** (12):751

[427] Creative Commons. CC0 1.0 Universal (CC0 1.0) Public Domain Dedication. Available from: https://creativecommons.org/publicdomain/zero/1.0/legalcode

[428] Creative Commons. Public Domain Mark. Available from: https://creativecommons.org/share-your-work/public-domain/pdm

[429] Geiger, C., Frosio, G., Bulayenko, O. (2 February 2018). The Exception for Text and Data Mining (TDM) in the Proposed Directive on Copyright in the Digital Single Market-Legal Aspects. Briefing paper. European Parliament's Policy Department for Citizens' Rights and Constitutional Affairs. Available from: http://www.europarl.europa.eu/RegData/etudes/IDAN/2018/604941/IPOL_IDAF243(2018)604941_EN.pdf

[430] Oxford Academic Journals. Third party data mining. Policy page.

Available from: https://academic.oup.com/journals/pages/help/third_party_data_mining

[431] Leval PN. Toward a fair use standard. Harvard Law Review. 1990; **103**:1006

[432] Authors Guild v Google, Inc, No. 13–4829 (2d Cir. 2015), Affirming Authors Guild v Google, Inc, 954 F. Supp.2d 282; 2013

[433] Authors Guild v. Google, 770 F. Supp.2d 666 (S.D.N.Y. 2011)

[434] Australian Law Reform Commission. (2013). Copyright in the Digital Economy. Discussion paper, June. Available from: https://www.alrc.gov.au/publications/copyright-and-digital-economy-dp-79

[435] Hargreaves I. Digital Opportunity: A Review of Intellectual Property and Growth. Independent report. United Kingdom: Department for Business, Innovation & Skills; 2011

[436] Copyright, Design and Patents Act 1988 UK; 1988

[437] Senfleben M. EU Copyright Reform and Start-Ups—Shedding Light on Potential Threats in the Political Black Box. N.D. Available from: https://drive.google.com/file/d/0B7NZMlL3kj5qQzN0R Xd2Z0JaR1JmemxhND d2VmgzSjhFQXdj/view and http://www.innovatorsact.eu/wp-content/uploads/2017/03/Issues-Paper-Copyright-Directive-2.pdf. [Accessed: June 10, 2018]

[438] Caldicott F. Information: To Share or Not to Share? The Information Governance Review. London United Kingdom: Department of Health; March 2013. Available from: https://www.gov.uk/government/uploads/system/uploads/attachment_data/file/192572/2900774_InfoGovernance_accv2.pdf>. [Accessed: May 2, 2017]

[439] Creighton B, Stewart A. Labour Law: An Introduction. 2nd ed. Sydney: Federation Press; 1994

[440] US Office for Civil Rights (OCR). Guidance Regarding Methods for De-identification of Protected Health Information in Accordance with the Health Insurance Portability and Accountability Act (HIPAA) Privacy Rule; 2012

[441] EMA. Data Sharing Policy; 2014

[442] US Department of Health and Human Services. Code of Federal Regulations. Title 45. Public Welfare. Part 46 Protection of Human Subjects. 2009. Available from: http://www.hhs.gov/ohrp/humansubjects/guidance/45cfr46.html

[443] Eze B, Peyton L. Systematic literature review on the anonymization of high dimensional streaming datasets for health data sharing. Procedia Computer Science. 2015;**63**:348-355

[444] Case T-235/15. Pari Pharma v EMA. Available from:http://curia.europa.eu/juris/document/document_print.jsf?doclang=EN&text=&pageIndex=0&part=1&mode=lst&docid=199041&occ=first&dir=&cid=249920

[445] Case T-718/15. PTC Therapeutics International v EMA. Available from: http://curia.europa.eu/juris/document/document_print.jsf?doclang=EN&text=&pageIndex=0&part=1&mode=lst&docid=199044&occ=first&dir=&cid=249920

[446] Case T-729/15. MSD Animal Health Innovation and Intervet International. Available from: http://curia.europa.eu/juris/document/document_print.jsf?doclang=EN&text=&pageIndex=0&part=1&mode=lst&docid=199042&occ=first&dir=&cid=253401

[447] European Parliament. Regulation (EC) No 1049/2001 Regarding Public

Access to European Parliament, Council and Commission Documents. 30 May 2001c. Available from:https://eur-lex.europa.eu/legal-content/EN/TXT/PDF/?uri=CELEX:32001R1049&qid=1517939157555&from=EN

[448] EMA Update on Clinical Data Publication. 29 January 2018. Available from: http://www.ema.europa.eu/docs/en_GB/document_library/Presentation/2018/02/WC500243177.pdf

[449] Commonwealth of Australia, Department of the Prime Minister and Cabinet. The Australian Government's Response to the Productivity Commission Data Availability and Use Inquiry. Report. May 2018. Available from: http://dataavailability.pmc.gov.au/sites/default/files/govt-response-pc-dau-inquiry.pdf

[450] The Privacy Act 1988 (Cth)

[451] The Antarctic Treaty. 1959. Available from: http://www.antarctica.ac.uk/about_antarctica/geopolitical/treaty/update_1959.php

[452] International Council for Science. 2016. Open Data in a Big Data World. An International Accord, Abbreviated Version, 1. Available from: http://www.science-international.org/sites/default/files/reports/open-data-in-big-data-world_short_en.pdf

[453] Allen BD. Principles on Full and Open Access to 'Global Change' Data, Policy Statements on Data Management for Global Change Research. Office of Science and Technology Policy. 1991

[454] ICSU-CODATA Ad Hoc Group on Data and Information. Access to databases: A set of principles for science in the internet era. 2000. Available from: http://www.icsu.org/publications/icsu-position-statements/ access-to-databases/

[455] Arzberger P, Schroeder P, Beaulieu A, Bowker G, Casey K, Laaksonen, et al. An international framework to promote access to data. Science. March 2004: 1777-1778

[456] Anonymous. Free for All. 2003 in context. Nature. 2003;**426**(755):748-757

[457] Zandonella C. Economics of open access. The Scientist. 22 August 2003. Available from: https://www.the-scientist.com/?articles.view/articleNo/22408/title/Economics-of-open-access/

[458] Brown PO, Michael BE, Varmus HE. Why PloS became a publisher. PloS Biology. 2003;**1**(1):1-2.r

[459] Sidler M. Open science and the three cultures: Expanding open science to all domains of knowledge creation. In: Batling S, Friesike S, editors. Opening Science: The Evolving Guide on How the Internet Is Changing Research. Collaboration and Scholarly Publishing. Springer Open; 2014. p. 81

[460] Granger CB, Ohman EM. Enhancing the value of clinical trials: The role of data sharing. Nature Reviews Cardiology. 2016;**13**:629-630

[461] Kiley R, Peatfield T, Hansen J, Reddington F. Data sharing from clinical trials—A Research Funder's perspective. New England Journal of Medicine. 2017;**377**:1990-1992

[462] Horton R. Offline: Data sharing—Why editors may have got it wrong. The Lancet. 2016;**388**:1143

[463] International Consortium of Investigators for Fairness in Trial Data Sharing. Towards fairness in data sharing. New England Journal of Medicine. 2016;**375**:405-407

[464] Longo LD, Drazen JM. Data sharing. New England Journal of Medicine. 2016;**374**:276-277

[465] UK Research and Innovation. Common Principles on Data Policy, originally published in April 2011 and revised July 2015. Available from: https://www.ukri.org/funding/information-for-award-holders/data-policy/common-principles-on-data-policy/

[466] Australian Research Council, Open Access Policy took effect from 1 January 2013. Version 2013.1. Available from: http://www.arc.gov.au/arc-open-access-policy [Accessed: June 10, 2018]

[467] The National Health and Medical Research Council (NHMRC). Open Access Policy (previously also referred to as the NHMRC Policy on the Dissemination of Research) took effect from 15 January 2018, 7. Available from: https://www.nhmrc.gov.au/_files_nhmrc/file/research/nhmrc_open_access_policy_15_january_2018_v2.pdf

[468] RDM at the University of Melbourne. Available from: http://research.unimelb.edu.au/infrastructure/doing-data-better/how

[469] University of Sydney. Available from: https://library.sydney.edu.au/research/data-management/

[470] Monash University. Available from: https://www.monash.edu/library/researchdata/about

[471] University of New South Wales. Available from: https://research.unsw.edu.au/research-data-management-unsw

[472] University of Queensland Available from: https://research.uq.edu.au/project/research-data-manager-uqrdm

[473] Australian National University. Available from: https://anulib.anu.edu.au/research-learn/research-data-management

[474] University of Adelaide. Available from: http://libguides.adelaide.edu.au/researchdata

[475] University of Western Australia. Available from: http://www.library.uwa.edu.au/research/research-data-management-toolkit

[476] Harnard S. Gold open access publishing must not be allowed to retard the progress of green open access self-archiving. Logos. 2010a;**21**(3–4):89

[477] Antelman K. Do open access articles have a greater research impact? College and Research Libraries. 2004; **65**:372-382

[478] Eysenbach G. The impact of preprint servers and electronic publishing on biomedical research. Current Opinion in Immunology. 2000; **12**:499-503

[479] Eysenbach G. Citation advantage of open access articles. PLoS Biology. 2006;**4**(5):157

[480] Gargouri Y, Hajjem C, Larivière V, Gingras V, Carr L, Brody T, et al. Self-selected or mandated, open access increases citation impact for higher quality research. PLoS One;**5**(10): e13636

[481] Harnad S, Brody T. Comparing the impact of open access (OA) vs. non-OA articles in the same journals. In: Digital Library Magazine. 2004. p. 10

[482] Harnad S, Carr L, Swan A, Sale A, Bosc A. Maximizing and measuring research impact through university and research-funder open-access self-archiving mandates. Wissenschaftsmanagement. 2009;**15**(4): 36-41

[483] Swan A, Brown S. Open Access Self-Archiving: An Author Study. JISC Technical Report. Key Perspectives, Inc; 2005. Available from: http://eprints.ecs.soton.ac.uk/10999/

[484] Kirsch A. Technology is taking over English departments: The false

promise of the digital humanities. New Republic. May 2, 2014. Available from: https://newrepublic.com/article/117428/limits-digital-humanities-adam-kirsch

[485] Wessels B, Finn RL, Linde P, Mazzetti P, Nativi S, Riley S, et al. Issues in the development of open access to research data. Prometheus. 2014;**32**(1):49-66

[486] Botstein D. It's the data! Molecular Biology of the Cell. 2010;**21**(1):4-6

[487] Dorch B. On the citation advantage of linking to data. Astrophysics. 2012. Available from: http://hprints.org/docs/00/71/47/34/PDF/Dorch_2012a.pdf

[488] Henneken EA, Accomazzi A. Linking to data—Effect on citation rates in astronomy. In: Digital Libraries; Instrumentation and Methods for Astrophysics. 2011

[489] Harnard S. Open Access/Open Data: Similarities and Differences, BRDI Symposium on Data Sharing, NAS, Washington DC, 1 December 2010b.

[490] UNESCO. Toward knowledge societies. UNESCO World Report. Conde-Sur-Noireau, France: Imprimerie Corlet; 2005

[491] McKeough J, Stewart A. Intellectual Property in Australia. 2nd ed1997

[492] Monotti A. University Employees and Intellectual Property. 2015. DOI: 10.2139/ssrn.3000693 Available from: https://ssrn.com/abstract=3000693

[493] ALRC Report 122. Copyright and the Digital Economy, at 11.57. Available from: https://www.alrc.gov.au/publications/11-incidental-or-technical-use-and-data-and-text-mining/data-and-text-mining

[494] Rosati E. The exception for text and data mining in the proposed directive on copyright in the digital single market. Technical Aspects. 2018. Available from: http://www.europarl.europa.eu/thinktank/en/document.html?reference=IPOL_BRI%282018%29604942

[495] Thomas M. Text and Data Mining Exception, EPP Group Hearing on Copyright, 8 June 2017. Available from: http://www.eppgroup.eu/sites/default/files/event-files/Ronja%20Füllenbach/201724/Thomas%20Margoni%20-%20EP_TDM.pdf

[496] Copyright Act 1968 (Cth)

[497] CSIRO. Australian Law Reform Commission, Copyright and the Digital Economy—Final Report, ALRC Report 122, Sydney, 2013, 11.68. Available from: https://www.alrc.gov.au/sites/default/files/pdfs/publications/final_report_alrc_122_2nd_december_2013_.pdf

[498] Castells M. The Information Age: Economy, Society and Culture Volume 1: The Rise of the Network Society. 2nd ed. Singapore: Wiley Blackwell; 2010

[499] Guibault L, Wiebe A, editors. Safe to be Open: A Study on the Protection of Research data and Recommendations for Access and Usage. Gottingen: Universitätsverlag Göttingen; 2013

[500] CJEU. case C-5/08, Infopaq International A/S v Danske Dagblades Forening

[501] CJEU. Case T-235/15, Pari Pharma v EMA

[502] CJEU. Case T-718/15, PTC Therapeutics International v EMA

[503] CJEU. Case T-729/15, MSD Animal Health Innovation and Intervet International

[504] ECJ Case C-5/08. Infopaq International A/S v Danske Dagblades Forening. ECDR 16; 2009

[505] European Parliament. Directive 2001/29/EC on the Harmonization of Certain Aspects of Copyright and Related Rights in the Information Society; 22 May 2001a

[506] European Parliament. Directive 2001/84/EC on the Resale Right for the Benefit of the Author of an Original Work of Art; 27 September 2001b

[507] European Parliament. Directive 2006/115/EC on Rental Right and Lending Right and on Certain Rights Related to Copyright in the Field of Intellectual Property; 12 December 2006

[508] European Parliament. Directive 2009/24/EC on the Legal Protection of Computer Programs; 23 April 2009

[509] European Parliament. Directive 2012/28/EU on Certain Permitted Uses of Orphan Works Text with EEA Relevance; 25 October 2012

[510] European Parliament. Directive 2014/26/EU on Collective Management of Copyright and Related Rights and Multi-Territorial Licensing of Rights in Musical Works for Online Use in the Internal Market Text with EEA Relevance; 26 February 2014

[511] European Parliament. Directive 93/83/EEC on the Coordination of Certain Rules Concerning Copyright and Rights Related to Copyright Applicable to Satellite Broadcasting and Cable Retransmission; 27 September 1993a

[512] European Parliament. Directive 93/98/EEC on Harmonizing the Term of Protection of Copyright and Certain Related Rights; 9 October 1993b

[513] European Parliament. Directive 96/9/EC on the Legal Protection of Databases; 11 March 1996

[514] World Intellectual Property Organization (WIPO). Berne Convention for the Protection of Literary and Artistic Works. Available from: http://www.wipo.int/treaties/en/ip/berne

[515] European Commission. Right Environment for Digital Networks and Services. Policy Statement; 6 May 2015

[516] European Commission. (14 September 2016c). Proposal for a Directive of the European Parliament and of the Council on Copyright in the Digital Single Market

[517] European Medicines Agency. (2 October 2014). Policy on Publication of Clinical data for Medicinal Products for Human Use, Policy 0070

[518] European Parliament. Report on Motion for a European Parliament Resolution on Towards a Digital Market Act. 2015. (2015/2147(INI))

[519] National Human Genome Research Institute. (March 1997). Summary of the Report of the Second International Strategy Meeting on Human Genome Sequencing

[520] SAS and Centre for Economics and Business Research Ltd (February 2016). The Value of Big Data and the Internet of Things to the UK Economy

[521] Vickery G. Review of Recent Studies on PSI Reuse and Related Market Developments, European Commission, Brussels. 2010b. p. 3

[522] Beijing Genomics Institute. Rapid open-source genomic analyses accelerated global studies on deadly *E. coli* O104:H4. Science Daily. 27 July 2011b. Available from: https://www.sciencedaily.com/releases/2011/07/110727171501.htm

[523] CERN. European Organization for Nuclear Research. Home page. Available from: https://home.cern/

[524] Data to Decisions CRC. About. Available from: https://www.d2dcrc.com.au/about/

[525] Digital Curation Centre. Home Page. Available from: http://www.dcc.ac.uk/

[526] European Commission. Database Directive. European Commission Press Release Database. 19 February 2018 Available from: http://europa.eu/rapid/press-release_IP-96-171_en.htm?locale=en

[527] Europe PMC. About. Available from: https://europepmc.org/About

[528] MIT Technology Review. New Disease Registry Gives Patients Some Privacy. 14 March 2013. Available from: https://www.technologyreview.com/s/512456/new-disease-registry-gives-patients-some-privacy/

[529] National Human Genome Research Institute. A Brief History of the Human Genome Project. N.D. Available from: http://www.genome.gov/12011239

[530] National Institutes of Health Commons. Big Data to Knowledge. Program Home Page. N.D. Available from: https://datascience.nih.gov/commons

[531] Open Data CERN. ALICE Data Preservation Strategy. 2013. Available from: http://opendata.cern.ch/record/412

[532] Open Data CERN. CMS Collaboration, CMS Data Preservation, Re-use and Open Access Policy. 2012. Available from: http://opendata.cern.ch/record/411

[533] Organisation for Economic Cooperation and Development (OECD). Technology and Innovation Indicators. Directorate for Science, Technology and Innovation. Available from: http://www.oecd.org/sti/msti.htm

[534] Lynn TE. China helps unravel new *E.coli* for embattled Europe. In: Reuters Science News. 3 June 2011. Available from: http://www.reuters.com/article/2011/06/03/us-ecoli-china-idUSTRE75224620110603

[535] University of Glasgow. Research Data Policy. Available from: www.gla.ac.uk/media/media_232425_en.docx

[536] University of Oxford. Research Data Oxford. Available from: http://researchdata.ox.ac.uk/home/introduction-to-rdm/

[537] U. S. Department of Health and Human Services. 'FDA's New Pilot Program Aims for More Transparency about New Drug Approvals' posted on 19 March. 2018. Available from: https://blogs.fda.gov/fdavoice/index.php/2018/03/fdas-new-pilot-program-aims-for-more-transparency-about-new-drug-approvals/

[538] Office of the Press Secretary, Remarks Made by the President, Prime Minister Tony Blair of England (Via Satellite), Dr. Francis Collins, Director of the National Human Genome Research Institute, and Dr. Craig Venter, President and Chief Scientific Officer, Celera Genomics Corporation, on the Completion of the First Survey of the Entire Human Genome Project, Media Release, the White House, Washington, 26 June 2000. Available from: http://www.genome.gov/10001356

[539] The European Federation of Pharmaceutical Industries and Associations (EFPIA). EFPIA and PhRMA Release Joint Principles for Responsible Clinical Trial Data Sharing to Benefit Patients. Media Release. 24 July 2013. Available from: https://www.efpia.eu/news-events/the-efpia-view/statements-press-releases/130724-efpia-and-phrma-release-joint-principles-for-responsible-clinical-trial-data-sharing-to-benefit-patients/